Professor Dieter Helm is Professor of Economic Policy at the University of Oxford and Official Fellow in Economics at New College, Oxford. He specialises in the environment, notably in climate change, biodiversity, water, energy and agriculture. Previous books have included *Burn Out: The Endgame of Fossil Fuels*, *The Carbon Crunch* and *Natural Capital: Valuing the Planet*. His next book, *Net Zero*, is forthcoming.

In December 2015, Dieter was reappointed as Independent Chair of the Natural Capital Committee. He is also an Honorary Vice President of the Berkshire, Buckinghamshire and Oxfordshire Wildlife Trust.

Praise for *Green and Prosperous Land*

'Dieter Helm has taken a good, hard look at the state of our natural environment and the result could be one of the most important books of the decade' *Country Life*

'Helm's solutions are refreshingly straightforward . . . The notion of the financial value of nature is long established. Helm takes this further to present a pure economic argument for conservation. We all need to listen to that' Simon Barnes, *Sunday Times*

'[Helm is] as eloquent with his recommendations as in analysis of the problem . . . This is an important analysis, argued with passion, intelligence and rigour. It is timely too, because – as Helm makes compellingly clear – of the urgency of the problem' *Financial Times*

'A trenchant manifesto for change . . . visionary, pragmatic and context-rich' *Nature*

'Delivers handsomely on the promise of its title' *New Scientist*

'Helm is able to explain how a price can be put on the intangible. Rather brilliantly, he does so through presenting future scenarios, imagining what the country will be like in 2050 if current practices continue, and then what the alternative is if an agenda of policies is introduced and properly regulated ... He makes a more optimistic future conceivable through domestic reforms ... There is an enormous amount to admire' *Times Literary Supplement*

'Hooray for this book! An economist dispensing with the usual nonsense, and applying his mind to the task of devising a sound economic plan for the protection and restoration of Britain's wildlife ... [This is a] brave and forthright attempt to begin a new conversation on how to pay to keep our wildlife' *British Wildlife*

'A tough-minded and eminently practical plan for the recovery of our natural capital and the protection of our renewables ... that might just make the Britain of 2050 a success story' *The Herald Magazine*

'A good read and an important one too. I loved it, as I agreed with much of it and was interested by all of it' Mark Avery

'This book is urgent. It should be required reading for all interested in turning the 25YEP into reality. I wonder if the next generation will recognise this book as a Rachel Carson-style moment that helped to kick-start the wholesale recovery of nature: I hope so' BTO News

'Written with intelligence and rigour, this is an important work' *The Week*

Green and Prosperous Land

A BLUEPRINT FOR RESCUING
THE BRITISH COUNTRYSIDE

Dieter Helm

WILLIAM
COLLINS

William Collins
An imprint of HarperCollins*Publishers*
1 London Bridge Street
London SE1 9GF

WilliamCollinsBooks.com

First published in Great Britain by William Collins in 2019

This updated William Collins paperback edition published in 2020

2021 2023 2022 2020
2 4 6 8 10 9 7 5 3 1

Typeset by Palimpsest Book Production Ltd, Falkirk, Stirlingshire

Printed and bound in Great Britain by CPI Group (UK) Ltd, Croydon CR0 4YY

To Sue, Oliver and Laura, as always, and to Amelie and Jake of the next generation in the hope that the natural environment they will inherit will be in better shape for them to enjoy.

They paved paradise
And put up a parking lot
With a pink hotel, a boutique
And a swinging hot spot
Don't it always seem to go
That you don't know what you've got til it's gone
They paved paradise
And put up a parking lot

Big Yellow Taxi by Joni Mitchell, 1970

I thought it would last my time –
The sense that, beyond the town,
There would always be fields and farms,
Where the village louts could climb
Such trees as were not cut down;
I knew there'd be false alarms
[. . .]
Things are tougher than we are, just
As earth will always respond
However we mess it about;
Chuck filth in the sea, if you must:
The tides will be clean beyond.
– But what do I feel now? Doubt?

Selected verses from 'Going, Going'
by Philip Larkin, 1972

CONTENTS

PREFACE

I have been thinking about the issues in this book for a long time. I grew up on the Essex marshes, and spent long hours around the sea walls and creeks of my grandfather's farm. It is the place of my memories, and places are how we remember nature. It was a small farm by modern standards, around 350 acres. It was a mixed dairy and arable farm, with the traditional farmyard chickens and ducks, a big vegetable garden, a small orchard and of course beehives. It had a patchwork of more than a dozen fields, butting up to the sea wall.

In spring there were flocks of lapwing nesting so densely that it was difficult to avoid treading on the eggs. There were lots of skylarks and the full range of farmland birds, and of course a stand of great elms. House sparrows literally swarmed in the farmyard, which was often dense with flies and therefore swallows and house martins. There were barn owls. In winter, the marshes came alive with wildfowl. There were flocks of brent geese, teal and widgeon. So great were the numbers that books were written about wildfowling and punt guns and all the paraphernalia of Essex marsh life.[1]

Psychologists will tell you that what happens in that magic time of childhood forms the subsequent person. It is why getting children and nature together is so vital for the future of the environment. It is hard to put into a person's mind what they never had in childhood. In my case, although most of my career has been spent in mainstream economics in Oxford, the experiences of those early years have never left me. It is one of the reasons why, in 2012 when I was given the opportunity to chair the Natural Capital Committee (NCC), I grabbed it.

By that time an enormous amount of damage had been done to the natural environment. After World War II, British agricultural policy, and then the Common Agricultural Policy (CAP), had transformed the land, polluting as it went. My grandfather's farm was sold and turned into one large field in the 1960s, with the hedgerows literally dynamited and mole drainage applied. That put an end to the lapwings, and most of the skylarks too. 'Progress' had arrived.

What happened to that farm was but a microcosm of what was happening everywhere at an accelerating rate from the 1960s. Alongside the intensification of agriculture, industrial development, housing and roads bisected the landscape and left fragments of nature in between. Population growth brought with it increasing consumption, and some of this has proved highly damaging. Prosperity came, built on a fossil fuel economy, bringing with it pesticides, plastics and petrochemicals.

The consumer boom drove a wedge between nature and people, and in a highly urbanised society fewer and fewer people experienced nature and, not surprisingly, cared less and less about it, except perhaps the bits they saw on television. There were exceptions and conservation successes, but the trend was abundantly clear. My grandfather's farm, with all its biodiversity and wonder, would now be regarded by most people as something that might appear in the fiction of H. E. Bates's *The Darling Buds of May*, or a nature reserve – an 'uneconomic' yet quaint relic of a more primitive time.

Many environmentalists had reached a point of despair by 2011 when the coalition government published its White Paper, 'The Natural Choice'.[2] The National Infrastructure Plan, the house-building targets, and the overwhelming emphasis on coping with the fallout from the financial crisis of 2007/08 set other priorities, with nature very low down the pecking order. A quick read of the 2011 White Paper confirms this: it is largely without content. With little to actually contribute to turning the tide on environmental damage, it took the classic *Yes Minister* approach: it set up a committee to think about it. This was the origin of the NCC.

Why, then, take on the chair of the NCC, apart from sentiment? Why try to work on the inside rather than protest on the outside? Or simply give up? There are several reasons. The past approaches have not worked, despite occasional Pyrrhic victories, and hence the NCC could hardly make matters worse. But the main reason was that I was optimistic that the NCC could really make a difference. For all the vacuity of the 2011 White Paper, there were two elements that could be built on: the clear aim to integrate the environment into the heart of the economy; and the overarching political commitment to leave the environment in a better state for future generations.[3]

Perhaps naively, I thought both worth taking seriously. I am an economist, not a scientist, and what interests me is the allocation of scarce resources. That is what economics is all about – making the best of what we have, and investing in the best possibilities to improve our lot. While humans have so far got by very well by pitting progress against nature, and especially in agriculture, this does not seem to me a good option going forward. The damage has gone too far, and our prosperity is likely to be compromised if we go on as we are. Put negatively, the environmental damage is going to make us all poorer. Put positively, we can be much better off if we protect and enhance our environment. It is not nature *versus* the economy; it is investing in nature to increase prosperity. My grandfather's farm might not have turned out to be so 'uneconomic' as was easily assumed in an agricultural context riven with perverse (uneconomic) subsidies.

This is beginning to be understood on the global stage, even if little is being done to address the problems. The climate change penny has dropped, and people are beginning to understand that the mass extinction under way is unlikely to have a happy ending for us. At the local level, the challenges of mental health, of obesity, and of the loss of beauty and wonder in our lives are getting more bandwidth. Added to this broad dawning of understanding, there are lots of specific costs to the pollution we are continuing to cause. Plastics are now headline news. Water companies have reached the end of the treatment road and recognise that it is cheaper to pay farmers not to pollute. The loss of soil is leaving farmers exposed. Poor air quality carries on killing people. None of this makes much sense even on narrow economic grounds.

Perhaps even more encouraging is the recognition that nature has value *in itself*, and not just for the ways in which it indirectly underpins our economy. Nature is *the* main organised interest in this country, way beyond football and trade unions. There are literally millions of members of nature organisations. Enjoying the great outdoors is the main leisure activity, whether it be a walk in the park or along the canal or riverbank, or visiting a National Park. People like nature and they care about it. They have what E. O. Wilson called 'biophilia'.[4] The BBC series *Blue Planet II* was watched by 17 million people in the UK. Gardening, that intimate engagement with plants and wildlife close up, is a national obsession. All of this great energy and enthusiasm can be harnessed to protect and enhance our natural capital.

Upon its creation as an independent advisory committee to the government, the NCC set about two main tasks: first, defining what natural capital is, identifying which bits matter most, and creating a conceptual framework around science and accounting; and second, putting the overarching generational objective into a practical and deliverable framework. Against the odds, and in the face of much scepticism from environmentalists, we did this.

The NCC has already achieved a great deal. It established natural capital as the way of thinking about our natural environment, as a hard and rigorous concept, and not simply another slogan that can mean anything to anyone according to their vested interests. Crucially, the NCC proposed a 25 Year Environment Plan, and this has now been published, with broad political support.[5] It remains to be seen whether it is fully implemented. But the signs are encouraging. Legislation is coming.

In the early years of the NCC I wrote *Natural Capital: Valuing the Planet* to provide an accessible account of what the concept means, how to measure it, and the broad policy implications that follow.[6] Now we have the 25 Year Environment Plan, I want to set out the prize that this could offer, and what the environment could look like mid-century. Most of all I want to show why this is in our economic interests, why it will enhance our prosperity, why we can be green and more prosperous at the same time, and why we don't have to accept as inevitable a world without our insects, our birds, our wild flowers and fungi, and our mammals, reptiles and aquatic life. We don't have to have the poverty of a silent spring and of monotone landscapes.

That is what this book is all about. It is deliberately broad in scope and content, providing a framework and illustrating what sort of outcomes there might be, and most importantly showing how we can not only deliver on all these individual projects, but also how they can be combined in a great national effort. Most of the examples are already well known to naturalists and ecologists. Many very good people have come up with myriad plans for their own patches. The aim here is to think big, to think about Britain as a whole, and to consider how it can be made to work better for the next generation. I make no pretence of having the scientific expertise to fill in the details – that is for others much better qualified than me. What I do lay claim to is showing how this all works economically and how to implement it.

There are those who decry economic approaches to the environment; who claim that they overlook the beauty and spiritual values and intrinsic nature. They make a good point when the target is a narrow and crude cost–benefit analysis. But they are wrong in two key ways: prosperity is a broad, not a narrow, concept; and the value to people of nature and all its beauty is every bit as important as the health benefits of clean water. The conventional metric of economic success, Gross Domestic Product (GDP), is a pathetically poor measure of what we get out of nature; and if conservation and enhancing the environment does not make economic sense then the evidence from the last two centuries at least is that it will be neglected. Sadly, appealing to intrinsic nature and spiritual values has not worked so far.

LIST OF ABBREVIATIONS

AI, artificial intelligence
AONB, Area of Outstanding Natural Beauty
BBOWT, Berkshire, Buckinghamshire and Oxfordshire Wildlife
   Trust
BEIS, Department for Business, Energy and Industrial
   Strategy
BSE, bovine spongiform encephalopathy
CAP, Common Agricultural Policy
CFP, Common Fisheries Policy
CLA, Country Land and Business Association
DDT, dichlorodiphenyltrichloroethane
DEFRA, Department for Environment, Food and Rural
   Affairs
EEC, European Economic Community
ELMS, Environmental Land Management Scheme
ESG, Environmental, Social and Governance
GDP, Gross Domestic Product
GM, genetically modified
GPS, global positioning system
HS2, a planned high-speed railway project
NCC, Natural Capital Committee
NFU, National Farmers' Union
NGO, non-governmental organisation
NRA, National Rivers Authority
OEP, Office for Environmental Protection
OFWAT, Water Services Regulation Authority
ONS, Office for National Statistics

RSPB, Royal Society for the Protection of Birds
SEPA, Scottish Environment Protection Agency
SSSI, Site of Special Scientific Interest
TB, tuberculosis

Introduction

OUR NATURAL CAPITAL INHERITANCE

Britain's natural environment is shaped by its past and its biodiversity. Few locations on the planet have had such a turbulent past visibly carved into the landscape. In the Hebrides, some of the oldest rock formations on the planet, dating back 3 billion years, have broken the backs of crofters for generations. The Carboniferous age left coal and limestone not only in the Pennines, but also in the pavements of our cities and the industrial landscape that coal enabled. In the Lake District, the glaciers' ghosts are all around, while the South Downs show the ripples of the distant collision of Italy and the African tectonic plate into Europe.

The more recent physical severing of the land link to the European Continent, as the rising waters in the North Sea broke through between what is now Calais and Dover, cut off the migration of terrestrial species. The Irish Sea opened up, cutting Britain off from Ireland too. The snakes never made it to Ireland as the ice melted. In a smaller Britain (and even smaller Ireland) without many migratory replacements, it made it all the easier to exterminate some of Britain's fauna. There are no bears, bison or wolves left. There is no land bridge to return on.

Being cut off has had its climatic effects too. Surrounded by sea, warmed by the Gulf Stream, Britain does not experience the deep freezes of Continental Europe. Its winters are comparatively mild. And its shorelines attract many winter visitors.

This is our inherited natural capital. It is what nature has endowed us with. Yet most of us are unaware of most of this for one very crucial reason. Our natural environment has been massively modified by humans over the last 8,000 years, and mostly in the last 200 years. Where once the Lewisian gneisses and the limestone and U-shaped glacial valleys would have been the hard constraints that people had to work with and around, now these hardly matter at all. We have so modified our world that, for many, nature appears hardly relevant. We may still rely on the land for agriculture, but agriculture is no longer the overwhelming driver of our economy. While, before 1800, the economy was mostly about farming and the trade in agricultural produce, with an empire built on food and crops, this is no longer the case. Farming now represents less than 1 per cent of GDP, and at least half of that is propped up by subsidies. A bad farming year no longer induces hardship and famine. In economic terms it just does not register. Fishing is now an even less consequential part of the economy, employing only a few thousand people.

Nature may not be man-made, but we as the ultimate eco-engineers increasingly shape it. Britain is a leading exemplar of the Anthropocene, a new geological age defined by human impact. There is nothing truly wild left. Much of the fauna has ingested plastic of one form or another, and the fashion for rewilding is best seen as just another form of eco-engineering, a switch from one man-made landscape to another. Wild, as a concept, has lost its practical meaning, even if its cultural power remains.

For all the angst this human transformation of nature causes environmentalists, it is not only a fact on the ground, it is also one that has proved remarkably successful from a human perspective. Over the last couple of centuries, we have broken out of thousands of years of virtually zero economic growth. The Industrial Revolution, and then the Age of Oil in the twentieth century, ushered in a wholly new historical experience. A cornucopia of new technologies raised the population out of poverty and into a material existence that has got better for each generation. Even two twentieth-century world wars could not dent the march of economic growth and prosperity. As nature declined, GDP kept going up.

For the bulk of the population, what was not to like about this? True, there might be fewer swallows and flycatchers, and the sound of the cuckoo might get rarer, but very many people have never seen or heard any of these anyway, and probably never will, except on a screen. They might watch the BBC's *Planet Earth* and be sad that so much is being lost (and angry about the pollution), but in our democracy access to housing and health services counts for much more. When it comes to actual spending, the environment comes way down the list of priorities, and where spending does come into play, it has often been to pay farmers to do sometimes dubious things to what is left of nature. If it goes ahead, the high-speed railway project, HS2, is likely to far exceed its original budget of £56 billion; the core annual budget for DEFRA (Department for Environment, Food and Rural Affairs) and its associated agencies – spent on foods and farming, rural interests, and the environment – is less than £3 billion. In other words, it would take more than 20 years of DEFRA environmental spending to exhaust the HS2 budget. Already, before even starting, HS2 has burnt through more than one year's total DEFRA spending.[1]

Faced with this onslaught, and the relative indifference of much of the population, those for whom nature really matters have been ploughing their own narrow furrow. Naturalists study in meticulous detail the declines of particular species and habitats. They band together to oppose building on sensitive sites, and they talk to each other in trusts, charities and campaign groups. It is largely a voluntary, amateur and charitable crusade, and it always has been. They feel under siege and try to hang on to what is left. They stand on the beach Canute-like and try to hold back the tide. They count the losses.

It has been a picture of comprehensive defeats, punctuated by the occasional success. These are often hugely symbolic, and where they focus on readily observable species, they garner a lot of support. Farmers may gripe about the impact on lambs, and grouse-shooters might complain about their precious game birds, but the recovery of the golden eagles, the reintroduction of sea eagles and red kites, and the sound of buzzards now over much more of the landscape are all hard-won victories for the small bands of environmental brothers and sisters.

The public can empathise with big birds of prey. They also see the merits of beavers and even lynx back in what passes as wilderness – the managed landscapes of Devon rivers and the Kielder Forest respectively. But what they do not see is the broader tide of destruction that tells a very different story – the insects that have gone; the soils that are depleted and soaked in chemicals; the rivers that are full of agricultural run-off; landscapes that are fragmented; wildlife corridors that are closed off; and the seas that are full of plastic.

In the agricultural battle against nature – to destroy everything that competes with the crops and livestock – agrichemical companies get better and better at doing their job. Now non-selective herbicides like glyphosate can kill off all the vegetation after crops have been harvested, ready for the next, and a host of genetically modified (GM) crops are specifically designed to be glyphosate-resistant. Neonicotinoids (new nicotine-like insecticides) are another chemical in the armoury, and the combination of glyphosate and neonicotinoids is now deemed by the farming lobby to be essential for maintaining crops and farm profitability, even as attempts to ban them gather momentum. Look closely at a crop of oilseed rape. Note the absence of insects and the brown, dead undergrowth. It is an example replicated for maize and other cereals, and is evident in the poverty of biodiversity in much 'improved grassland' too.

The technology is advancing at an ever-faster rate, as genetic engineering, precision applications and chemical advances get better at eliminating those 'enemies of agriculture'. The collateral damage is not something that matters much: the crop is what yields the profit. The farmer does not pay for the consequences to the pollinators, for the river life impacted by the chemical run-off, and for the 'silent spring' predicted so long ago by Rachel Carson.[2] She focused on DDT (the insecticide dichlorodiphenyl-trichloroethane), and her silence was about birds. She was right in her dire warnings, and on a scale she could not have imagined. It is a silence not just of birds, but insects, amphibians, reptiles and small mammals. The farmers' response is predictable: if they are to be persuaded to pollute less, they must be paid to do so. The pollution impacts are other people's problems.

Yet technology does not need to lead to an ever-greater destruction of nature. It is not the technology itself but some of its uses that is the problem. The tide of destruction is eating away at the very economic growth that has been bought partly at nature's expense. This recognition is also the consequence of new technologies. The extent of microplastics pollution and its consequences for marine life is now beginning to be understood because we can measure it. We have much better technologies to measure air quality, and medical advances allow us to see the link between the pollutants we put in the atmosphere and people dying from the consequences of inhaling dirty air. Just as it took several decades to prove the link between tobacco and lung cancer, so it has taken these new technologies to pinpoint the scale of the impacts on us of the destruction of nature. The impacts on mental health of a loss of nature are now becoming evident and measurable too.

In the past, diffuse pollution was often hard to pin on any one polluter. That is no longer the case. We can increasingly see down to the smallest areas who is doing what. The anonymity of the polluters that allowed them to deny specific responsibility is now being gradually blown away by GPS drones and other high-resolution mapping. While we might forgive those who know not what they are doing, it is much harder to forgive them when we and they do know. And they (the developers, the waste criminals, the packaging companies, manufacturers, service industries and farmers) do now know.

Over this century these impacts will play out and undermine our prosperity unless we actively head them off. The trade-off between more economic growth and less nature that has been the hallmark of human history so far is no longer benign. Destroying nature is beginning to eat into economic progress. Climate change is the obvious example, but in hogging the lime-light it has eclipsed the myriad other impacts. The costs of polluted waterways, of polluted seas, and of soil degradation, the loss of pollinators and the impacts on humanity of the loss of nature to anchor our lives by, relentlessly keep going up. One incremental loss after another may eventually trigger systemic consequences as key thresholds are crossed. As we create an increasingly brown world, we create a less prosperous one too.

Among the many reasons why nature matters, one is that it is part of the economy. It is a vital element of the resources that the economy allocates, and the economy can no longer get by with less and less of it. Technology brings with it an increased capacity for destruction, but it also brings routes to a better and greener world – and a more prosperous one too. We can have a greener and more prosperous country. Conserving (and enhancing) nature increases our prosperity. Economic growth, properly measured, is driven by developing human ingenuity, placing in our hands technological tools that previous generations lacked. It need not be in conflict with the environment. We can be green *and* prosperous.

There is no lack of ideas and projects to make this transition to a greener and more prosperous state. At the national level we know what to do. The river catchments need integrated management, reducing costs at the same time as improving outcomes. The way forward in agriculture is pretty clear too. Just stopping the perverse subsidies and enforcing the law would be a good start. Making polluters pay, and focusing subsidies on the public rather than private goods would greatly improve economic efficiency and transform the agricultural landscape, capture and retain carbon in the soils, and protect the pollinators. Enhancing rather than encroaching on the Green Belt would bring nature next to people, with big health and leisure benefits. Ensuring that there is net environmental gain from development would transform the impacts of new housing. Landscape-level wildlife corridors would give nature a chance to recover.[3] The railway lines, road verges and canal paths are obvious ways to build green corridors that millions of people can enjoy. Getting serious about Marine Protected Areas, including prohibiting fishing in them, would allow fish to bounce back and provide more sustainable stocks. Turning the coastal paths around Britain into major wildlife corridors would be good for people, tourism and nature.

At the local level, there is a cornucopia of economic and environmental opportunities. Initiatives here are often specific and highly focused, including restoring village greens; protecting and enhancing urban parks and green spaces; planting trees along the streets; getting children to participate in local environmental projects; enhancing the biodiversity of churchyards; cleaning up the litter on beaches; taking responsibility for local footpaths; and planting wild flowers in every garden.

In between the local and the national, the environmental organisations all have a checklist of preferred measures, from restoring particular habitats, to making road verges and railway lines havens for nature, to bringing back beavers. The general bodies have lots of great ideas for plants, birds and bugs. The national bodies, like the Wildlife Trusts, have plans for key habitats, from the Brecklands and managing the grazing now that the rabbit populations have collapsed,[4] to restoring wetlands in the Upper Thames like Otmoor by keeping the floodplains of the River Ray wetter,[5] creating and enhancing green spaces in cities, and managing and enhancing woodlands.

All of this makes very good economic sense. It can all be done. This is not only a prize worth fighting for because nature matters in its own right, but represents good mainstream economic policy. We can stop doing stupid things like wasting £2 billion per year on paying farmers to own land;[6] wasting money on cleaning up water for drinking, which should not have been polluted in the first place; wasting money on creating hard flood defences when natural flood management can be much cheaper; and wasting money on cutting down urban trees, as in Sheffield. All of this money can be much better spent on actually enhancing nature. This is why we should do it – because we should care about nature, and because we will collectively be better off as a result.

Part one of this book sets out these great opportunities – the prize. The prize is what nature could look like by the middle of this century. It is all about what we could have, what a greener Britain could look, smell and sound like. It identifies the value of halting the declines and moving towards a richer natural environment, and explains how we can all be more prosperous as a result.

Set against this great green prize is the brown alternative: what happens if we don't seize the opportunities, and what happens if we allow the destruction of nature to continue. The prize of sustainable economic growth is not the same thing as the fool's gold of GDP. It is all about harnessing technology and human ingenuity to make us all better off, by maintaining the natural environment and seizing the opportunities to get much more out of nature. The brown alternative of business-as-usual is literally a waste of money. It is also ugly and often nasty, as beauty is translated into lifeless monoculture fields and bleak housing estates. The sounds and sights of nature are diminished, replaced by ever-more noise and vistas of the man-made. The scale of the destruction of nature coming down the track if we do nothing should terrify everyone.

Part two is the practical part. It is all about how to secure the prize, what can be achieved, and why it is sensible economics to do so. Pragmatically, it involves five key areas of the natural environment: the river catchments (chapter 3); the agricultural land (chapter 4); the uplands (chapter 5); the coasts (chapter 6); and towns and cities (chapter 7). For each you are asked to imagine what an enhanced nature might look, sound and feel like. For each a practical framework to achieve the greener outcomes is provided, and why we will be more prosperous as a result is explained. To whet your appetite, and to move from the wonders of the imagination to reality, in every one of these areas a few practical examples of initiatives and projects already under way, and potential new ones, are identified.

It is all about river catchment system operators and ensuring the polluter and not the polluted pays; about a new agricultural policy based on public money for public goods, not perverse subsidies for owning land; protecting and enhancing the uplands for their beauty, health and leisure, and the biodiversity, and again not damaging them through perverse subsidies; opening up the coasts and coastal fringes for their full public potential, and stopping destructive fishing practices, most importantly in Marine Protected Areas; and greening towns and cities with trees, parks and Green Belts to improve air quality, childhood experiences, and health and leisure. What is not to like about this, not just from a conservationist's perspective, but also for the economic prosperity of Britain?

Part three turns to the money – how to pay for it all. Chapter 8 considers public goods, why they matter, why the market won't deliver them, and how they should be paid for. Chapter 9 looks at the polluter-pays principle, compensation and net environmental gain, and perverse subsidies. The place to start is with the sheer inefficiencies of current policies. An efficient economy is one that internalises all the costs and benefits of economic activities into prices and decision-making. In an efficient economy pollution is charged: it is inefficient not to charge for pollution, resulting in a lower level of economic prosperity. This is both 101 economics, and rarely followed. Not even carbon has a proper price yet. Making polluters pay is the single most radical and effective policy that could be adopted, for economic prosperity and for the environment. The British countryside would be radically different, and radically less polluted, were this simple economic principle adopted. It would not cost anything to the economy in aggregate, and at the same time it would yield lots of revenue, some of which could go to repairing past damage and enhancing our natural environment.

Instead of demanding more public expenditure, conservationists would be better advised to home in on this fundamental economic principle. Why should it be any more acceptable to pollute than to steal? Both take something from others that they do not pay for. Polluters steal people's health and they force the polluted to pay for what has been done to them. Expecting more public expenditure is something that might motivate protests and campaigns, but most conservationists know that if they wait for the Treasury to open its coffers they will be disappointed. While money is needed, getting to a more efficient baseline is an urgent necessity, making us all better off.

The converse of making polluters pay is to get rid of perverse subsidies. More than £3 billion is spent annually on subsidising Britain's farmers, £2 billion of which goes on paying them to own land. This absurd policy has been perverse not only for the natural environment but for the farmers themselves, inflating land prices. It came about as a result of trying to get away from the even more absurd consequences of subsidising the prices of agricultural products, resulting in the infamous European wine lakes and butter mountains, and the intensive sheep grazing that has done so much damage to the uplands. Getting rid of perverse subsidies would save a lot of money. It could be better spent. But even if it were just withdrawn, Britain would be greener.

Next comes the fraught subject of compensation for damage to the environment. While there are conservationists who believe that there should be no damage at all, the reality is that there will be. Faced with a population increasing by around 10 million by mid-century, and with more than 200,000 new houses per year for over a decade, more land will be concreted over. Add in the new roads, railways, and energy generation and networks to service all these extra people and the wider growing economy, and damage is inevitable.

Can this damage be squared with enhancing the natural environment? Only if there is compensation over and above the damage to the natural environment elsewhere. This is the *net environmental gain principle*: any damage must result in not just offsetting it, but by a positive margin. The positive margin is the precautionary principle in action.

Nowhere is it more important to apply these three principles than to climate change and net zero. But to meet the climate imperatives, and at the same time be mindful of the natural capital dimensions, requires us to integrate all of these into the wider environmental context. Net zero might be an environmental disaster if it means planting the wrong sorts of trees in the wrong places. Chapter 10 shows how the smart use of natural carbon sequestration and the creation of natural capital markets can bring the net zero agenda into this broader creation of a green and prosperous land. Markets help to ensure that polluters do in fact pay, public goods are efficiently provided, and that compensation is paid. Money is currently spent in silos, notably the agricultural subsidies. Winning the prize, and making sure we hang on to it, requires cementing the money into a comprehensive and integrated framework. Chapter 11 sets out how to do this within a Nature Fund. This acts a bit like sovereign wealth funds do for oil- and gas-producing countries. It should include the economic rents from these non-renewable activities like North Sea oil and gas production, mirroring other sovereign wealth funds, but it can also bring together the monies from pollution taxes and charges, from subsidies directed towards public goods and the net gain payments. Crucially it would be for nature, not general public spending.

The net gain principle set alongside the polluter-pays principle together ensure that there is enough money to pay for an enhanced natural environment. Add the money previously spent on perverse subsidies, instead going to environmental public goods, and the numbers stack up. We can have a greener and more prosperous Britain, without extra public expenditure.

A Nature Fund would need to be protected from the host of vested interests and from political opportunism. These interests are not just those opposed to the conservation of nature. They include nature organisations, which are notoriously fragmented and quarrelsome. With a pot of money, the Nature Fund will become a target for each and every interest to look after its own, whether specific species or specific habitats and locations. Its constitution matters, as do the rules of engagement. A Nature Fund should encourage cooperation and coordination for the prize as a whole.

The way to do this is to bring the opportunities together into an agreed practical plan to make it happen – a plan of how to integrate the myriad opportunities into coherent actions, and the necessary institutions to deliver this wonderful opportunity. It is about the full delivery, in spirit and letter, of the 25 Year Environment Plan published in 2018.[7] Some will say that this is too radical, but the real radicalism is in doing nothing, in allowing the business-as-usual to continue. This radically worsens the opportunities of the next generation, who will not only be deprived of swallows and flycatchers but, in the process of the continued destruction of nature, find the basic necessities of their lives increasingly compromised.

The 25 Year Environment Plan needs to integrate the principles behind it into the fabric of the economy and government. These are the two aims of the earlier 2011 White paper, 'The Natural Choice':[8] putting the environment at the core of the economy; and leaving the natural environment in a better state for the next generation. Although much may be achieved immediately and a number of reforms will help us along this path, to stand the test of economic crises and recessions and the sheer power of the hostile lobbyists, there needs to be an overarching legal and constitutional framework. As with climate change, politicians are good at the rhetoric, and they may well mean what they say, but permanently delivering it requires something more. The 2008 Climate Change Act changed the game. It is very hard to get out of its targets and the carbon budgets. We need something similar, a proper Nature Act that enshrines the principles in the 2011 White Paper and the 25 Year Environment Plan.

There is a choice: we can impoverish ourselves by continuing down the current path, or we can have a greener and more prosperous land, and one that is pleasanter too. The book concludes with this choice.

PART ONE

The Prize and the Risks

1

THE PRIZE

Imagine what our natural environment could look like in 25 years. Imagine bright colourful hay meadows full of wild flowers, bird-song and butterflies. Imagine cities with green trees along the streets, green parks and green Green Belts. Imagine the sounds of uplands, of golden plovers and curlews. Imagine beaches without plastic, and the loud noise of winter waders in the estuaries and marshes. Imagine wildlife corridors all around the coastline and across the land and along the rivers, roads, railways and canals. Imagine a marine world full once again of fish and free from the harrowing of the seabed by trawling. Imagine colour and beauty restored to the landscape. Wouldn't it be wonderful?

This prize is not just a dream. It is perfectly practical and achievable, within our reach, and it would greatly enhance our lives and our economy. We don't have to 'go back to nature', become austere and abandon capitalism. None of that is likely to happen anyway. Instead we need to embrace the most important type of capital: natural capital – the stuff nature gives us for free. We would be much more prosperous as a result. To make this possible, stand back and think big.

The prize comprises two parts: holding the line against further deterioration of existing natural capital; and creating and enhancing more of it. That is what leaving the environment in a better state for the next generation means. Not to go down this path is to court a significant loss of prosperity and make the next generation worse off. The question is just how much worse off. This chapter is about that prize; the next is about what happens if we don't halt the destruction.

No more declines

The natural capital that really matters is the renewables – the stuff that nature keeps on giving us for free for ever, provided we don't deplete it below a threshold so it cannot continue to deliver its free bounty. Nature at threshold risk is the stuff of red lists and endangered species, and some of it is well known. To hold the line means that the sounds of cuckoos and turtle doves and nightingales and corncrakes are going to continue – for ever. But it also means protecting those renewables that are less obvious to the casual eye, and those assets we take for granted but that are actually in considerable danger. It is about the things we no longer see so often, like insects and butterflies, and about the once-common that is slipping from our grasp. How many people realise that the rabbits, which were ubiquitous, have now almost vanished from some areas? That the hares may follow? And how many have failed to notice that the swallows are harder to sight now? It means fertile and productive soils, lots of pollinators, clean water and clean air, and natural flood defences too. These rely on a host of creatures at the more microscopic level, and beneath the soils and under water.

The focus is often on the more iconic species at risk, since these are usually easy to measure and easy to design conservation strategies for. In almost every case, what is required is a habitat within which they can thrive, and an end to persecution. Species protection is all about these underlying critical natural infrastructures, which are every bit as important as man-made infrastructures in energy and transport. Although it might not actually matter greatly in the scheme of things if there are no bitterns or ospreys, it would matter if the reed bed ecosystems are gone and there is more eutrophication of rivers and lakes. Protecting particular species on the brink of their thresholds is typically good conservation generally, and the result is all sorts of other species benefits.[1]

Holding the line is not straightforward for the obvious reason that we are going backwards. Simply stopping more direct damage would not stabilise the natural environment. It is clearly on a downward path, notwithstanding a host of projects to turn things around in specific areas and for specific species. So much damage has been done over the last half-century that resilience is low. Even where there are attempts to halt the declines, as in the case of river quality, the cumulative damage means the under-lying conditions could continue to worsen. In the case of rivers, the fly life continues to decline and groundwater pollution will worsen even if the polluting stops now. It is not enough to cease further damage. We need to stop the slide through remedial actions – the natural capital maintenance we should have done long ago.

There are various ways of going about this. We could start at the species end or we could start at the habitat and ecosystem end. In practice it will be both. This book looks in detail at each of the main habitats – the river catchments, the landscapes and agriculture, the uplands, the coasts and the urban countryside. But first let's just take a preliminary look at each to get a handle on the overall prize.

Stopping the environmental damage in river catchments starts with the chemical inputs into rivers and the silting from soil erosion. As urban centres developed and the Industrial Revolution got going, rivers were treated as sewers. The Great Stink of London in July and August 1858 is but one example of what was going on in all the great rivers that had the misfortune to flow through towns and cities. The Taff in Wales and the Mersey in northwest England died because of mining and industrial effluent.

Both of these forms of gross pollution have been tackled at source, but sewage still ends up in rivers and industrial pollution remains in some pockets. The river sediments contain lots of heavy metals, and many estuaries – like the Thames – have serious residuals. Dredging to develop the new Thames Gateway container port revealed its scale. Halting the decline means not only stopping further pollution, but also dealing with the continued and long-lasting damage it has caused. We have to deal with not only our mess, but that of previous generations too.

When it comes to sewerage, existing systems continue to over-flow in heavy rain through the storm overflows. Stopping the declines means increasing the capacity to contain sewage and prevent overflows. The Thames Tideway aims to do just that, carrying it all to the east of London to the Beckton Sewage Treatment Works. What happens there continues to be a problem, and the estuary remains the final repository. For many sewerage works, it means going down the natural capital route with reed beds and other natural options, and dealing with the sewage at source too. This is both cost-reducing, so our water bills don't go up, and it creates great habitats for birds, insects, amphibians and aquatic life. The phosphates the water-treatment works pump out into the rivers need to be reduced, partly by stopping them at source from getting into the river in the first place, and partly by better treatment.

The decline of heavy industry and the development of sewerage systems have put a stop to some of the grossest pollu-tion, but river pollution is a moving target. Since the middle of the twentieth century, intensive and agrichemical agriculture has done immense damage. Stopping the further declines here means the creation of significant buffers between the rivers and the arable fields, limiting fertilisers near rivers, putting an end to maize and cereal crops close to rivers to stop the silting, and seriously controlling the application of pesticides and herbicides. It means stopping the treatment of sheep with chemicals near rivers upstream, and it means strict controls of slurry storage to prevent it ending up in the rivers. All are economically good things to do anyway, and this prize will make all our rivers assets rather than liabilities.

Agricultural impacts on the land continue the degradation of the environment more generally, perversely incentivised by the subsidy regime. The decline in insect life is one of the major impacts, and this has contributed to the falling populations of farmland birds. The soils are often in a poor state and are in many areas deteriorating, and this is bad for farming productivity. Hedgerows and field boundaries do not look after themselves. Doing nothing allows the degradation to go on. Stopping the further damage in agriculture requires quite radical surgery. Fortunately, in such heavily subsidised industries the costs of changing practices are low, and especially so when compared with the benefits. Arguably, these improvements can be made and less public money can be spent – much more for less. The prize is a healthier and more vibrant farmed landscape at lower cost, and hence we will be doubly better off as a result.

Because they are harder to plough up, because the weather is less benign to farming, and because the soils are poorer and thinner, the uplands often remain the last bastions of once-widespread wildlife. Once-common lowland birds, like red kites and even house sparrows, have been pushed back to the uplands, back behind the natural constraints that limit intensive farming. Unfortunately, even though upland agriculture is barely, if at all, economic, it has been environmentally damaging. This can and has to stop. Intensive sheep grazing has seriously damaged much of the remaining habitats, stripping the vegetation and exposing peat to the elements. Stopping further damage means reducing sheep intensity, as well as preventing slurry, sheep-dip and other pollutants from entering the rivers. Because the sheep are of very little economic value, the costs of this surgery are negligible. Sheep sale value minus all the various subsidies equals zero, or even less than zero. There is economic gain to be made here.

Stopping the declines along our coasts again comes back in part to agriculture. Most environmental things do. It requires dealing with the run-off of fertilisers, phosphates, pesticides and herbicides, and also dealing with the declines caused by over-fishing, by fishing that damages the seabed, and by a wide range of pollution. As with farming, subsidies and especially regulation are an important part of the current system, and the economic value of Britain's fishing catch, net of supports, is very low. In many areas the obvious answer is simply to ban fishing in exclusion zones. This will mean more fish and a larger sustainable catch than that provided in a business-as-usual scenario. In other areas it needs sustainable fishing plans, which are properly enforced, so that stocks can recover.

In the emerging aquaculture industries, the initial 'wild west' of the salmon farms has had serious environmental costs that the producers first denied, and still neither fully pay for nor take sufficient mitigating action against. Indeed, in the west of Scotland this economically inefficient damage is accelerating. Stopping the further damage means sustainable regulations and making the polluters pay. This is all the more important as aquaculture in general is growing and can make a greater contribution to food production over the coming decades, provided the environmental impacts are taken fully into account.

In the urban areas, halting the declines means stopping the further erosion and loss of green spaces, and the chipping-away and degradation of public parks and gardens. It means preventing further loss of urban trees, most notoriously exemplified by Sheffield City Council cutting down thousands of mature trees in the name of utility works. The lack of a full statutory duty to preserve urban green spaces is a serious threat, as councils struggle to pay for social care and other increasing demands on their budgets. Green streets and green parks have very large economic benefits.

What all these measures, which will be elaborated on in subsequent chapters, have in common is that they are all ways of increasing prosperity *immediately*. They are all sensible economic policies, as well as making a better and greener world. Improving rivers improves our drinking water, and stopping further pollution reduces our water bills since less treatment is needed. Indeed, so great are the economic benefits that some water companies are already paying farmers not to pollute, and to keep the ground covered with crops and grass over winter. Sewage in the river from overflows directly affects people's welfare. It is not only a health hazard, it deters people from the riverbanks, from exercise and therefore from the health and well-being benefits.

Measures to clean up agricultural pollution would result in seriously large economic gains. Much of the pollution is encouraged and paid for by us as taxpayers. It is heavily subsidised and, as we shall see in chapter 4, reforming agricultural policies to ensure that subsidies are only for the provision of public goods is sound economics. When it comes to the uplands, the subsidy element becomes overwhelming. We pay taxes to subsidise the overgrazing of sheep that are simply not economic. We even subsidise sheep that get live-exported to Europe, with all the animal welfare consequences that such transportation brings. Stopping the damage by reducing grazing intensity would increase the economic value of the uplands, and if the subsidies went towards public goods instead, the economic prosperity of the hill farmers would improve. They are trapped in a system that keeps many of them both poor and marginal.

Stopping overfishing, particularly of shellfish, around our coasts improves the value of the fisheries, and helps to solve the classic free-rider problem that the 'tragedy of the commons' reflects.[2] It will increase fish stocks generally inside and outside the protected areas. Unregulated fishing is a disaster for the industry and the public and, as with the upland farmers, inshore-water fishers do not come off well. They are at the economic margins. The economic prosperity of coastal communities is much more about services, tourism and amenities, and these in turn improve the health of the population. But even where it is about catching fish, protected areas excluding fishing is in their interests.

Stopping the environmental decline in cities is an economic no-brainer. The health benefits of access to green space are well documented. It bears directly on mental health, on the quality of the air and hence on limiting respiratory diseases, and it increases physical activity and therefore helps to fight obesity. The costs of these diseases and the bad health outcomes are considerable; the costs of holding on to green spaces is trivial in comparison.

No more declines means more economic value – now. In narrow terms, it is worth achieving. Prosperity goes up if we halt the damage. Yet it is not going to happen on its own. The reason why we can go on depleting the natural environment is that there is little pressure to pay for its capital maintenance. Where physical infrastructure is concerned, it is obvious that failure to carry out the necessary maintenance is economically costly. The potholes in the roads not only cause damage to cars and bikes, they undermine the roads themselves. Eventually they have to be fixed, and because the early damage is often left unchecked, the eventual repair costs escalate. Similar issues arise with the maintenance of water pipes, sewage-treatment works, railway lines and signalling, and electricity distribution cables.

Exactly the same economic logic applies to the natural environment. Failure to maintain natural capital stores up problems for the future, and stores up extra costs too. We can pretend, like the company that allows its buildings and machines to deteriorate and reports inflated profits as a result, that we can spend the gross surpluses, when economics tells us we should do our accounting properly, and set aside the costs of the maintenance. It is simple: not to do proper capital maintenance is to live beyond our means, and store up trouble, leading to lower living standards for the future. This is precisely what we have been doing: living off nature's bounty without recognising the thresholds and safe limits.

It works for a while. Sometimes it works for a long time. But eventually it catches up with us. The farmers who fail to take care of their soils will run into trouble eventually. The Fens will one day cease to deliver,[3] just as swathes of the badlands in the USA did in the 1930s, and China's expanding deserts are today. The loss of pollinators will cost farmers dear, and the loss of the urban parks is already having a detrimental impact on health. Just because we do not account for these costs properly does not mean they are going to go away.

The first part of the prize – no more declines – is best seen as basic housekeeping. It will save us from a lot of costs later and provide natural capital to future generations that is at least as good as we inherited ourselves. This book sets out the sorts of measures necessary to achieve this – all practical and economic.

Enhancements

The gains from stopping the declines pale almost into insignificance when compared with the gains from enhancing the natural environment – not just holding the line, but improving our ecosystems across the board. This is the real prize for the next generation.

If you ask what the main physical infrastructure networks of Britain will look like in 2050, in every case the answer is both different and much enhanced compared with now. Take the electricity system. By 2050 it will be digitalised and decentralised, and linked into the transport system and electric cars. It will be transformed from the passive, centrally controlled electricity grid of today. Take communications. By 2050 it will all be fibre; we can expect to have massively enhanced 5G mobile and fibre networks. Train networks will be more integrated at the international level, and there may be High Speed 2 (HS2), Crossrail 2 and full electrification, whether overhead or with batteries. Roads will be intelligent digital highways. We have a National Infrastructure Commission to look into all this and come up with a 30-year plan to present to each parliament.[4]

When it comes to the natural environment – the critical infrastructure on which all else depends – this sort of ambition is largely absent. There are two possible reasons. First, it might be widely assumed that there is not much economic gain from an ambitious transformation. Second, the ambition itself might be thought to be beyond our capabilities. People have lowered their sights: they simply expect it all to get worse, and at best not to get much worse.

Both of these are wrong. The economic gains from enhancing the natural infrastructure are considerable, and may be greater than some of those projected for physical infrastructures. A major enhancement is well within our grasp, and the costs are not that great in getting there, especially when compared with the costs of some of the physical infrastructure ambitions described above. If, for example, HS2 were to cost in excess of £56 billion and Crossrail 2, say, £25 billion, think what more than £80 billion of environmental enhancements might look like in comparison. Add in some all-too-predictable cost overruns and these two projects will cost well over £100 billion. It is unlikely that the gains from the environmental enhancements would be less than those claimed for HS2 and Crossrail. It is not just a failure of imagination that holds us back, but also a basic failure to do the economics properly.

Part three of this book tackles the economics head-on, showing why the benefits exceed the costs, and in many cases way beyond the narrow margin for HS2. The trick turns out to be all about how to measure economic prosperity properly. Once the costs are seen to be less than the benefits, the funding and financial frameworks can and should fall into place.

But before we get into the economics, let's raise our eyes to the prize itself: what our natural environment could look like in 2050. As with the measures necessary to halt the declines, more of the detail is provided in subsequent chapters; here we take a high-level look at the opportunities.

There are two ways of going about this exercise. The first is to focus on the outputs. This looks at what we can expect to get out of the natural environment in the future. The second is to look at the underlying state of the assets, and the opportunities these assets provide for future generations. The first is very much about utility and hence is utilitarian; the second is about the capabilities and choices people will have about how they choose to live their lives. It is therefore a distinction between direct and narrow benefits and the broader opportunities natural capital offers to future generations.

The two are of course related. You need the natural assets to get the utility; the ecosystem services and the natural assets that are going to be given priority are those that have the greatest direct benefit to people. The differences come in the practicalities as much as the philosophy. Natural assets come in systems, not discrete lumps, and hence mapping the outputs onto the assets is far from straightforward.

Let's take a look at the two approaches and see how the prize might be defined. Taking the outputs approach, there are some obvious direct-benefit prizes. In 2050 we can have much cleaner air. Children can grow up in cities without clogging up their lungs with particulates. By 2050 the air should be 'clean'. Drinking water could be of better quality, drawn from cleaner rivers and aquifers. There should be increasingly diverse plant and animal populations. Wildlife should be thriving. People should get more out of nature, and benefit from landscapes that are more beautiful. These are all ambitions included in the 25 Year Environment Plan.[5]

The great advantage of starting with the high-level outputs is that they are measurable. The content of air in different locations can be directly measured. The health outcomes can be measured too. The quality of drinking water is measured all the time already, and we can measure whether it is getting better. The number and diversity of plants and animals can be measured too. How many people spend how much time doing what in nature is measurable. We can also measure mental health and obesity and relate all these to the time spent with and experience of nature (or the lack of it).

These outputs are every bit as measurable as the time saved by HS2 or Crossrail; by the speed of internet access, and the use time people get out of the internet; by the impacts on carbon emissions of renewable energy technologies; by the convenience and use of electric car charging and other outputs from physical infrastructures. Natural capital infrastructure is on an empirical par with physical infrastructure.

The fact that these things can be measured gives the 25 Year Environment Plan traction. Governments can be held to account for identified failures. There may be many environmentalists who claim that we cannot measure the beauty and wonder of nature, or the spiritual values and so on. They are right. But the trouble is that this does not get us very far. The Treasury can easily wriggle its way out of the capital maintenance and investment in the enhancements. Whether the benefits of the prize can all be measured or not, the fact remains that the costs can, so there is no avoiding the question of how much should be spent on the various competing outcomes and ends. There is a good reason why the Treasury thinks in numbers.

In narrow utility terms the value of these prizes can be assessed and compared with the value from investing in other infrastructures in the economy. Just as the value of HS2 depends on the other infrastructures that connect with it and support it, so too on the environmental side. HS2 will not work unless other bits of the road, railway and airport transport networks interconnect with it, and unless it has fast broadband fibre to facilitate its operations. Similarly, clean water depends on what happens in river catchments and in agriculture. The specific projects get their economic rationale from the coexistence and interaction of the rest of the networks. Ultimately, none of them works unless there is a natural environment to support them.

This creates a big problem for the application of crude cost–benefit analysis. Take HS2. It makes little sense to calculate the costs and benefits of the link between Birmingham and London without including the rest of the high-speed rail network to the north. Similarly, whether or not HS2 is connected to HS1, and hence the main European cities, makes a big difference to the potential benefits in the cost–benefit calculation.[6]

Carried across to the natural environment, these problems arise because the environment comes in ecosystems. Everything is connected to everything else. Hence the outputs depend on the overall environmental context. This means that achieving these headline outputs in 2050 will require attention to be paid directly to the underlying environmental infrastructures – to the state of the catchments, the farmed land, the uplands, the coasts and the urban countrysides. Even taking these separately is a questionable heuristic, since the catchments depend on the uplands *and* the farmed land, and the costs depend on what happens in the rivers *and* the estuary *and* coastal towns and cities.

We have to start somewhere, and the pragmatic approach is to divide things up into our five categories, while always accepting that it is going to be at best a roughly right answer.

The attention to the systems leads into the second perspective, starting with the natural capital assets, and setting the prize as having these in much better shape by 2050, rather than trying to calculate the utilities of each bit. Natural capital is about making sure that the next generation has these assets, so they can choose how they want to live. They can do their own utility calculations: it is not for us to prejudge these.

Taking each of our five categories in turn, again as a preview of what follows in the book, the catchments natural capital in 2050 could be much enhanced by looking to natural capital solutions to both river quality and flood prevention. Many rivers are a sad shadow of what they were before they were tamed. Since the Middle Ages and sometimes even earlier, they have been straightened out and controlled for energy through weirs and hard physical flood barriers.[7] The results are not only far from pretty, they are often inefficient. Imagine a river catchment where the upstream is allowed to meander, creating oxbow lakes and slowing down its flows. Imagine trees taking up more of the shock of heavy rain. Imagine reinstating flood meadows to hold the water in winter.

These natural capital measures would restore and rebuild what has been lost, improve flood defences and avoid the costs of more hard concrete. This is something that can start now. The Cumbria catchment has been designated as a pioneer for the natural capital approach, and has already identified lots of opportunities. The new concrete canal being built around Oxford might not be needed, or could be constructed at a reduced scale, were money instead spent upstream on trees, meadows and better land management.[8]

Natural capital approaches would greatly contribute to biodiversity outcomes, and these in turn would open up additional health and recreational benefits to people. Imagine the wonders that restored water meadows might bring in snake's head fritillaries, cowslips, barn owns, curlews, redshanks and lapwings. All of this is possible not only in the Upper Thames, but throughout our river catchments, and it is much more cost-effective even in the narrow flood defence context. The Severn lends itself to a similar approach, as does the Ouse above Pickering.[9] The more pertinent question is whether there are any major river catchments where it *would not* be a sensible approach to prefer major enhancements to the natural environment at lower cost and with less emphasis on the alternative hard solutions.

Consider the cost–benefit comparison between all that concrete and natural capital approaches. The reintroduction of beavers could help slow down flows. Imagine if all of the main river catchments had thriving beaver populations in their upper river stretches. Imagine rivers as green corridors through towns and cities.

Turning to the broader landscape and agriculture, imagine if the monochrome fields were replaced with an enhanced patchwork quilt of many colours. Imagine if the harsh vivid green of 'improved grassland' were replaced by the complexity of shades of green that unimproved land still hangs on to. Imagine if rye grass were not the only species, but rather that sweet vernal grass, Yorkshire fog, crested dogstail and other grasses were once again peppered across our landscape. Imagine if the countryside were colourful again, and the simple delights this world has were set against the stresses of everyday life. Imagine if the hedgerows were put back, and the dry-stone walls repaired. Imagine if beauty was brought back into the landscape – and most of the landscape, not just the protected areas.

To do this requires a wholesale reconfiguration of agricultural policy. The vested interests would no doubt protest that all of the above is just a romantic ideal, and a dangerous one at that. They would point to the need to produce food, and even argue that food security is of overriding importance. They would want to claim that this ideal is not remotely realistic. But they would be wrong. For what the vested interests cannot claim is that current agricultural policy is remotely economic, or even that it focuses on the core food products or provides for food security. The fact is that it isn't economic. It is chronically inefficient, greatly distorting production. It is hard to think how the economic costs of the current agricultural systems could be more adverse. The vested interests would probably not want to admit that the net economic value of agriculture as it is – the agriculture that has produced the monochrome landscapes, destroyed insect life and led to great declines of farmland birds – is in fact approximately zero.

In chapter 4 the startling arithmetic will be set out, and it is this that needs to be compared with the prize of the colourful, beautiful, vibrant and noisy landscape we could have instead, with all the economic benefits it would bring.

The prize would have pay-offs beyond the landscape and biodiversity. The river catchments cannot live up to their potential, and hence their part of the prize, without dealing with the agricultural pollution and silt. The coasts cannot escape the plumes of algae from river mouths. That is why it all keeps coming back to agriculture: it is the key to an enhanced environment. Without a radical change the ambitions will be disappointed. The fact that it makes economic sense to do this brings the prize within our grasp.

Of all the natural capital that agriculture relies upon, soil plays a central role. Even holding the line here is a big ask. The Fenlands will carry on losing soil for a long time to come.[10] The prize is a healthy soil. Soil, like many marine habitats, may be largely out of sight, but it contains a mass of biodiversity, and it is the foundation of the food chains of almost everything else. The bacteria and fungi make plant growth possible. It harbours invertebrates and insect larvae. The prize of healthy soil is an economic necessity if farming is to continue, and if the broader biodiversity is to thrive. Even in the narrow context of carbon emissions the soil is critical. Improving the carbon content, which farmers have been depleting, increases the soil's ability to support crops and helps in the battle against climate change. Economically it is yet another no-brainer.

Many of our uplands are a shadow of what they once were. To the untutored eye the rolling hills signify 'wildness' and 'raw nature' – they are anything but. These are managed landscapes, and they have been managed with specific interests in mind. These are mainly extensive agriculture and game in a mix of small marginal farms and large private estates. Our uplands are overgrazed by sheep and manicured for the shooting fraternity. Imagine if the heather moors were managed not just for grouse and deer, but also for the wider public benefit. Imagine if the hen harriers were not persecuted, so people could watch the male bird pass its prey in mid-air to the female, and watch as the birds hunt low over the land. Imagine if the wild flowers were given a chance by much reducing the uneconomic sheep densities. Imagine if deciduous trees thrived alongside the Scots pines and the larches, and dark and dense timber forests were diversified.

The costs of transforming our uplands are even lower than for the lowlands. Reducing grazing densities saves money. For the deer-stalking, the grouse and pheasant shoots, the problems are rather different. They are about incorporating the costs these activities give rise to, reducing the deer numbers and the destruction they cause, regulating the deposits of lead shot and the poor management of feed for the game birds, and enforcing the law. As so often happens when businesses do not pay for the pollution and environmental damage they cause, they get over-extended. Making the polluters pay would improve the management of the uplands. Making those who break the law face the consequences and pay the proper costs for crimes would be a big win for the economy and the overall economic prosperity of the uplands.

When it comes to the coasts, we are already on the way to opening up a path around the whole of England. Imagine what will have been achieved when this is finally in place. Imagine the economic gains it will bring to those whose health and well-being benefit, and to the tourist industry (which is much more economically significant than agriculture and without large subsidies). Imagine if the beaches were cleared of all their plastic rubbish; if the fish and the seabirds had enough to feed on; if fishing were managed for the long term; and if the cold-water corals and the underwater wonders were allowed to return to where they were before fish farms polluted them and trawling and dredging scoured them away. Imagine if there were no longer any need for Surfers Against Sewage, and it was no longer possible to see the algae plume from the Thames right out into the North Sea (joining the plume from the Rhine).

It might even be possible to make an economic merit out of cleaning up the beaches. It could be a form of national service, or a task taken on by local communities and local schools. They could take ownership of keeping their patch of the coastline clean, and in the process gain from the community involvement and mental health benefits – as well as the exercise it would involve. Many economic activities are outside the formal measured GDP, but they matter for prosperity.

Finally, imagine what our towns and cities could be like if we invested in their green infrastructure. Imagine how much healthier and more vibrant they might be. Imagine if every child had access to a green space within a few hundred metres of their home. Imagine if today's developers actually built houses with proper back gardens. Imagine allotments for many more people, green roofs and green walls, and new and enlarged parks. Imagine if the parks were vibrant healthy environments, with lots of biodiversity, instead of the mown monochrome lawns. Imagine if plants were encouraged alongside railway lines, road verges and urban canals, and trees planted in every street. Imagine if nature's much more messy beauty replaced the ugliness and sterility that straight lines and tidiness bring.

Britain's gardens comprise an area the size of the Norfolk Broads, plus Exmoor, plus Dartmoor, plus the Lake District. Acres of Britain are gardens and they have an enormous potential as wildlife havens.[11] Indeed, they already are: gardens can be much more biodiverse than intensive agricultural land. Imagine if every garden had a small pond and a patch of wild flowers, besides the conventional palette of garden plants, fruits and vegetables. Imagine if all of these were chemical-free. This would be a great refuge for bumblebees and honey bees, lacewings and spotted flycatchers, swallows, frogs, newts and toads, and hedgehogs too. It would also bring many who have nature-deprived lives, and especially children, face to face with the beauty of nature. They might even dig up their concrete driveways and allow water to be absorbed by the ground, reducing flooding and creating sustainable drainage.

Putting all this together would create much greater genuine prosperity. It would be the right thing to do, because it would be both the economic thing to do and, in the process, would deliver the environment that many environmentalists who reject economic approaches would want too. It would also be ethically right, fulfilling our duty as stewards of the natural environment on behalf of future generations. There would be hen harriers and golden plovers and curlews and flycatchers, and there would be all sorts of plants, insects and other fauna.

It would not be a wild world, and it certainly would not be a 're-wilded' world. It would be every bit as managed as it is today. Even those areas left aside would be deliberately chosen for intentional neglect. Deer would be culled, hedges would be reinstated and managed, rivers would be built around natural capital deliberately put in place, and city streets would be planted with trees. The prize is not an abandonment of the land to the 'forces of nature', but the replacement of a badly managed natural environment with a much better managed one. We have witnessed the disastrous consequences for people of taking the nature out of their lives, and we can redress this, but we cannot take the people out of nature.

Wouldn't it be wonderful if this was what we could pass on to the next generation?

2

BUSINESS-AS-USUAL

Imagine waking up in May 2050. You might remember the May mornings before 2020. This was a time of bright yellow oilseed rape fields. There were still some swallows, a few swifts and the occasional cuckoo. In the right place you might have heard a curlew. If you were really lucky you might have seen a spotted flycatcher. In 2050 it will be very different if we go on as we are. By then, all these birds will be rarities. There will be even fewer insects, agriculture will be more intensive and the fields barren of anything but the chosen crop.

There will be 5 million more houses, and little left of the Green Belt, except perhaps in name. Lots more roads, railway lines, solar panels and wind turbines will have industrialised the countryside. There will be very few wild salmon left, but lots of fish farms and more Trump-style golf courses. Nature will be ever-more confined to reserved areas – like zoos in an increasingly urban and industrial landscape.

There will be compensations. You will have communications technologies that cannot even be imagined today, just as I have an iPhone now, which was unimaginable a couple of decades ago. Everything will be digital, with robots, 3D printing and artificial intelligence (AI) fulfilling many of your needs. You will know your genome, and have medical treatments available to you that again are hard to imagine now.

Some economists continue to think that the natural capital you will have lost is a price worth paying for all these new benefits. But much of this can't be simply substituted, because natural capital is not like that, open to a marginal loss here and a marginal loss there. Nature isn't marginal, and it does not come in discrete bits to trade off against discrete bits of man-made and human capital. Worse still, it might bite back: you may know your genome, but you might not have any antibiotics that work.

This is the silent, grey and impoverished natural world we could leave to the next generation. It is what it might look like if we don't act now, and confront the stark reality that we face if current trends continue. We cannot and should not shy away from thinking through what will happen if we carry on damaging nature and allowing our stock of natural capital to continue to decline. It is not just about the loss of nature, and all the spiritual and emotional underpinnings to what makes us fully human, but about our economic prosperity, which depends on nature and natural capital. The land would be a dull, brown and unprosperous land – and a lot less appealing to share pictures of on whatever replaces Instagram by then. We really would need a virtual and screen-based reality to console ourselves with.

Being brown, not green, means a lower level of sustainable economic growth, and perhaps even no growth at all. It is against this background that the case for nature is to be seen as a great opportunity to make us all better off: better off in a narrow economic sense, as well as a wider sense. May 2050 could be noisier and more vibrant and exciting than May 2020, and more prosperous too. But not unless we make this happen.

A damaged inheritance

The decline of nature in Britain has been extensively documented by some of the world's best naturalists. There are books about the decline of particular species, and studies and reports on the more general declines of life on farmland, uplands and in the soils. Even where things appear to have got better, as with water and urban air quality, some of this is not what it seems.[1]

Much of this evidence is specific to particular species and habitats, and it is supplemented by anecdotes and personal memories, and in novels and films. It is a spiritual and aesthetic loss, as well as a scientific one. Laurie Lee's world of *Cider with Rosie* in the Slad Valley in Gloucester, Flora Thompson's *Lark Rise to Candleford*, and the novels of Thomas Hardy describe a landscape full of colour and variety, with wild flowers, songbirds and elements that could almost be called wild, even though they are all man-made.[2] The early landscape painters and the Romantics eulogised nature and developed concepts of the ideal landscape and the picturesque, and Wordsworth underscores the special powers of the natural world to heal our minds – a point made repeatedly down the ages.

This art and literature, often dismissed as 'romantic', has a hard scientific foundation. Over the twentieth century the colour and vitality of the British landscape has been replaced by monotones of green, yellow and brown. There are dark and dense conifer forests, vivid green fertilised fields of grass, and the yellow and brown of cereal landscapes. The people have gone too: farmland, which makes up 70 per cent of the country, is now managed largely by fertilisers, agrichemicals and machines, and in time it might be autonomously farmed by robots. To the silent spring of the birds has been added the silence of people.

It has not all been downhill. The pea soup fogs have gone from the cities and the gross pollution of the mid-twentieth century has been gradually unwound. There are few rivers now that could be called biologically dead, as the Mersey and even parts of the Thames have been until relatively recently. Sewage is no longer dumped at sea, and DDT has been banned.

Some species have recovered, and these are often trumpeted as 'successes'. The peregrine falcon is becoming quite common again (albeit as much in cities as in the uplands where illegal persecution remains); the buzzard has broken out of its south-western enclaves; and the odd salmon has even made it up the Thames. The red kite is back in the Chilterns and mid-Wales, and is spreading fast. The cirl bunting has been pulled back from the brink of extinction in the southwest of England. Even the pine martens are showing tentative signs of recovery, and the fortunes of the otter have been transformed.

The optimists get terribly excited about these very visible improvements. Such success stories can be tracked, filmed and shown on screens, unlike the bulk of the biodiversity that lies beneath our feet in the soils. But welcome though they are, they don't tell us much about the underlying adverse trends; nor do they indicate some quick and miraculous improvement. Like the climate sceptics who point to the odd colder year, or even just a cold snap, they mistake exceptions for the trend. It simply is not true to suggest that as people get richer, they reverse the declines and get back to anything like what has been lost. Ecosystems are complex; they require firm foundations, and many of the building blocks have been knocked away, diminishing resilience to what is coming. There is not much chance of simply going in reverse gear back to the *status quo ante*. We can't just have a couple of hundred years of industrialisation, take a big environmental hit, and then, Humpty-Dumpty-like, try to put it all back together again. Nature doesn't work like that: much has gone for good – because of us, and the inefficient short-term economy we have built.

The fundamental building blocks of natural capital – the soils, groundwater, the river catchments and the air – are not getting much better. Soils are still deteriorating from a terrible baseline; groundwater will continue to deteriorate for at least another 60 years even if we limit current pollution;[3] the carbon in the atmosphere has exceeded 400 parts per million and does not appear to have peaked;[4] and the mayflies in many rivers are now scarce. Statistically, adding more and more aliens as the globalisation of species plays out may increase the narrow measure of species biodiversity, but this is not the same thing as improving ecosystems. Counting species does not tell us much about the health of our environment. Zoos have lots of species, but not lots of nature.

While it is true that the chemicals applied to the land are sometimes used to a lesser extent than they once were, and in a narrow sense water quality has improved, in a dynamic ecosystem stopping pollution inputs does not halt the decline in the underlying assets. A tanker can stop its engines, but it will plough on for a long way before coming to a halt.

What is missing, and what matters, is the *aggregate* measure of the overall state of our natural capital, as well as the constituent parts, and the overall state of the natural environment that has been lost since the Industrial Revolution, and especially since the coming of industrial agriculture. A full picture will have to wait until proper national natural capital balance sheets have been developed and populated with good data. In time and with the explosion of new digital technologies to do the measuring, this will be possible and the numbers for the past can be added, in the way in which numbers for populations and economic performance in past centuries have been added to the national statistics by painstaking research.

In the absence of an aggregate, the best that can be done is to piece together the evidence for the main categories of our natural capital. This is something that naturalists and conservationists and ecologists have been doing for a long time. There are bird atlases, plant atlases, insect and butterfly atlases, and reptile and amphibian atlases, and there are *New Naturalist* studies on specific species and habitats. The non-governmental organisations (NGOs) have brought much of this together in the 'State of Nature' reports, led by the RSPB (Royal Society for the Protection of Birds).[5] Steps to develop more comprehensive databases, using the full panoply of digital mapping techniques, will shortly give us a real-time and extremely detailed understanding of exactly what is going on.

This is not the place to try to provide a comprehensive summary. It is both beyond the scope of this book, and well beyond the abilities of an economist to construct. The direction of travel is, however, pretty clear, and it is this that we need to bear in mind in being realistic about the baselines, the scale of the challenges, and the disastrous consequences that will follow if we do nothing to hold the line.

More declines

The easy bit is the non-renewables which, as the name implies, can be used once.[6] Nature has endowed us with them – they are natural – but they do not renew themselves except over geological time. They include the coal, iron ore, tin, oil and gas upon which our economy has been built and remains utterly dependent. Unsurprisingly, we know a lot about them. There are detailed measurements of the volumes mined and extracted, and there is also price data. This least interesting dimension of natural capital is the easiest to measure. It is also the dimension of which, by 2050, much will have been exhausted or, in the case of coal, oil and gas, hopefully left in the ground. In chapter 11, we will see that we should compensate future generations for what we have consumed, and for the legacy of carbon and other mineral pollution we have left behind from our largely selfish use of these non-renewables.

When it comes to the really important stuff, the renewables – the natural capital that nature can keep on giving us for ever – there are two obvious starting points. The first is the bits we are familiar with: the birds, plants, mammals, fish and invertebrates. The second, the one we concentrate on throughout, is the habitats and ecosystems, including the river catchments, the farmed lands, the uplands, the coasts and the urban areas.

How bad could the river catchments get in a business-as-usual scenario? Think of the stresses they already face. If you drink tap water in London it is often said that it may have already been through up to seven people.[7] That water will have been abstracted from rivers and cleaned of all the chemicals that have leached into it, and will be again after your sewage has been collected, processed and discharged back into the river. It might also include raw sewage from storm overflows. The sewage, before it is treated, will be contaminated with pharmaceutical products. Take a look in the cupboard under your sink. See the cleaning fluids you put down the sink and the toilet. Take a look in your bathroom at all the products you use. Many of these end up down the plughole, and we all just expect the environment – in this case the rivers – to absorb them. You turn on the tap and you expect clean water to flow. You water your garden and wash the car with this costly, treated water, and you don't want to pay much for it.

Yet that is just the beginning. We go on tipping more and more fertilisers, pesticides and herbicides into our watercourses, and allow the silt to run off the land from intensive farming practices. Industry adds its pollution too. Add all the plastic and other rubbish that gets thrown in and you can see the results alongside any major river.

Now add another quarter-century of all this. Add more and more chemicals, and more demand for more water for everything from land irrigation to servicing the expanding population. The National Infrastructure Commission[8] recommends a new water grid to connect major rivers just to meet demand (and without much regard for the environmental consequences of the mixing of waters).[9]

Now add climate change on top. You may be confused by the various claims about the impacts of climate change. Droughts, floods and plagues make the headlines, and dire warnings may induce scepticism or, worse, fatalism, but behind the hysteria lie some very inconvenient predictions. Heat in summer means more demand for water.[10] Floods in winter mean more silt and more pollution. The river life is adapted to what we have, not the climate we might get. For the river catchments, business-as-usual for another quarter of a century looks bad.

Agriculture plays a big part in both water demand and pollution and much else. A common theme in all these sad tales of decline is the impacts of modern farming not just on specific species, but on farmland birds generally *and* on the state of our rivers *and* on inshore marine environments *and* on the emissions and air-quality consequences *and* on the loss of invertebrates and mammals *and* the serious decline in the soils. It is beyond doubt that it is the intensification of farming, and in particular the application of chemicals, that is a primary driver of this major environmental damage.

By 2050, targeted chemicals should be able to get rid of almost anything that competes with or damages crops. Indeed, many can now. Almost all arable weeds (and in some robotic applications every individual weed) can be killed off with the non-selective herbicide glyphosate. That is why one well-known brand is called 'Roundup'. As glyphosate comes under increasing regulatory scrutiny, replacements are on their way. Without a change of direction in agriculture, by 2050 herbicides will be completely and selectively engineered for specific crops, and pesticides will finish off specific insects. Ultimately nothing will be left for wildlife to eat. By 2050 it will largely be over.

The uplands will not escape these pressures in the business-as-usual scenario. Being home to a lot of biodiversity now does not mean they will continue to be so. The economics of marginal upland farming is already precarious. If and when the main elements of the CAP wither away, and in the absence of proactive efforts to protect and enhance the uplands, things could go downhill very quickly. This farmed landscape could revert to ranch-style extensive farming, to intensive game-shooting and to development. Worse still, it might simply be abandoned. The rewilders might like this idea. Let the scrub grow back and then the woodlands re-clothe the hills. Except it will not be like this. The uplands are farmed landscapes. It is farmers who have shaped the landscapes that so many people, and so much of nature, enjoy. Farmers created the hedgerows, and the ditches and the lanes and the meadows. Grazing stock is the essence of the uplands. Woodland birds and woodland mammals might benefit, but this will not conserve the nature and landscapes we so admire today. By 2050 the uplands may be playgrounds still, but not the playgrounds we know now. Few think that zero subsidies will produce a helpful answer, except those who simply want us humans to abandon the land.

The impacts of farm pollution are exacerbated by other developments. Fish farms bring direct pollution to our coasts, and perhaps even more pernicious is the harvesting of sand eels and other small marine life to feed the farmed salmon. Direct pollution from shipping, from oil slicks and the washing of tanks at sea (including now palm oil), to the illegal dumping of waste and chemicals, all contribute to the declines. Plastics have become ubiquitous in our seas and along our coasts. Their sources are all largely out of sight, diffuse, and able to escape the law.[11] These are largely out of control. By 2050, with lots more trade and shipping, with lots more fish farms, and with global warming impacting on already stressed ecosystems, there may be no puffins, few gulls, and below the surface a more lifeless habitat. By 2050, eels and wild salmon might be an occasional rarity, as their populations decline below the thresholds for renewing themselves naturally.

The threats to our urban environment out to 2050 are about both its size and its content. There can be little doubt there is going to be a lot more 'urban' in 25 years' time. More greenfield and brownfield sites[12] will be built on, new villages and towns will be built, and the built land area will absorb more and more of the Green Belt. There will be quite a lot of semi-urban sprawl for the 'executive homes' so beloved and profitable to the building companies. It is not inevitable that all of these developments will have less biodiversity than the land they concrete over. But concrete they will, and without strong net environmental gain compensations, the aggregate impacts are probably going to be worse. For every showcase green development project, there are many that are anything but.

In terms of the content of urban areas, the temptation to concrete over the green spaces in our towns and cities will become increasingly intense. The parks and gardens are going backwards for a variety of reasons, and over the next quarter of a century, if we carry on as we are, these will gradually disappear. What remain may be turned into amusement parks, and nature will get squeezed out. Brownfield sites, even where they have surprisingly high levels of biodiversity, will go under concrete.

What is coming next

The above stock-taking is a picture of general declines, with some noticeable exceptions. Almost all of the causes are known and persistent, and all can and should be dealt with. Yet what dramatically raises the stakes are the new challenges the natural environment is facing. Without positive action, all the trends described above will continue. It will be a picture of gradual declines, punctuated by sudden population collapses and occasional trumpeted successes. As resilience is tested, one day you will look up and there won't be any swallows and swifts in May. The scary thing is that you might not even notice. For the next generation, it may be a case of not missing what they have never seen, except in pictures and films.

These extrapolated trends could get a whole lot worse without immediate action. Over the next few decades through to mid-century, Britain faces a rising population, and rising consumption. These together mean *more* houses, *more* developments and *more* hard infrastructures. On a business-as-usual basis, the results will in aggregate be negative for the natural environment. It is not only the present baseline that needs to be addressed, but also the 'known unknowns', and resilience against the 'unknown unknowns' of the future.

More people

Britain is one of the most densely populated countries in the world, even though large areas are sparsely inhabited. There are the great conurbations, and then there are the Scottish mountains, the Pennines and mid-Wales. Although London and the surrounding area is being overtaken in scale by the mega cities of Southeast Asia, the southeast is as densely populated as parts of the Netherlands and Hong Kong. The corridor that runs north to Birmingham and Manchester is dense too, and HS2 would make it more so. The new Oxford–Cambridge corridor, with more than 1 million new houses planned, could add another dense conurbation. The clamour to build on the Green Belt is getting ever louder.

In the 1970s and especially the 1980s, the assumption was that Britain's population would peak and then perhaps gradually decline, and in the process it would age. The assumption was that Britain would go the way of Japan and Germany – with an ageing, static or even declining population. British women have already gone through the so-called 'demographic transition', and the silver lining to the silver age should be less pressure on resources. The depopulation of the rural areas that followed the great urbanisation of Britain in the nineteenth century, indeed since the enclosures, would continue relieving environmental pressures. We could, it was thought, become an older, less populated and greener country.

This has been turned on its head by immigration. For much of its recent history, and especially in the nineteenth century, Britain exported people (and Ireland more so). The displaced rural populations colonised the USA, Canada, Australia and New Zealand, and countries throughout the British Empire. It was the safety valve as mortality rates fell.

Britain started the twentieth century with a population of around 25 million, and ended it with around 60 million. Nature was bound to suffer as a result, especially as the 60 million were many times wealthier than the 25 million. Immigration picked up as the Empire slowly wound down, with notable flows from the Caribbean and then Uganda and East Africa, and from India and Pakistan.

The initial numbers were quite small, but the game changed in the twenty-first century. European immigration was added to the non-Europeans, notably after 2004 when the Eastern European countries joined the EU, and freedom of movement applied to them. Britain made few objections at the time, and assumed that immigration from Eastern Europe would be marginal – perhaps 50,000 per annum – and would enhance economic growth.

The immigration figures started to edge up from the mid-2000s, reaching a gross 600,000 per annum in 2014/15, with net migration peaking at over 300,000. Such levels are unprecedented in British history. Net migration is still around 250,000 per annum (the average since 2004), with non-Europeans taking up the slack as European net migration falls.[13]

Few societies find it easy to cope with what now could be described as mass immigration, and for Britain it was a crucial factor leading to the Brexit vote. The political ambition is clearly now to limit the number of European immigrants. Whether this objective is met, those who are here in the main expect to stay, and there will still be positive net immigration for years, and perhaps decades, from non-European countries.

There are two effects on the natural environment. The first is the aggregate resources, including housing and infrastructure, that will be required to address the needs of a growing population. The second is the impact on composition. By 2020 the population is expected to reach 67 million, rising to 77 million by 2050.[14] Although this population will continue to age, it will have more young people than anticipated a couple of decades ago. The European immigrants have turned out to be young and well educated. For the European and non-European immigrants, birth rates are typically higher than for the rest of the population. We have built population growth into the long term.

Without mitigating action now, the environmental consequences of some 10 million extra people will be a repeat of what happened throughout the twentieth century. They will place 10 million more demands on the environment for consumption – for water, energy, housing and food. They will have a higher standard of living than those in the twentieth century, and therefore they will consume more per head. This is the equivalent to adding one more London, and one that is wealthier at that. None of this suggests that immigration is a bad thing: these extra people would have an environmental impact wherever they live, just as we do. The important point is that if we want a green and prosperous land, we have to factor in the inevitable consequences of a growing population.

More houses

With the growth of population has come an assumption that Britain needs more houses, and all the main political parties have committed to building more. The Conservative and Labour parties are competing to come up with ever-higher targets. These extra houses could pose a great challenge to the natural environment, and the impacts depend on where and how they are built and what supporting infrastructure is provided. On a business-as-usual basis, it could mean more ribbon development, more incursions into the Green Belt, more loss of greenfield land and more traffic and associated infrastructures. Every city, town and rural village is getting houses added and, with housing a political imperative, there is so far scant evidence that the environment is going to do anything other than suffer, as it did in the 1930s with the creation of ribbon development and suburbs, and in the 1960s too. There is little beauty in this business-as-usual world.

The increase in population does mandate more houses, but the demand for houses is more complicated. Britain has a high level of owner occupation (even if it is falling), and owning a house is the main way in which citizens acquire wealth by what is in effect forced savings. British people want to *own* houses, in addition to needing housing. It is still a core part of the 'British dream' for young families, in a way that young Germans would not appreciate, even as fewer can afford it.[15]

The emphasis on ownership reinforces a further trend, which is household break-up. More people are choosing to live alone and still own houses, and this is reflected in a fall in occupancy rates. Whether there are enough houses to go around depends on how many people live in each of them.[16]

The point about occupancy rates drives a wedge between the simple equation of population and the number of houses needed. It gets worse: as people get richer they want bigger houses; they want more privacy and seclusion, and they may even want more than one house. The constraint on housing demand is income. House builders know this. It is one of the reasons why they prefer to build large 'executive homes' and not affordable small ones.

Changes in housing size and occupancy in turn have implications for the environmental footprint. A row of small tenements or blocks of apartments and flats in inner cities have radically lower environmental impacts than those of larger houses and housing estates on the periphery of towns and cities. Dense urban housing creates fewer carbon emissions and less traffic, and brings economies of scale and density. Imagine a world where most people lived in cities, and most of these in the city centres. It would be a world of public transport, not private cars, and of radically greater energy efficiency. It would leave most of the rest of the land open and green, and indeed it would create more scope to green the suburbs with lots of natural capital for these urban populations to enjoy.

What these considerations illustrate is that housing left to market forces will be an environmental disaster and will replicate some of those disasters now being witnessed in a number of rapidly developing countries. Market forces drive up demand for houses in line with income. If the next decades witness 2 to 3 per cent GDP growth per annum, it is not hard to see that much of the Green Belt, and lots more green fields, will be concreted over by 2050. If each development does not have to pay for the environmental and social costs it imposes on the rest of the population, it will impose them. Imagine how quickly the Green Belt would fill up if the landowners could sell to the highest bidders without worrying about planning permission and paying for the environmental detriments caused. Paying for top lawyers and using consultants, lobbyists and PR companies to influence legislation and planners' decisions has worked for them in the past, and it could go on doing so. Indeed, it is.

This is why planning is essential to housing and housing development. Britain needs to decide how many houses should be built, what sort of houses should be built, and where they should be built. That was the step taken in the 1947 Planning Act, and with the creation of the National Parks (which were largely planning bodies – more on this later). It has now fallen away.

It is perfectly possible to house the growing population without a net detriment to the natural environment. Indeed, the environment can be enhanced as part of the process. Nor is it necessarily the case that house prices have to rise, provided that the impacts of developments on the rest of the natural environment and us are properly priced, compensation is paid and prudently spent on new and enhanced natural capital, and, overall, houses are not protected from taxation to make them particularly attractive ways of accumulating wealth. But to do this requires much more efficient policies, to which we will return later.

More infrastructure

There are probably not many people who think that Britain's physical infrastructure is in good shape. Sitting in a traffic jam on the M25, experiencing the delays on the Great Western main line, trying to make a mobile phone call on Exmoor, let alone trying to get a decent broadband connection, are daily reminders that all is not well with Britain's infrastructure.

Along with these basic service failures there are additional pressures. Water supplies are taken for granted, but the pressure on abstractions and the growth in demand with new housing have considerable implications for the natural environment. The attempts to reduce carbon emissions are leading to the need for new electricity transmission lines, new wind and solar farms, and new nuclear power stations.

It is not hard to argue that Britain's infrastructures are generally not fit for purpose, even before we add the extra 10 million people and all the houses that are planned. If we do add these, and work out how much transport, energy, water and sewerage, and communications demand they will add on top, the scale of the new infrastructure development requirements that emerge is very large – with potentially massive implications for the natural environment.

Infrastructure comes in lots of shapes and sizes. There are massive projects like HS2, Crossrail, Hinkley nuclear power station, the Thames Tideway and new airport runways. Then there are significant increments to the existing systems: to roads, electricity and gas networks, and to the water and sewerage systems.

On top of all this, there are the connections to all the new houses. Travel around many smaller towns and villages, and you will see 500 houses being added here and there on the outskirts. Semi-rural Oxfordshire is littered with them – from the housing developments at Didcot linking up to the A34, to the housing estates added to villages without many amenities – in effect dormitories. One or two cars per new house on the existing roads is going to have obvious consequences, and yet the developers have only limited liabilities to address these.

Many conservationists take a hostile stance towards new infrastructure and new housing developments. Across Britain there are community initiatives to try to halt the bulldozers. Dismissed by the housing industry and their lobbyists as driven by 'nimbys' ('not in my back yard'), these campaigns are typically about much more than the impacts on their individual properties. To many these look like a repeat of tagging housing on to existing communities in the 1960s, or, worse, the ribbon developments of the 1930s that helped to precipitate the planning legislation of the 1940s. They have much to fear and much to protest about if they want to protect their local communities.

The problem for these objectors is that they will mostly lose. Central government has pushed through a series of planning acts to tip the balance away from local communities, encouraged by the massive lobbying of developers. There are now national plans and national strategies, and local authorities are in effect told to get on with it.[17]

While there are good reasons for particular campaigns and objections, something more is needed if the impacts are not to be seriously damaging to the natural environment. This requires not only a return to planning, but also the urgent application of the 'net environmental gain' principle to infrastructure and housing developments, properly and comprehensively measured.

It also requires an intelligent approach to technologies. Electricity transmission lines no longer need to be a blot on the landscape. They can go underground. Roads and railways can be fully digital. The need to travel to work can be tempered by video links and ever more efficient communications. The comprehensive roll-out of broadband and fibre could reduce the demands for other physical infrastructure. Better measurement and management of energy supplies and water can reduce demand too. It is possible (and in the above examples it is necessary) to improve infrastructure and at the same time protect and enhance the natural environment, but only with an integrated and planned approach. The unconstrained application of market forces will not deliver this.

More consumption

The pressures of population growth, housing and infrastructure are multiplied through the rising levels of consumption. As GDP goes up, so does consumption. Indeed, most of the increases in economic growth in Britain are driven by spending ever more. Britain has a very high propensity to spend all of its income – and indeed more than its income – by increasing debt levels. In 2018, this was reflected in the average household spending £900 more than their income.[18]

Some numbers help to bring a perspective to this challenge. If GDP grows at 3 per cent per annum, it will double in less than 25 years. It is just the power of compound interest. Britain probably won't quite make 3 per cent, but, as a rough guide, by 2050 a doubling is a plausible assumption to make.

Imagine what this would look like in 2050. Although the extra income would be spread over more people, think what you would spend twice your current income on. The better-off might buy bigger homes or even more second homes. The bulk of the population will buy more holidays, more clothes and more services. Most of this stuff has the potential to further damage the natural environment and create even more waste.

It is this that leads more radical greens to question whether we should be allowed to keep on spending so much or whether a more frugal lifestyle is required to 'save the planet'. It is not hard to empathise with this sentiment. Looking beyond Britain, growth rates in China, India and increasingly in Africa are more like 5 to 7 per cent per annum. China has spent nearly 30 years growing at around 10 per cent per annum, which is a doubling of the size of its economy every seven years, and this is reflected in the new affluence of the emerging Chinese middle classes who now turn up in Britain in significant numbers as tourists. Whatever the benefits of all that extra consumption to the

Chinese people, from a global environmental perspective, the spectacular GDP growth of China since 1980 has been a disaster for climate change, water resources, the state of the seas and for biodiversity. And it is one that continues to gather pace.

There are two dimensions to this extra consumption that impact on the natural environment: how much is spent; and what it is spent on. How much is spent should not be based on the 2 to 3 per cent GDP growth number, and there is a lot to be put right before economic growth can be accommodated, including the impacts of all the fiscal deficits, trade deficits and quantitative easing that pumped consumption up artificially high since the financial crisis of 2007/08. Current growth and spending levels are not sustainable: we are living beyond our means. It is not that these numbers cannot rise without damage to the environment. They can. Rather, it is that the numbers need first to be adjusted so that they are in fact sustainable.[19]

The amount of consumption growth *after* these corrections depends on technical progress, and there is lots more of this to come. Rebased, what will the resultant incomes be spent on? This depends on prices and planning. Current spending does not properly take account of all the external negative impacts on the environment – the externalities – and it should. What this requires is that these externality costs are reflected in the prices we pay online and in the shops. Food is artificially cheap because farmers do not pay for the pollution they cause. New houses are artificially cheap to build because the builders do not pay for all their wider impacts and the infrastructures they require. Packaged goods are artificially cheap because we don't pay for all the cardboard and plastic. Once all these externalities are included – if the polluter-pays principle is properly applied – what we spend our money on may turn out to be rather different than business-as-usual suggests.

An even quieter spring?

Business-as-usual is not a stable equilibrium, a world where we just live with the damage done in the twentieth century and allow it to worsen in this century. The damage is dynamic and, if allowed to run on, it will not bode well for the natural environment. More people, more houses, more physical infrastructure and more consumption is a world in which the chances that nature will hold its own are slim without action now. There will be some successes, but this is a world of instant gratification in almost all human activities.

The housing lobbyists argue that there is lots of land, and that building on more of it leaves lots left. Similarly they argue that the Green Belt is large, and a few more houses make little difference. Tracks up hillsides for wind farms, trucks to fish farms and cutting down a few ancient woodlands for HS2 are collateral damage for a claimed greater economic good.

This marginal argument, a marginal difference for each project and each marginal development, when set against a much larger whole plays out in business-as-usual. At each point along the way, one more housing estate is too small to make much difference to the whole. But it is a deadly argument. The trouble with this marginal argument is easy to see, but almost entirely ignored. Each time the marginal card is played there is a bit less left of the ecosystem and habitat of which it is a part. And so it goes on, until there is nothing left. In the words of the song by Joni Mitchell, *'you don't know what you've got 'til it's gone'*.[20] You will hear developers say that the Green Belt is not really very green anymore anyway because it has been intensively farmed. But why has it been intensively farmed? Because each new marginal addition to the chemical arsenal has been added on a case-by-case basis.

The tyranny of the marginal is the route to an increasingly

silent spring. It is what business-as-usual means. Lots and lots of marginal losses end up with a catastrophe for insect life and for farmland birds. To seriously head off the damage that business-as-usual will bring – through more people, more houses and more hard infrastructures – the starting point needs to be the public goods, and not the marginal changes. It is these public goods that are being eroded in a death by a thousand cuts. Make no mistake, business-as-usual is likely to tip many ecosystems over the edge. By 2050 there could be very little left, and in a world with perhaps 500 or more parts per million of carbon in the atmosphere. The intensification of farming, industry, towns and cities could result in a silence of nature – of the birds, of the remaining insects and most of our mammals, reptiles, fish and invertebrates. It doesn't have to be like this, but it will unless we act, and act now.

PART TWO

Building a Greener Economy

3

RESTORING RIVERS

What could rivers, nature's plotlines, be like in 2050? How might they be enhanced? The water quality could be good and free from pollutants. They could follow more natural paths, with meanders and oxbow lakes, rapids and gentle floodplains. They could flood from time to time, creating and sustaining the floodplains. The wildlife could be plentiful, with otters and dippers and kingfishers and grey wagtails. Salmon and other migratory fish could be better able to breed. There would be abundant aquatic plants and invertebrate life. The rivers would be accessible for boats and children and recreation. There could be river paths for walkers, stretches for canoes and for anglers and birdwatchers.

How could we achieve a much better outcome by 2050, and why would it enhance prosperity? The main steps are obvious: protect and enhance the peat bogs and upper river catchments; go for natural capital solutions in the upper valleys; keep farm pollution and soil from entering the rivers; reduce phosphorus, pharmaceutical and other emissions from water-treatment works and, better still, stop them getting into the sewerage system in the first place; stop storm overflows pouring raw sewage into the rivers; manage abstractions more effectively, and address leakage; stop industrial pollution entering the rivers and limit surface run-off; and, finally, open up access so we can all enjoy greener and more prosperous rivers.

Do all this and our rivers will thrive, and we will all be better off as a result. Each and every one of these steps is practical and can be implemented now. They all fit together. What is needed to get from here to there is to treat the catchment as a system, and to take a whole-system approach.

Protecting the upper rivers

Rivers start with a trickle from springs on hills and moorlands and mountainsides, and become streams. It is here that the rain tends to be most persistent and floods start. What matters is the ability of the headwaters to hold onto the rainfall and to turn a downpour into a trickle. Damage to river catchments at the source is mapped onto the rest of the catchment.

Run-off is a big problem for many of our rivers, and it has been exaggerated by farming practices. Moorlands drainage and over-grazing has done much damage. Farmers seeking to improve their upland grazing have added drainage. Overgrazing exposes peat and fragile soils, and once the vegetation is stripped off, the waters run much faster. On lower elevations, river catchment sources have sometimes been ploughed up for crops, further increasing soil exposure.

These problems are among the simplest and cheapest to fix in a catchment. The sheep densities can be reduced, the drains blocked up, and the ploughing of the uplands limited. Digging peat can be stopped, and peat bogs restored. All of these measures have economic costs, notably to sheep and, to a lesser extent, cattle farmers, and to maize and other crops lost. But the economic equation is heavily tilted in favour of these measures. Upland sheep farming (more on this later) is at or below the margin of economic viability in any event and heavily dependent on subsidies. Without the subsidies it would be very different, and since the subsidies are public money, redirecting them in the uplands to better water management practices would be a net economic gain.

Indeed, so great are the economic benefits to the water industry just in the narrow terms of managing water quality that water companies have been taking direct action, including through the management of land owned by the companies in the headwaters and by payments to farmers to change their practices. United Utilities helped on its land in the Forest of Bowland Area of Outstanding Natural Beauty (AONB) to rewet and restore blanket bog and add woodlands, and South West Water has been helping the Exmoor Mires Project to conserve and enhance peat bogs at the top of the Exe and Barle river catchments – in both cases out of self-interest. To give an indication of the economics, the Exmoor project has been estimated to have benefits that exceed the costs by a very high eight times.[1]

In ploughing up some of the steeper slopes, and in particular planting maize on them in the Somerset Levels catchment, soils can be left very exposed, and indeed maize farming has directly contributed to the silting-up of the River Parrot and River Tone, which in turn helped to worsen the great flood of the Somerset Levels in 2014. The farmers then demanded that the Environment Agency dredge the rivers to remove the silt that they had contributed.[2]

These costs, and the value of the lost soil to the farmers themselves, easily outweigh any possible profits from the crops.[3] The Somerset Levels – the 'summer lands' – are mostly below sea level and the sea level is rising with climate change. It is an integrated catchment system, not a series of discrete bits to be addressed separately by farming policy, flood defences and dredging, and conservation measures. Natural capital approaches are integrated and offer much better economic returns. Cultivating maize on exposed slopes should be banned on both economic and environmental grounds.

Stopping farm pollution

Once the trickle becomes a stream and then a proper river, it becomes vulnerable to direct pollution. Few upper river catchments have a lot of industry, so the main pollution comes from farming. Upper river valleys are typically given over to grazing and pasture, rather than cereals, and hence it is livestock farming practices that pose a threat.

Perhaps the worst is the release of slurry into rivers, depleting their oxygen and destroying their biodiversity.[4] There are two principal ways this can happen. First and most reported is the failure of slurry-holding pits and tanks, usually as a result of poor maintenance. Such incidents are surprisingly common and often devastating. But there is also the spreading of slurry: while the intention is to retain the liquid manure on the fields to promote grass growth, it can nevertheless run off into streams and rivers. This is particularly problematic if the slurry is applied in winter to frozen fields. The frost makes it possible to get tractors and machinery onto the land, but it also forms a barrier to absorption. The lethal (for the fish) combination is slurry-spreading on frozen ground, quickly followed by heavy rain.

Slurry, badly managed, is a serious threat to the natural environment, but it is not the only way in which animal husbandry can adversely impact on rivers. Sheep-dipping to tackle a range of parasites, worms and foot rot is another detrimental element of (non-organic) farming practices, and it involves water. The residual liquids, after the dipping, have to go somewhere, although their disposal is regulated. Too often this has been out of sight in the watercourses, with sometimes devastating results.[5]

All these activities can be mitigated, often at minimal cost. The release of slurry and maintenance of slurry tanks are already subject to regulation. Spills are illegal and the problem arises not from the regulation but rather the inadequate penalties and enforcement. As budgets have been squeezed, the Environment Agency, Natural Resources Wales, and the Scottish Environment Protection Agency (SEPA) have retreated from the effective policing of the rivers. Catchment system management requires catchment system regulation and enforcement. A large number of incidents go unreported, or when they are investigated it is often too late to identify the source. The fines are clearly not a serious deterrent to farmers. Properly resourced policing and significant fines could all but eliminate these sources of river pollution. The use of drones and new advances in digital technologies to detect diffuse pollution will help to transform detection. There would be costs to the Environment Agency and the other bodies, but the balance of the damage versus these costs points towards more enforcement. The polluters may be fairly diffuse, but the pollutees are diffuse too, all down the river. Slurry in rivers can and should be stopped. Diffuse pollution should be limited. Both make good economic sense. The fact that the costs of the damage may well exceed the value of the total economic output of the farm tells us a lot about the perverse economics of much farming practice. Pollution is under-priced; agricultural output is therefore also under-priced.

Once the river gets to its middle stage, the ratio of grassland to arable land usually shifts towards arable. Conventional arable farming adds several layers of pollution and stress to rivers. It uses intensive fertilisers, pesticides and herbicides, and as with maize and the Somerset Levels example, it leaves the soils exposed to run-off and the depositing of silt in the rivers. It may also take water from the river for irrigation.

Farmers operating in these middle river areas are themselves vulnerable to the flooding that their activities can help give rise to, and hence they want to get the water quickly off their land and into the river, so the rate of run-off is artificially increased by ditches that take the chemical cocktails directly to the river much faster and hence in more concentrated forms. This raises flooding risk downstream, exporting the dangers to others. This was a process once managed through water meadows and vegetation cover along the rivers, in part because this made economic sense in a predominantly mixed farm system, but also because ploughing up riverside meadows required heavier and more powerful tractors and machinery. That can now be done. Once flooding was a resource for farmers to exploit in order to enrich their land. Now it is a menace to get rid of as quickly as possible.

The results are economically very inefficient and the economy would be much better off if many of these practices were curtailed or even stopped altogether. The central issue from an economic efficiency perspective, which we keep coming back to, is that some farmers are polluters who do not pay for the damage they cause others. Instead, they are polluters who expect to be paid not to pollute.

As discussed in greater detail in the next chapter, this should be reversed. If farmers paid for the pollution they caused, they would use chemicals in smaller quantities and target them more accurately. In the case of flooding, if farmers paid for the services that the river provides in taking excess water away, the ditches might not be so deep. They could also store more water. Finally, in a polluter-pays model, silt exported to rivers from riverside ploughing and cropped fields would come with a bill, and fewer of these fields would be ploughed.

With a polluter-pays policy, and hence the right relative prices, the rivers would be in a much better state. Biodiversity would go up, abstraction would go down, more ponds and reservoirs would be created, and the land would be wetter, especially in winter. It is all just good economics, and leads to a much more sustainable farming industry.

Dealing with the industrial legacy

Coal mining has wreaked havoc with rivers for a couple of centuries, and whole river systems have effectively been killed off by the spillages and run-off from mines. Mining tends to attract industrial processing to locate nearby, which adds to the pollution.

When it comes to mining and heavy industry, it is only relatively recently that polluters have been expected to pay. It is a surprisingly new idea. Mining has historically taken the same approach as that taken by the farming industry: the rivers are there as free waste-disposal systems.

As with farming, the economically efficient answer is to make the polluters pay. But it would still leave a horrible legacy. The toxic chemicals remain evident in the silts and muds of the rivers, and will do so for a long time to come. There have been many measures to deal with the legacy of asbestos in buildings, yet in the case of mercury, lead, radium and other nasty chemicals and substances in river muds, few such measures have been applied. Instead they just lie there in the sediment, largely out of sight, and off the agendas of the regulatory bodies. Roughly 2,000 miles of over 400 of our rivers may be affected by substances like cadmium, zinc, lead and arsenic. All have their unique pollution fingerprints – from examples like Bleaklow in the Peak District and the efforts to save the peat moorland from acidification, to the coal and industrial wastes affecting the coasts of the northeast.

In many, perhaps most, cases, there is little that can be done to make the polluters pay for legacy pollution, since the companies are typically long gone. The burden falls to the state to sort it out. In the case of coal mining, there is the Coal Authority, still grappling with the coal industry legacy, the flooded and polluted waters in old pits, and the groundwater problems.[6]

The economics of cleaning up these past legacies is often finely balanced. It very much depends on the precise pollutant, how stable the deposits are, and how fast the rivers can 'cure' themselves by washing the heavy metals out to sea – and then pollute some other marine environment.

Most of the mining has now gone. The ordinary economics of the markets has done for coal and most other mining, although open-cast mining still poses a threat and the use of water for fracking requires regulation. There are still the clay pits, and tin mining and even cobalt and lithium extraction may return in Cornwall. These aside, the main problem is no longer so much about the mining, but dealing with its legacy.

As mining and heavy industry have declined (often to be replaced by imports and production doing its environmental damage elsewhere), the various pharmaceutical and chemical concoctions that make up our daily lives and end up being washed down the sink and flushed down the toilet are among the new challenges. Contraceptive pills lead to oestrogens impacting on fish life. Antibiotics can be toxic for the bacteria and algae that form the basis of aquatic ecosystems. Anti-depressants can change bird behaviour. Shampoo, soap and washing powders increase phosphorus content in water courses.

The pharmaceutical industry is a major threat when it comes to our rivers and water supplies. As with earlier industrial pollution, the rivers are treated as waste-disposal systems, especially when the companies can pass on what ought to be a producer responsibility to the consumer. They supply the drugs and products, we use them, the rivers then collect them, and water companies try to remove them from our drinking water and wonder what to do about them in our sewage.

A radically different approach is needed before we end up leaving the next generation with major new damage and another industrial pollution legacy. The catchment-based approach starts by trying to limit what goes into our environment. Drugs are tested for their effects on human health, but less so for their waste disposal. Producer responsibility, and therefore polluter liability, could change the game. Imagine if GlaxoSmithKline were liable for the environmental damage caused by its products. Imagine if Unilever were responsible for the disposal of all its beauty and personal hygiene products. The result would be a radical shake-up of the chemical composition of their products. They would have a direct incentive to minimise the risks.

But what about us, the consumers? The problem with a pure producer responsibility approach is that it leaves us free to dump our waste, without any thought as to how we do this. We should learn the lesson from municipal waste disposal and recycling, making the householder responsible for the safe disposal of their rubbish. We have separate bins, and there are regulations about the safe disposal of white goods and batteries. These may be imperfect processes, but they go in the right direction. Sewage is just another form of rubbish. To secure a better environment, household waste needs to be considered holistically. All of it needs to be regulated. In the case of sewage, consideration should be given to using pricing too. As technology advances, it will be increasingly possible to monitor the content of our wastewater and sewage. We can meter water coming in. In due course we may be able to analyse what is going out with real-time information. Might you change your behaviours if you really knew what was in your waste and the damage it might do? And if you paid for the consequences?

The water companies

Water companies are obviously key players in the river catchments. Water is for the companies a 'crop', to be harvested as a renewable that nature will keep giving them for free from rivers (and groundwater sources). The companies want 'clean' water and hence want to limit pollution from others. Cleanness in drinking water is a chemical concept: it does not necessarily mean that it is biodiversity-rich, and indeed there are many organisms that water companies would rather not have in their water supplies. We want to drink clean water, pure H_2O, not a host of other things that live in the river environments. Solving jointly for clean water *and* for biodiversity is not the same thing as just wanting the former.

In providing us with clean drinking water, water companies abstract water, which reduces flows, and they discharge our sewage and the waterborne waste of industry, suitably treated. The management of river flows and the consequences for river biodiversity is a complex business, further complicated by the building of dams and other water-storage facilities. Reservoirs on the middle rivers (and sometimes the upper rivers too) have economic and environmental costs and benefits, all dependent on the catchment system as a whole. Water abstraction is rarely marginal: it has a system impact.

The abstraction problem arises partly because there is no price for water.[7] Once water becomes a valuable resource, it pays to address the 30 per cent leakage rates from water company pipes, and the companies have a stronger incentive to encourage water efficiency. Universal metering plus abstraction charges transform the incentives. Water may be freely provided by nature, but it has alternative uses. It should be priced at both the abstraction and the consumption points, and in the process capture the leakage costs in between. Otherwise it will be inefficiently used. Indeed, it is.

Water pipes leak treated water. With a marginal cost of water of mostly zero, it does not make economic sense to have a zero leakage policy. Yet the incentives to fix the leaks are distorted by the low cost of abstraction. Because there is no price, the choice between fixing the leaks on the one hand, and taking more water from rivers, groundwater and lakes on the other, is skewed towards the latter and, as a result, in times of shortage it is the rivers that suffer because of the leakage levels. It is not the water companies' fault: it is the incentives they face. The water regulator can tell the companies to cut leaks, but this is a crude approximation of what is needed, which is a proper balance, reflecting all the environmental costs, of the alternatives, and the locations too.

This feeds through into the storage question and the crazy idea that we need high-quality water fit for drinking for use in watering the garden, cleaning the car, and a host of other non-consumption activities. So-called grey water is not only perfectly adequate for these other purposes, it is also of much lower cost. In some cases, such as using rainwater from water butts in the garden, it is better for the plants. The more expensive the purified water, the greater the incentive to do the right thing and store water.

What is missing is a grey water *system* and comprehensive metering. The former is probably not economic, except at the household level, although there is potential. Hence it is all about decentralising water, as part of a decentralised utility system. Future houses should be able to generate their own electricity, provide a place for work instead of commuting, and store quite a lot of water. They can have smart energy and smart water.

Sewerage is where the historical damage from water companies' activities has been most apparent. In the past, rivers were sewage-disposal systems, and most of it was simply dumped in the rivers and out to sea. Over time this has been somewhat refined, but it is still the case that the capacity of sewerage networks cannot always cope in the event of storms. When it rains a lot, the sewerage systems overflow into the river. The argument is that it will consequently be very diluted (because of the storm flows). Yet this is far from convincing, and little consolation for those whose houses are flooded with it.

Fixing the sewage problem is not only about having big enough sewerage works. It is also about how the effluent is treated, and what happens to the resulting sludge. As with the deployment of natural capital approaches to the supply of water through the management of uplands, so sewage lends itself to natural methods too. It is just a form of muck and, like muck, it can be broken down and taken up by plants. It can be an asset. Reed beds are one method of doing this, once natural processes have begun degrading it. The methane, a by-product of decomposition, can be used for energy supplies. The insect life is a bonus, especially for birds.

As with abstraction, this is a problem of incentives. Water companies are not charged for disposals, and they have skewed incentives to prefer hard concrete infrastructure solutions rather than natural approaches. This is because of the way the economic regulation of their physical asset base works. It is much easier to solve once a whole-catchment approach is taken, but much harder when the water companies are regulated in a silo and neither benefit from the impacts on biodiversity of natural capital approaches, nor face the costs of their activities on the catchment as a whole. In order to get a better environmental and economic system, the water companies need to be brought directly into the catchment system economics. Below I explain how this can be done.[8]

Towns, housing, roads and sustainable drainage systems

Housing, concreted urban centres and roads bring further pollution and flooding problems to rivers, and they are as much a part of the catchment and its management as the farmers and the water companies. Run-off from roads is often nasty and fast, and housing and factories displace water that would otherwise have soaked into the ground, to be gradually absorbed. Towns and villages were traditionally built to have access to water, and they are often built right up to the riverbanks, which are in turn concreted over and reinforced. The houses and infrastructure reduce the ability of their land areas to absorb rainfall, and increase the speed and rate of run-off.

The solution here is better planning, regulation and pricing. Planning needs to steer development away from floodplains and to require porous roads and driveways to reduce run-off. Better still, unpaved and unconcreted driveways can be planted to encourage biodiversity. Plants absorb water too. The costs of the run-off need to be incorporated into the economics of new developments, thereby creating an incentive to build houses in the right places, and with the right porous green footprints.

Like the mining and the abstraction along rivers, the economic incentives on house-building produce perverse environmental outcomes. Flood insurance should reflect the risk of flooding, but it doesn't. Instead the flood risk is socialised, so that house prices do not fully capitalise this risk. If others pay some of the costs for locating near a river that floods, more houses will be built in the wrong places. Even worse, the Environment Agency prioritises reducing the risk of flooding to those most at risk. You buy a house in the wrong place, you get your flood risk insurance subsidised (through schemes like Flood Re), and then public money is spent on protecting you.[9]

Town populations have other great economic interests in the state of the rivers. Rivers are an immediate source of leisure for them, and they need access to the clean water. Green banks and riversides bring wider physical and mental benefits too. Many benefit from the tourism that rivers bring. Towns like Ross-on-Wye, Hay-on-Wye, Lechlade, Eynsham and Carlisle all have significant leisure industries and the associated services. The tourism is often more economically important than agriculture, and hence the economics points to an enhanced river environment.

The lower sections of rivers are the floodplains, and, with access to the sea, major cities and ports tend to be located in this part. Newcastle, Bristol, London, Newport and Exeter are just some examples. Floodplains are meant to do what their name suggests. They are meant to flood. The problem is that major conurbations and flooding do not mix, and hence the modifications to rivers downstream tend to be pervasive. The Thames in London was once 10 times wider in places and had lots of tributaries. To manage this process the rivers are channelled, the banks are concreted over and flood defences are put up, including flood barriers. Rising sea levels as a result of climate change will exacerbate these problems.

There has been quite a lot of success in dealing with the grossest city pollution. The Victorian sewers and now the Thames Tideway are major capital works, as are the ring mains pipelines around London. They have made a big difference to the natural environment too. London's Thames has much more biodiversity than even a couple of decades ago. Much of this has been helped by the closure of large-scale industry in the floodplains. The great industrial complexes on the north and south banks of the Thames to the east of London have largely gone. Teesside and Tyneside are an industrial shadow of what they once were. The economics of cities on floodplains is stacked in favour of 'hard works' – the buildings are just too valuable. Yet even in these cities much could be done to soften the impacts. The London Wetland Centre brings biodiversity into the heart of the city, and estuary wetlands help mitigate tidal surges and pollution. Much can be done in the estuaries to absorb high tides, before they get anywhere near the barriers and urban hard infrastructures.

Putting it all together: Coordinating catchments

The various individual measures set out in this chapter would transform our rivers. They would stop the declines in their natural capital, and start us on the path to an enhanced river environment. Stopping the slurry, better planning with porous urban surfaces, fewer sheep, making farmers pay for pollution and silt run-off, grey water storage, fixing the leaks, meters and abstraction charges are some examples of sensible economic policies.

We can do even better by bringing these measures together into a coordinated framework, and ensuring that the public goods of the river systems are properly protected and enhanced. In other great infrastructure networks, coordination is hard-wired into the industry and regulatory structures. The national electricity grid is coordinated through a System Operator, which ensures that there is enough electricity-generating capacity and that the system as a whole works. This is now being gradually extended to the regional levels, with Regional System Operators in electricity too.[10]

When it comes to our rivers, no one body is in charge of the systems *as a whole*. The water companies are in charge of sewerage and water supplies, and regulated by OFWAT, the economic regulator of the water sector in England and Wales. The farmers are in charge of the way the land is used, and have been subsidised by the CAP. The local authorities are in charge of planning. The Environment Agency is in charge of largely publicly funded flood defences and it does some regulation.[11] Natural England, the public body responsible for protecting and enhancing England's natural environment, is involved in environmental regulation and management, notably under agri-environment schemes and in protecting Sites of Special Scientific Interest (SSSIs) and nature reserves. The Wildlife Trusts are in charge of nature reserves. Then there are the numerous river trusts and other voluntary bodies. Each looks after its own patch.

It is a mess, although it works after a fashion. Specific natural assets are protected. But farmers are subsidised to pollute and do not pay the full costs of abstraction. The water companies make their money from free abstraction and by adhering to the sewerage rules, rather than considering the wider water environment. OFWAT focuses on consumers and tries to push down water bills. Local authorities are under pressure to deliver housing targets, and house-builders have a big say in what is developed and where.

All of the various parties in the catchment know that there are considerable gains from coordination, and from taking a natural capital approach to the river catchment systems as a whole. The answer is to follow the electricity system model and create a proper system operator for each of the river catchments, in charge of a catchment plan, and with the opportunities to auction the various public monies and the agricultural and other subsidies.[12]

The sheer scale of spending on our rivers is sometimes under-appreciated. Add together what the water companies spend on cleaning up the water for drinking purposes and treating sewage, including dealing with the pollution from farming, *and* the spend by the Environment Agency on flood defences and enforcements *and* the farm subsidies *and* the local authority costs, and the result is for many rivers a big number. Now compare how little we get for all this money. It is incredibly inefficient.

A system operator starts with the river catchment *as a whole*, as an integrated system, and not a series of marginal discrete projects. It takes the subsidies and other spends in totality. In consultation with DEFRA and in accordance with environmental law protections, it comes up with the required high-level outputs. It auctions the functions out where possible to those who can add the greatest environmental and economic benefits. As we shall see in chapters 4 and 10 respectively, the farmers could be asked to bid for environmental improvements for their subsidies, and bid too to sequestrate carbon. Water companies could avoid spending on cleaning up the water if the waste was tackled at source. The Environment Agency (or ideally lots of others) might bid for flood defence monies against bids from natural capital flood defence providers, from the Wildlife Trusts to farmers offering to hold flood waters.

To some this might smack of heavy intervention and regulation. But as with the electricity analogy, it is a smart combination of coordination and planning on the one hand, and using markets and prices and all the great ideas of the many river players to get value for money on the other, and in the process we can get a lot more nature out of our river systems.

What would the system operator offer as its catchment plan? Looking at the system as a whole, the catchment system operator starts with the water flows and the flood water modelling. This is readily achievable – we already have sophisticated flood-risk maps. The catchment system operator would be the centre of modelling excellence, and make the models publicly available.

Those in new housing developments who benefit most from flood defences should pay for them through their insurance premiums. If people want to live on floodplains, they should face the costs and not smear the costs of the risks over people who don't. This will give those at risk a very strong incentive to look for the cheapest options, and these will, as in our examples above, include natural capital answers. They will be bidders in the auctions of flood risk management solutions, either individually or through insurance companies.

Under this model, the Environment Agency (or whatever takes over its functions) would not have to rely on short-term Treasury monies for flood defence and be driven to hard capital answers. The money would come not from the Treasury but from those who benefit, and those who cause the problems.

The catchment system operator would take a view about pollution down the *whole* river. Instead of simply requiring water companies to clean up the pollution, the polluters would be encouraged to address the problems at source. This requires a careful mix of regulation, building on the EU Water Framework Directive, and incentives through pollution charges. The water companies would pay for the phosphates they discharge into rivers. That in turn would make people think hard about what goes down the sink and the toilet, as this cost would be reflected in their water bill, especially if real-time data eventually allows us to see what is going down our drains.

Some more enlightened water companies have already started to act, and in the process have taken on certain system operator functions. Wessex Water has set up EnTrade, an online platform providing an auction to farmers to keep the land covered around Poole Harbour.[13] As noted, United Utilities has been in the game of paying for improvements in its upper catchments, and South West Water has engaged in the Exmoor Mires project. All of these are examples of what is possible, but they are hamstrung by the incentives they face. OFWAT regulates them, and natural capital and the environment is not its prime objective. Worse, its focus on minimising bills and on the financial structures of the companies can undermine the full potential of these sorts of schemes. Financial rather than environmental resilience is what motivates OFWAT, even as environmental factors are tacked on as secondary duties. Water is an example of regulation and regulators standing in the way. Ironically for all the emphasis on keeping water bills down, the sheer inefficiencies of the ways water regulation works make the costs higher than they need to be.

Part three sets out in detail the full framework for paying for the environmental enhancements. The point here is that even without more money, things could be a whole lot better, greener and more prosperous. To get from here to there is not a matter of making marginal changes. It will require a wholesale reform of the key institutions and the incentives the water companies, farmers and developers face. OFWAT, the Environment Agency, Natural England and the farming subsidy regime are simply not fit for purpose. It could be so much better: cheaper, greener and more prosperous.

What is not to like about this?

4

GREEN AGRICULTURE

Farmers manage over 70 per cent of the UK's land area. Features that we value today for their biodiversity, such as hedges, water meadows, and ridge and furrow, are all man-made. We have modified even the most ancient of ancient woodlands, and we are now modifying the climate as well. There is nothing natural left. Humans have changed each and every environment. We are eco-engineers for the entire planet.

We have to fix farming. Without changes to farming practices, the natural environment farmers manage will continue to decline. Intensive farming is, from an environmental perspective, a desert of monocultures. It can be less biodiverse than the built environments. Despite all the subsidies, farmers are not doing well, and many smaller farms are in danger of going under. Since World War II, 70 years of subsidies have not brought prosperity to the bulk of farmers. Modern British agriculture is bad for the environment, bad for farmers and bad for taxpayers.

It does not have to be this way: some farming treads lightly on the land and maintains and sometimes even enhances the natural environment. We can do much better, for both the environment and the farmers. Current farming practices are almost everywhere uneconomic without subsidies and when the full costs are taken into account. It would be quite hard to make the outcomes worse from an economic perspective. Once the true scale of the disaster of modern British agriculture is recognised, we can set about putting nature back into our countryside, to the benefit of not just the environment but for farmers and taxpayers too. It is one of those really rare examples of win–win–win.

How we got into this mess

Farming today is the product of a long process of the symbiotic development with transport and market access, and technical advances since the late eighteenth century. Railways, crop rotation, enclosures, fertilisers and tractors transformed an organic and labour-intensive agriculture, largely delivering local self-sufficiency, into what is now a global, capital-intensive industry.

This intensification really got going with the *Dig for Victory* objective of maximising food production during World War II, the 1946 Hill Farming Act,[1] 1947 Agriculture Act, the Common Agricultural Policy since 1973, and the 1975 White Paper, 'Food from Our Own Resources', all encouraging the relentless march of agri-chemistry and farm mechanisation. From the 1947 Act onwards, agricultural policy and technology went hand in hand, with the Ministry of Agriculture, Fisheries and Food and the National Farmers' Union (NFU) working hand in hand too to fix guaranteed prices to both reduce price fluctuations and maintain farm incomes prior to the CAP taking over the role.

The intensification is likely to gather pace with the next wave of technologies. The chemicals get more effective at eliminating each and every competitor to the crop. The widespread use of glyphosate heralds the end of what is left of arable weeds, and the dead fields are inert and bird-free, except for the specialists of this brave new world, like woodpigeons and rooks. If and when glyphosate is banned, or when weed resistance to it begins to pose a significant threat, substitute chemicals can be relied upon to take its place. The result will be a more silent and browner environment. The countryside becomes more and more industrialised.

To these incremental technological advances, two new and transformational ones are being added, together already further changing the face of agriculture. These are digitalisation and genetics. Digitalisation enables both precision farming based on big data, and a further switch away from labour to robotics, 3D printing and AI. Genetics means that centuries of careful plant and animal breeding can be leapfrogged in a test tube. The very building blocks of species can be manipulated and changed, and all at a fast pace. These two changes are probably each more profound than the switch from horse power to tractors. Together they herald a very big revolution. The impacts of this intensification depend on location and the specific geologies, and on the particular incentives in the subsidy regimes. These can be classified into the consequences for water systems, the loss of soils and their biodiversity, and air pollution.

In chapter 3 we saw how agriculture can pollute rivers with chemicals and silt and its impacts on flooding. Whereas water pollution is relatively well understood, what is happening on the land is less obvious. The biodiversity that really matters is the stuff we cannot see, and much of this is in the soil. The evidence we have on the decline of our soils as a result of modern agriculture is alarming. It has been suggested that many soils have only around 100 harvests left in them, and that some urban soils are in a much better state.[2] As the Secretary of State for Environment, Food and Rural Affairs put it at the launch of the Sustainable Soils Alliance in October 2017:

> If you have heavy machines churning the soil and impacting it, if you drench it in chemicals that improve yields but in the long term undercut the future fertility of that soil, you

can increase yields year on year but ultimately you really are cutting the ground away from beneath your own feet. Farmers know that.

Part is simply caused by its physical loss, and in some areas of the country, like the Fens, the declines are exacerbated by the dry conditions and wind-blown erosion. Given too that the Fens have large peat deposits, the carbon emissions from soil losses are significant, and the costs of reducing these emissions through changing farming practices should be offset against the costs of doing so in the energy sector. The general carbon emissions from agriculture are something the Committee on Climate Change has not yet properly tackled – surprisingly, given that the costs of foregone agricultural outputs are likely to be small given the subsidies.[3] Its 2019 'Net Zero' report started to redress this gap, and further reports are expected to follow.[4]

The thing about soils is that they are renewable, up to a point. The continuous interaction of fungi, bacteria and invertebrates breaks down organic materials that come from the residues like stubbles, manures, leaves and other vegetation. Many of these resources for renewing the soils have been drying up. Manure is no longer a major fertiliser: the Haber-Bosch process for manufacturing fertilisers has put paid to this.[5] Manure is increasingly a waste to be disposed of. If the carbon concentrations in the soils diminish, the invertebrates and other soil life are starved of their supplies of raw materials, while the chemical doses kill off much that we cannot see with our eyes. It takes a microscope to see what happens when chemicals like neonicotinoids are applied, and how pesticides do their job, which is to kill invertebrates, and indirectly some vertebrates too. Typically we don't know the impacts, because they are incremental and take time to work through the biodiversity, and so we don't know where the critical renewables thresholds (in other words, the thresholds from which the renewable resources cannot recover) lie. That is why we need safe limits, and why the precautionary principle is so important.

These impacts on soils are bad for both the natural environment and for farmers. The soils support the base of the food chain, supporting the worms and the insect larvae, which in turn support the insects and the birds and many mammals. Without healthy and biodiversity-rich soils, the supporting structures of life suffer.

The above-ground impacts are controversial too. The effect of neonicotinoids and other pesticides and herbicides on bees is a case in point. Bees forage on lots of different flowers, and not just the oilseed rape treated with its seed coating. Oilseed rape flowers in the spring, and then for the rest of the year bees feed on other plants, which may or may not be affected by other chemicals and pollutants from other sources, like power station and car emissions.

It is relatively easy to put a bee in a test tube and subject it to specific chemicals, but this tells us very little, unless of course the bee dies quickly from a low dose. In general they don't, and the impacts are much more subtle. Given the other pressures on bees, including the parasitic varroa mite and the loss of wild flowers from the countryside, the more insidious impacts come from a general weakening of colonies.[6] Chemicals are part of degraded ecosystems and testing should take all these various effects *jointly* – and not separately – into account in large-scale, long-term field studies. Proving a direct link to the scale of declines and the use of specific chemicals is all but impossible.

What then should we do? The obvious answer is more research, more experiments and more data. But this will get us only so far, and in any event, it takes years to fully appreciate the complex chemistry and biology. The second approach is to invoke the *precautionary principle*: to limit and possibly ban the chemicals until proved safe, whatever that means. As we shall see in chapter 9, there are good reasons for deploying this principle, providing it is pragmatic and allowing for some risk.

Bees are only one of many pollinators, and the impacts of the chemicals are not restricted to them. What the chemicals tend to do is kill insects indiscriminately, starting, for example, with aphids and flea beetles that feed directly on the crop plants. These insects are food for predators and, in a natural environment, equilibria develop between predators and their prey. The trouble comes when the prey kills the predators by passing on the poisons. The classic example is DDT, which became concentrated in the prey of those at the top of the food chain, such as the peregrine falcon, almost wiping them out in the process.[7] This example is well known because it is an iconic bird. But it is just one example of how the food chain works. Without proof of the harm, the farmers are understandably keen to hang on to the latest chemicals in their arsenal upon which they have become reliant. Indeed, farming lobby groups have defended most chemicals that were eventually banned, just as they do now for glyphosate and neonicotinoids. Many farmers aren't precautionary: they prefer to use until proven dangerous. This is a very predictable reflection of the incentives they face.

To this concentration of pesticides and herbicides in the food chain is added the wiping-out of critical links in the chain. Agrichemical farming has been a disaster for insect-eating birds. There may be problems migrating for cuckoos and flycatchers and swallows, and turtle doves may be shot as they pass through Malta, but the lack of abundant insects in Britain has to be one contributing factor.

Just how much damage has been done can be seen in a groundbreaking study of insect populations in German nature reserves, close to intensive agriculture.[8] Over an extended period, this study found that more than 80 per cent of the insects have gone. For the more visible effects, note how much cleaner car windscreens are in summer now compared with even a couple of decades ago. There may be some dispute about how far the extermination of insect life has gone, but there can be no doubt that a lot has gone, and that this must impact on farmland birds, especially those that depend on insects for their chicks (in the case of many seed-eating birds) and as a direct food supply. Such large-scale losses cannot be without large-scale consequences.

Slugs and snails are a continuous hazard for crops, especially those in the brassica family like oilseed rape. This has led to blanket slug-pelleting with metaldehyde. The results are that those creatures that feed on slugs and snails are going to have less to eat, and what they do may carry the poisons up the food chain to them. For the thrushes, hedgehogs and frogs this is bad news, and it is one reason why they can do better in gardens and towns, although gardeners continue to resort to slug pellets too. The metaldehyde shows up in rivers and, as with the impacts on terrestrial wildlife, the effects on aquatic life are uncertain, and are often part of a broader picture of environmental stresses. It is not so much that one particular chemical kills, but rather that it, plus all the others, plus all the pressures on habitats, together do the damage. It is the bee example again. For water companies, metaldehyde is hard to remove in treatment works, and as a result a number of companies are paying farmers to limit its application.

Intensive chemical farming changes the way farming is done. In traditional practices, there would be stubble left over winter, and many cereals would be sown in the spring. Before modern combine harvesters, lots of seeds would be wasted on the ground, and before modern herbicides, there would be many more arable weeds, leaving their seeds too. Winter stubble was once a key resource for birds, either directly or indirectly, as small mammals and insects lived longer to provide the food for predators such as barn owls.

Modern chemical farming on cereal lands now goes more like

this: after combining in late July or August, the land is sprayed with glyphosate to kill off all the vegetation. It is then sown (no plough), with the next crop getting established before the onset of winter. It then starts growing earlier and faster in the spring, aided by fertilisers and protected from insects, rusts and fungal infections. In the case of maize, the crop is planted late in the spring, harvested in the autumn, and the fields can be left bare to the elements all winter. For maize fields after harvest there is almost nothing for wildlife to eat. Oilseed rape, barley and wheat fields are similarly brown deserts post-harvest.

To make this system work, and in particular to optimise the use of ever-larger machinery, fields need to be modified. The hedgerows that once formed part of the enclosures and land management systems, and provided shelter and protection, are an impediment to the use of machinery. The farm gates have to be wider, and where possible the hedgerows are removed. Over the last few decades, an awful lot has gone and it is only recently, after the damage has been done, and controls put in place, that the losses have been stemmed. But the horse has bolted.[9] As with the brown, green and yellow single-species deserts that have been created, this hedgerow refuge has been decimated, and the result is that much of the rich biodiversity of the hedgerows has been lost. Where they remain, the flail has largely replaced traditional hedge-laying and management, and so the remaining hedges are generally of less value to wildlife.

As planning and regulatory controls have belatedly tried to limit the losses, the flail provides an opportunity to chip away a bit more of what is left every winter. Ironically it was farming that created many of these hedges through the enclosures, and it is farming that has been removing them. Farmers even resist limits on hedge-cutting during the bird-breeding season so that they can use labour and machinery in the otherwise quieter periods pre-harvest.[10] It is a more profitable approach.

In the north and the west, where cattle and sheep are fed partly on grass, artificial fertilisers play a central role too. The grasslands have been 'improved', moorland has been enclosed, and the rich plant and insect life has been impoverished as a result. But for public outcry, it would have gone further. The classic example is Exmoor in the 1970s, as the farmers started to plough up the moor.[11] Farmers were actively encouraged on this path and subsidised to take more marginal land into direct cultivation.

There are now virtually no natural meadows left in Britain. Some 97 per cent have gone, leaving only fragments in nature reserves. This is not just a tragedy for the plants that have gone, and the rich tapestry of colours that have been replaced by a uniform vivid green, but also for everything that depends on them. Evolution has produced very complex symbiotic relationships between the plants, insects, fungi, birds and mammals of the grasslands, and when the plants are gone, a host of these relationships collapse. They can be gone before we have had a chance to even understand what we are losing.[12]

For many, notably in the mainstream farming lobby, this loss of nature is just an unfortunate side effect of the greater benefits that come from making the land more productive and producing more food, which it also claims is cheap. Cheap, secure British food is held up as a great economic achievement, and the damage to the natural environment a price worth paying. That after all is what successive governments (and then the EU) have exhorted and paid them to do. It is not their fault that they have done what they were incentivised to do.

Except all this turns out to be simply wrong: the economic costs typically outweigh the economic benefits, once the madness of the economics of modern farming is revealed. Being brown rather than green in farming is achieved at great economic cost. Very little of this intensive chemical farming is actually economic. It thrives on three things: subsidies, tariffs, and the avoidance of paying for the pollution it causes. No other economic activity combines such a perverse set of incentives, or produces so little economic value for its true costs. It is the taxpayers, not the farmers, who hold the prices down. It is simply not true that increasing levels of intensification are economically efficient. To see why this result holds, and why the route to a prosperous countryside is not through the current approaches to farming, we need to dig deeper into the crazy economics of British farming.

The crazy economics of British farming

British agriculture contributes around 0.7 per cent GDP, has a turnover of around £9 billion, and receives around £3 billion of direct subsidies via the CAP. Farms are exempt from business rates, and farmers enjoy cheaper red diesel and are exempt from inheritance tax. Exemptions from pollution charges and the cost of the carbon emissions and the air pollution impacts of ammonia amount to an extremely large implicit subsidy. Farmers receive compensation for the death of livestock from specific diseases, such as BSE (bovine spongiform encephalopathy), TB (tuberculosis), and foot-and-mouth.[13]

British agriculture is protected from foreign competition through tariffs. Without protection most of it could not compete with cheaper imports, whether Argentinian beef, New Zealand lamb, or Canadian and Ukrainian grain. We have *more expensive* British food to protect British (and European) farmers from competition. Whatever the rationale, this is not *cheap* food.

One way of trying to get a handle on this is to calculate some of the costs that others pay as a result. Water companies spend millions on getting rid of the chemicals to produce water fit to drink, which we pay for in our water bills. The Environment Agency spends millions dealing with the silt run-off from fields.

Energy companies invest in renewables to mitigate carbon and pay the Carbon Price Floor and other levies, while farmers get half-price (carbon-subsidised) diesel.[14]

There has never been a full economic assessment of all the agricultural pollution costs. It is likely that they exceed the value of the CAP subsidies. Add in the inheritance tax concessions, business rates exemptions, and the special privileges in planning law, and it is not implausible to suggest that the £9 billion gross output has an economic value that is close to zero. Then add back the higher prices British customers pay because of import tariffs.[15] The actual value of British farming could even be negative.[16]

Perhaps even more extraordinary is that the results are not that good for the farmers. In order to protect and enhance our environment we need profitable farms and a thriving industry. The average British farmer is 60 years of age. It is very difficult for any young person to enter the industry. Why? Because much of the CAP subsidy is paid for owning land that is farmed. This is the 'basic farm payment', and farmers get it per acre of their farms. Inevitably this is capitalised in the land price, which is driven up to capitalise the subsidy value. Add in the other factors driving up land prices (including the inheritance tax and the development uplift that goes to landowners rather than to the public) and the result is land prices which cannot justify the yields from the crops and livestock. In 2018, good-quality agricultural land was around £10,000 per acre, and even marginal hill farms in Exmoor were over £5,000 per acre. This means that, allowing for the risks, farmers need to earn around £1,000 and £500 profit, respectively, per acre per annum in order to earn a reasonable rate of return on their capital invested in the land, given the volatility of prices and outputs. Most don't. To add to the crazy economics, in order to incentivise young farmers to enter the industry, the EU has introduced subsidies to offset these high land prices partly caused by the CAP.

It would be hard to make up such an economically inefficient and costly system of supports. What it does mean is that the claimed benefits to the British population from the CAP are even smaller than they at first glance appear. Put simply, cheap, secure food is neither what we have, nor the result of an efficient industry, but rather of taxpayers subsidising the costs of food, and consumers and taxpayers paying for the pollution caused in producing it.

The benefits of a green countryside

The less-than-impressive economic benefits of modern agriculture need to be placed in the wider context of the value of the countryside to its multiple other users. Recall that agriculture employs very few people, and the number is likely to diminish further with robotics. Many of the very few it employs are migrants. Working on farms is now a minority activity in the countryside.[17]

The big rural employer and the biggest economic industry in much of the countryside is tourism and leisure activities. Like farming, tourism is location-specific. Very few tourists go to the Peterborough area to enjoy the intensive-agricultural landscape (although they may go to see the remaining fragments of Fenland in nature reserves), but they do flock to the southwest, the northwest and the Pennines. Part of the attraction for these visitors is the patchwork quilt of the fields and the hedgerows – what many urban dwellers think of as 'farming'. It is an illusion that the farming industry itself likes to project. The NFU website shows happy cows and big hedgerows. It does not show brown fields, intensive chicken and pig farms, or indoor dairies. The harsh realities of much of modern farming are kept out of sight of the general public. They would certainly deter tourists.

For most of British history, the countryside was often seen as an uncivilised place, and nature as something to be tamed. The idea that you would want, as a sophisticated urban dweller, to go anywhere near the countryside and its 'country bumpkins' is a relatively new one, except perhaps to hunt. Nature was an enemy to be pushed back, to be civilised.[18] It was only in the eighteenth century that the idea of nature as pure and attractive, rather than ugly and dangerous, caught on, to be then rapidly developed by poets and painters. The countryside could be sublime to Burke, inspirational to Wordsworth, and picturesque to Gilpin and Constable.[19]

With the change in the idea of the countryside came tourism and the romanticism of the 'simple life', 'close to nature'. Thus began the movement that rapidly became an industry. There would be grand tours for the rich to the British countryside, as opposed to the classic worlds of Italy and Greece.[20] The Victorians would collect the countryside – its bird eggs, stuffed specimens, butterflies and rare ferns – rather like the parallel craze for stamp collecting. Later still, the countryside would be a retreat for people to 'go back to nature', and in the 1960s and 1970s the refuge for cults and eco-communities. The modern version is 'rewilding' holidays to places like Romania, and to spend electronic-device-free time with 'nature'.

The countryside is now firmly established in the public mind as something that can be beautiful, as something worth fighting for, where nature can give peace, tranquillity and soothe the soul.[21] By the 1960s, the countryside (and especially the coast) had become the location for mass British tourism, and for the workers as well as the upper classes. In practice, this meant Blackpool, Minehead and Skegness, and was captured by companies like Butlins. In the 1970s this changed with the coming of the package holidays and the British obsession with the beach holiday in the sunshine of Spain and Greece. Cheap travel could provide leisure opportunities which had been unimaginable before the 1970s. The result was that British holidays went into a steep decline, but one from which they are now recovering. Withdrawal from the EU, falls in the value of the pound, and climate change may increase the attractiveness of British holiday destinations in the coming decades.

From the Romantic movement on, these wider public interests in the countryside came to challenge the idea that the land is a matter of purely private property rights, and gradually these have been attenuated. For most of the history of agriculture the challenge to the sole rights of the owners had been about who should own the land, rather than the multiple public claims upon it. Land reform is a long-running political saga, going back centuries, and brings into play the rights of tenants against landlords, and the rights to the commons, which were trampled on in the enclosure processes with the repeated parliamentary approval of specific enclosures.[22]

This public interest is in the *public* goods, and the ownership question arises in terms of who should have access to them, and who should pay for them. In terms of prosperity and economic values, these public goods stand in equal stead with other competing private claims, related to food production, and the consequences for biodiversity and for the landscapes that people value – and they have a link from these to tourism and other economic benefits that arise from the way the land is managed. The private goods of food need to sit alongside these public goods, as indeed they have to in most of the rest of the economy.

The easy assertion that public monies should be for public goods leads on to the question about what these public goods are. These are discussed in greater detail in chapter 8. The public interest in these public goods is manifest in almost all aspects of the countryside – in access and footpaths, in biodiversity, and in the landscape itself. It ranges from the scientific through to the cultural and aesthetic. The reason why some areas are more highly prized than others is partly because there are landscapes and reservoirs of nature that have survived modern agriculture in a sea of intensification. The argument then becomes a form of natural apartheid: the best use of the countryside, it is argued, is to protect *some* islands of beauty and nature in a sea otherwise given over to intensive food production. Translated further, it is fine to carry on degrading some bits of nature as long as other bits are enhanced elsewhere.

The value of land is not just the revenues from tourism, although, as noted, these trump agricultural economic value in aggregate by a very wide margin. The natural environment is a key part of our health and well-being. What moulds us, what calms us and what gives us good air and exercise, is a natural environment. It is not wilderness, for the simple reason that there is no wilderness. Rather it is nature, shaped by us, and our imaginations, in turn shaped by the way we live our lives and the cultures, histories and art that inform us.

For the health and well-being benefits of a natural countryside there have been a number of heroic empirical stabs at getting at some numbers. These numbers are at best roughly right, which is a lot better than being precisely wrong. They tell us something of prime importance: the public goods from the land are much bigger than the true value of the agricultural production, once all its externalities have been accounted for. The numbers overlap with the tourist revenues, and we should not double-count. The tourist and health and well-being studies tell us that, by a considerable margin, what matters for prosperity most is these public goods rather than the purely private ones of private landowners.

A new sustainable and prosperous agriculture and agricultural policy

Can we combine food production with these public goods? Can the farming industry prosper in an enhanced environment? These are the challenges for the new British agricultural policy and the 25 Year Environment Plan. To imagine a mid-century rural environment that is richer in natural capital than it is now and with a thriving agricultural community, a number of conditions need to be met.

The starting point is an output measure: the biodiversity should be increasing and not falling as it is now. This means more farmland birds, more wild flowers, more insects and more mammals. To achieve this, the input, natural capital, has to be first maintained and then improved. It means restoring soils, and the ecosystems that exist in them, and on which the food chain is built.

What would the farmland look like if this increase in natural capital were to be manifest, and available for the public to benefit from, while still producing food? The most important point to make is that an increase in natural capital is incompatible with an agriculture that seeks to eliminate everything but the specific crops.[23] The chemicalisation of the soils, the war on insects and the ever-bigger fields are not sustainable. For if the trends in farming continue, there will be the application of increasingly effective chemicals to eliminate all the pests and diseases and speed plant growth.

It is remarkably simple: the further chemical elimination of pests and diseases and the further application of artificial fertilisers cannot be compatible with increasing natural capital. The countryside will become even more like a general industrial park. The war against nature will continue until everything but the crop is eliminated, so that there are fewer insects, birds and mammals left, other than those that are strictly necessary for the crop – and even these might be industrialised, as with bees that pollinate California's almond harvest.[24] It is dishonest to claim otherwise. Better to admit that natural capital will continue to decline for as long as this transformation, which started in the nineteenth, is allowed to play out in the twenty-first century without paying for the pollution costs it causes, and without regard to the provision of public goods. That is the gloomy scenario of chapter 2.

For most farmers, reducing reliance on chemicals and reducing the size of fields is anathema. They have become overwhelmingly dependent on them, especially given the resistance that the chemicals have induced. *Farmers Weekly* published a telling article early in 2018, 'Six of the Best', which lists what it considers the most important advances in arable farming over the past 40 years.

1974	Glyphosate, now the most widely used herbicide in the world
1975	Self-propelled sprayers, which offered 'high-capacity spraying'
1976	Azole fungicides, the largest class of fungicides
1980s	Oilseed rape combined with 'huge subsidies' for growing it as we joined the European Economic Community (EEC)
1996	GM crops
2001	Voluntary initiative on pesticide use, heading off the threat of legislation for a pesticide tax.

Source: *Farmers Weekly*, 12 January 2018

From the perspective of nature and natural capital, five of the six have been major contributors to the decline of nature. GM crops are yet to have much impact, but even here the combination of Bayer's Roundup (glyphosate) and other chemicals on the market *and* GM crops is important (often referred to as 'Roundup Ready GMOs'). A key feature of this genetic modification is that it makes the crop resistant to the pesticides and selective herbicides.[25]

None of the above can be un-invented, and the list is a partial one that *Farmers Weekly* chooses to highlight. It does not include fertiliser developments, plant breeding, or the increase in farm machinery size and capabilities. Nor does it include the coming of digital and GPS precision technologies, which can bring one potential silver lining: precision applications can reduce doses. Organochlorines, organophosphates and neonicotinoids are also missing, and DDT is pre-1974.

To some, the answer is obvious: go organic. The prospect of a wholly organic system of farming is, however, remote. Today it represents less than 4 per cent of agricultural land, and most is permanent pasture. Yet it is an approach that has caught on elsewhere. President Macron claimed to be targeting over 20 per cent organic farming in France by the mid-2020s.[26] There can be little doubt that nature would on balance benefit: directly on the agricultural lands, but also in reduced river and air pollution. Just because a wholly organic agriculture is out of our grasp does not mean we cannot shift towards more organic methods, reducing the chemical inputs, protecting the soils, and maintaining the natural capital they represent.

The apartheid between the intensively chemical world and the non-chemical one cannot continue. It is not enough to plant field margins that are not sprayed, surrounding the intensively sprayed fields. The result is that there are arable fields that are practically devoid of nature, except for the field margins, which are supposed to be reservoirs for nature.

Although better than the whole field being dead, there are several problems with this approach. The first is that the nature in the field margins has nowhere to go. The rest of the field is like a concrete barrier, with little or nothing to eat in the intensive areas, and with tramlines made by machinery to bring predators and prey together. For arable weeds and other wild flowers, the main area of the field is intentionally out of bounds. In some cases, there is a neat line of herbicide applied along the edge of the crop to stop these so-called arable weeds spreading, a sort of prison wall for nature. The result is at best mini-nature reserves on the edge of deserts. The second problem is that the margins themselves have a tendency to end up as roadways for tractors and farm machinery: mowed, compacted, and of little natural value, but just green enough to earn the subsidies.

In theory, farmers are supposed to abide by the more general requirements of 'cross-compliance' for the receipt of the basic farm payments, which have formed the bulk of the CAP subsidies and are most important for more intensive agriculture. Cross-compliance has lofty aims: farmers are supposed to be taking environmental considerations into account. But take an aerial picture of the great cereal lands of Britain and ask yourself how exactly farmers are 'cross-complying'. There are few inspections and few withdrawals of subsidies as a result. It is in reality very much a voluntary matter. The lesson for future agriculture policy is that we cannot rely on farmers 'self-complying'. Many don't for obvious economic reasons. Most farmers are in it for profit, not nature. Cross-compliance is a cost, not an income.[27]

Wildlife corridors

It does not have to be like this. The field margins do matter, along with the hedges that can be brutally flailed. Not only can they be improved, they can also be linked, creating wildlife corridors. Plants, birds, mammals, reptiles, amphibians and insects need to be able to move around, just as freshwater fish need to be able to navigate up and down their rivers. Nature does not do well in small islands, a point made by E. O. Wilson decades ago as a result of his island experiments.[28]

Wildlife corridors come in various shapes and sizes, and they straddle the patchwork quilt of farm ownership. They are all different, and yet they all need coordination. There are some great examples of this working. Wiltshire farmers on the Marlborough Downs have clubbed together to create a significant wildlife corridor, funded by the Countryside Stewardship Facilitation Fund for three years. There is now an impressive range of local partners participating in the scheme.[29]

Many more exciting and significant wildlife corridors could be created, with benefits orders of magnitude bigger, because of the area impacts on the diversity.[30] The obvious starting point is to take the river catchments and follow the river corridors, as discussed in chapter 3. There are the lines of hills, which will be covered in the next chapter on uplands. Both of these are reflected in river pathways, such as the Thames path, and in upland ways, such as the Two Moors Way in the southwest, and the Pennine Way. Imagine if every river and every range of hills was a thriving wildlife corridor. There would be long-distance paths and wildlife corridors throughout the landscape, linking towns and cities to the countryside. All practical, all cheap, and all with significant economic benefits.

In the lowlands and on intensive land, wildlife corridors and public bridleways and footpaths offer considerable possibilities, and where the hedges remain, these can often be connected at little cost. There are Salt Ways, Pilgrims Ways and a host of what Robert MacFarlane called the 'old ways'.[31] There is no obvious reason why farmland that is deliberately set aside and hedgerows should not be required to link up as part of the basic cross-compliance of the emerging subsidy regime, as large-scale public goods. This patchwork quilt once linked villages. It could do this again with a little imagination and very little cost. Imagine taking a map of each locality and using a thick green pen to mark up every one of these micro-corridors, and then imagine all the 'use and delight'[32] the local population would derive from them along the footpaths and cycle ways which could be restored and enhanced. Children could even use them to get to school. This marked-up map would help identify which hedgerows to protect and enhance and where public money would provide the largest public goods.

Food production and self-sufficiency

The objection that farmers raise to the above is that these nature-friendly steps are all very well, but they will not get the food produced, and the result will be that more of Britain's food is imported. They argue that farming is about food production and food security *first*, and only then nature. As NFU President Minette Batters recently put it, 'You cannot go green if you're farming in the red.'[33]

It is an easy – and, from the farmers' point of view, under-standable – argument, but it is full of holes and pitfalls, including for the farmers who advocate it, and especially when it comes to food security. Let's start with food production. There is no right answer to how much of what sort of food should be produced on British farmland and, despite the rhetoric, the maximisation of production has never been a serious aim except in the most desperate years of World War II. Production could be maximised by a number of steps, which would be rightly rejected by the population, including those buying the food. Mega-intensive cattle, pig and dairy units, and larger-scale and more intensive and industrial battery chicken factories are not acceptable because they involve an intolerable level of animal cruelty and pollution. Farming intensity and practice is always subject to minimum standards and rules. Food security is not an absolute priority, but just one consideration among many.

Recall too, the fact that farmers do not pay for the pollution they cause. If they did, their costs would be higher and their output lower. By tolerating the idea that the polluted and not the polluter should pay, agricultural output is higher than it should be on economic efficiency grounds. If farmers paid the true costs of their farming practices, and if there was a level playing field in terms of tax, benefits, and the removal of subsidies for land-ownership, the shape of British farming would be very different from what it is now. Nature and natural capital would be correspondingly higher. The resulting economic equilibrium would be altogether more benign.

Would this be a problem? Only if Britain were cut off, or if it faced the possibility of being cut off, from foreign food supplies, or if the land reverted to scrub as farmers abandoned it. The former prospect is absurd: it is just silly. In the event of a major war, the new digital technologies would render Britain defenceless pretty quickly, and the nuclear button would probably be the only serious, credible defence. The electricity industry and all the computers, robots and data networks would be taken out long before anyone could starve to death because Britain could not produce its own food. Re-running the (non-nuclear) blockades of World War II is to imagine that technology has not marched on since the days of Spitfires, the Battle of Britain and the Atlantic Convoys.

But just for a moment imagine that Britain seriously wanted to be self-sufficient in food production using its current methods. The obvious steps would be to invest in our own chemical production of fertilisers, pesticides and herbicides, and in tractor and machinery manufacture. Britain imports most of this now: under siege it could not, and hence there should be an immediate programme of national agricultural industry development. Storage would be crucial and national stores would be set up around the country, stockpiling basic essentials and of course chemicals. Better still would be to have a rationing regime ready to go, following the rationing that lasted into the 1950s.

With this investment in primary industrial processes, the next step would be to take a hard look at what is happening on the land. Out would go non-food-maximising activities. There would be a significant switch from animals to cereals. The hill farms would stop game production and shooting. Biofuel crops would probably go. And so on. For the inconvenient truth for the farming lobbyists who play the 'food security' card is that quite a lot of farming is not for food at all in the conventional sense that food security requires. These lobbyists would have a lot to lose if they thought through the full implications for their farms of what they advocate. They would be growing potatoes, not acres of oilseed rape, and breeding pheasants.

A moment's reflection tells us that we are not remotely pursuing the sort of agriculture which would be able to give us food security, and to do so would be not only a great economic burden, but also not the best defence policy. It would be better to invest in cyber security for the electricity industry, without which the economy and now much of the farming industry would collapse in a matter of days, if not hours.

Food security is largely an empty slogan of lobbyists. It should not be taken seriously. A better question is what proportion of our food *consumption* should be home-produced and what proportion imported. For example, we might want to reduce food miles for welfare and carbon reasons. If this is the aim, then the live *export* of animals would probably be stopped. All those sheep going to Europe would stay here. Stopping live animal exports is one of the better policies if food security is what matters. Indeed, stopping exports generally would be conducive to increasing domestic food security, feeding ourselves before people in other countries. But when it comes to wheat and other grains, quite a lot of British farming may be uncompetitive without farm subsidies and its avoidance of paying for the pollution it causes. To increase the percentage of British food consumed at home, we could also stop importing avocados, beans, mangoes and all-year-round fruit and vegetables. It would make for interesting politics, and is hopelessly unrealistic, even if it might reduce the air miles.

Farmers' lobby groups argue that the CAP has given us cheap food, and if production falls food prices will go up. This again is nonsense. Food costs are *higher* not lower because of the CAP, and the reason is tariffs. If we produced less and imported more, under a free-trade regime, food prices would fall, not rise. That is not necessarily a 'good' thing: it depends on the full costs of production. But whether it is or is not desirable should not be muddled up with the error of claiming that the CAP produces cheap food.

A better agricultural sector and countryside

Imagine if the £3 billion CAP subsidy were diverted from the basic farm payment to the provision of public goods primarily from the agricultural sector. Imagine too if a full suite of pollution charges was introduced for artificial fertilisers, pesticides, herbicides and to capture the emissions of carbon and ammonia from farmland. Imagine if the tax system were common to all of industry, including the taxes on diesel and other carbon-intensive fuels and business rates.

This is what a normal industry looks like, and it is what normal agriculture could look like. It would be massively more economically efficient. All the costs would be priced into production, on a common basis.

It is enough to make some farmers choke on their breakfast. 'How could they survive?', they would try to get their MPs to shout in Parliament, and lobby the media. But stand back and consider what the public benefits would be. Three things would happen pretty quickly. Land prices would fall, decapitalising the

CAP subsidies. Land would be within the reach of young farmers to get into the industry. And marginal land would be taken out of production, unless explicitly subsidised to produce public goods. The composition of agriculture would change, as chemical inputs became more expensive, soils better protected and water abstraction reduced, all as a result of having to pay for the pollution.

What is not to like about this? There are two negatives. *Some* of the existing farmers would, like the coal miners in the 1980s and 1990s, face a sharp change of fortunes; and they claim that food output would fall, at least initially. The first is less than it seems. The loss to farmers caused by the adjustment depends on the aggregate subsidy and its distribution. Supposing that £3 billion continues to be spent on the agricultural sector. There is *no net loss* to the sector *as a whole*. The £3 billion is income to *some* farmers. It is just that they are *different* farmers. The money now goes to those who produce more public goods, and not to those who tend to produce more harm than good. There could be special support for those who choose to leave the industry, as indeed is set out in the 2018 Agriculture Bill.

It turns out that the beneficiaries of the 'public money for public goods' method of distributing subsidies tend to be the less chemical-intensive, and more marginal farmers. These are the small family mixed farms of the lowlands and the hill farmers. They have more to offer to the public good precisely because their farms have retained a better environment. They are the ones with the hedges and the stone walls, the water meadows and the moorland. With land prices at a more normal level, the basis for a sustainable farming industry is created, and one that is much more viable for farmers than the one produced by the current crazy economics of agriculture. They could also be paid for sequestrating carbon.

The second claim from the lobbyists is that there would be a flood of imports. Yet this also is less than it seems. For while protectionist tariffs are detrimental, common standards at the border are not. If imports have lower welfare standards, include pollution that is not paid for, receive state aid, and are the result of higher carbon emissions, these can and should be dealt with at the border. That includes imported carbon emissions caused by foreign production and transport. Those avocados and mangoes and winter strawberries would (and should) be more expensive. Free trade is not distorted trade. It is economically efficient to insist on the same standards and a common border carbon price.[34]

With the subsidies spent on the public goods and with polluters paying for the damage they cause, nature in Britain would be radically transformed. The challenge is to sort out which public goods should have what amounts spent on them, and who should get the money. How to go about this is set out in chapter 8. In the meantime, let's take a closer look at the uplands, whose farmers will stand to benefit most from a new, more economically efficient agricultural policy.

What is not to like about this?

5

THE UPLANDS

When most people think of the British countryside, and the nature that goes with it, they typically have the uplands in mind. They contain a lot of what is left of our biodiversity, and they have some spectacular scenery and much beauty. They also tend to be open, so people can go and enjoy them, in contrast to the fenced-off lowlands and intensive agricultural lands.

There are lots of uplands, and they include much of Scotland and its mountains and moorlands, the Pennines, the Peak District, the North York Moors, the Lake District, Snowdonia, the Brecon Beacons, Exmoor, Dartmoor and the South Downs. In England and Wales the key uplands are National Parks, and many of those that are not are often listed as AONBs. In Scotland, there is so much to choose from that only a small proportion of uplands are National Parks, including the Trossachs, Loch Lomond and the Cairngorms.

Uplands are special in part because they have few other uses. They have not been built upon, and farming has always been extensive and with much lower revenues than the lowlands. It is a harsher environment and typically a harder life for those who choose to make their living there.

Large swathes of Britain's uplands were once closed off to the public, with 'Keep Out' and 'No Trespassing' signs prominently displayed, for the benefit of big estates, and their associated grouse moors, pheasant shoots and, above all, deer stalking. The 'land question' about access and ownership has been one long battle to open up these upland areas. In Scotland it is still a visceral part of its politics, as it has been since the Highland Clearances evicted significant numbers of tenants during the eighteenth and nineteenth centuries.

They have typically been badly managed. The combination of sheep, deer and grouse has not been as beneficial to the uplands biodiversity as it might have been, and given the poor economic returns of sheep, the scope for improvement without significant economic cost is considerable. The uplands contribute very little to food security, and little to genuinely economic food production. They overwhelmingly depend on subsidies. The taxpayer is the main source of income, and as taxpayers we can get much better outcomes. The uplands offer great potential to deliver a much greener environment at no extra cost. They can be much greener and we can be much more prosperous as a result.

The rewilding fallacy

The most immediate visual impact in most uplands is the lack of trees, and the barren appearance. This is not a natural characteristic. On the contrary, it is the direct result of how the landscapes have been managed. With little or no competing land uses, much of the uplands can only be grazed. And grazed they have been: the lack of vegetation is a product of the millions of sheep, some cattle and lots and lots of deer. The sheep are farmed for the wool and meat, neither of which has much economic justification. The deer are encouraged and protected by the sporting interests.

Reducing the grazing pressures on the uplands is the single most important measure that could be taken, and one that is likely to encourage greater economic prosperity, rather than the reverse. The sheep are the lawnmowers of the uplands, in both the sense of close grazing and because they keep the land 'tidy'.

For some the answer is just to get rid of them and to 'rewild' the landscape, and save money in the process. The idea is that nature will then take its course, with first scrub and then gradually the emergence of natural woodlands. It has a superficial appeal as a core part of greening the landscape. What could be more natural than leaving nature to its own devices?

The answer is that 'natural' is not a reversion to some past baseline equilibrium of predominantly forest cover, followed by juniper and willows on the highest mountain screes. Our environmental engineering has so modified the land that any new equilibrium that emerges will be very different. There are no wild cattle to open up the glades, and no wolves to control the deer (to which we return below). In creating the uplands environment that we have now, the land has been opened up by the sheep and deer instead, and by the creation of field systems and the clearing of the forests.

To return some of the native Scots pine Caledonian forests,[1] and to allow oak woods to regenerate in some places is a good idea, but even in this case the process of getting from here to there will have its own dynamics and require a lot more environmental engineering. The deer would have to be intensively and repeatedly culled. The farmland birds of the uplands have adapted to the open landscape. The return of trees will be good news for some species and bad news for others.

It would not be obviously beneficial to simply withdraw, except in circumstances of *deliberate* neglect. The species balance would need to be readdressed too – both in dealing with the aliens who would thrive in this new world, and in thinking through the predator–prey relationships. To those in favour of rewilding in a more radical way, the task is to re-engineer the biodiversity. This means bringing back the animals and plants that have been lost. Less recognised, it also means losing others that have adapted to our man-made uplands but that might not escape the new predators.

The crucial species to reintroduce would be the top predators and very large herbivores to keep forest clearings open. At Knepp Castle in West Sussex there is a lowlands experiment to do just this, with cattle roaming without fences within the estate, building on the earlier example in the Netherlands.[2] But this is just the start: the new wild will need wolves, lynxes and beavers too. All are proposed, but the top predator – the wolf – has its obvious detractors who see it as dangerous not just to sheep and other livestock, but also to people. There would need to be a lot of wolves to control the deer. Wild animals do not have an automatic desire to stay out of the way in remote places – like foxes that look for food wherever they can find it, in towns and cities that are sources of abundant waste protein. In the case of wolves this is apparent in both Germany and France, and a reaction is inevitable.

In Alladale in Scotland, a plan to introduce wolves is one that sees the Scottish uplands as a giant wildlife park, fenced in from the outside world (as is Knepp Castle).[3] It would in effect be a large-scale extensive zoo, the Alladale Wilderness Reserve. This is not rewilding. It is very controlled, environmental engineering on a grand scale, in part because one person can own so much of the land. The animals that would be most strictly controlled are people, as paying safari travellers. The Alladale Wilderness Reserve has so far done much good conservation work, and has taken a more creative path compared with the conventional estate management for game. These are considerable benefits, as at Knepp, but wild it is not.

For some rewilders, the key is about getting rid of human influences, as if there is a state of nature apart from us which must be protected from us. It is a bit like the Chernobyl nuclear disaster site, where nature has recolonised the exclusion zone around the old power station.[4] Nature has indeed thrived in what might be regarded as the ultimate sanctuary, where people are kept out.

Rewilding means that all the numerous positive human environmental improvements, all the hedges and ditches, and all the hay meadows, would be allowed to fall back into scrub and woodland. This might be what is happening anyway as the hedgerows are neglected and the bracken spreads. But this is not the only option: the hedges and ditches and ponds could instead be managed for nature, and the hay meadows preserved and enhanced for nature. Getting rid of silage and returning to traditional hay meadow management maintains habitats that would not thrive on neglect. This active management of nature by us, and with us very much in mind, is the opposite of rewilding. It is a man-made and man-managed nature, for which we take responsibility. It allows us to create something better for the future, and to maximise the benefits to us that will follow.

None of this active approach rules out managed neglect of particular areas. The key difference in the managed case is that this is a *planned* decision and not an accident, and it is precise in its location and not general. It is a location-specific, controlled withdrawal of one type of land management in favour of another.

The rewilding approach has a determinism to it which tends to ignore the transition as well as the desirability or otherwise of the end state. The management now in place would be dropped, and the results might not be quite what the advocates imagine. Culling herbivores, like deer, is a key part of the management not just of the highlands, but of almost all woods and forests, and where it does not happen the results can be really damaging. Nor would it necessarily live up to our sense of beauty. Indeed, it is integral to rewilding that landscapes we have come to love would gradually disappear.

Our woods and forests, which the rewilders would allow to expand rather than deliberately create, have been invaded by both native and alien species. The 'wild' of Britain did not have fallow deer, sika deer or muntjacs. It had only red deer and roe deer, themselves food for the top predators. The aliens have tended to prefer the south and the lowlands, but they have nevertheless cleared much of the woodland and forest undergrowth. This habitat is important to many species. But it is also crucial to the forest itself, and undermines its ability to regenerate naturally. In the 'wild woods', large animals would push down trees and create clearings, into which first foxgloves and other glade-loving plants would flower, then the brambles and scrub species would take over, to be followed by new saplings pushing through. The deer have cut out this entire process. Any rewilding project probably needs a mass deer cull first. Pure rewilding would require the elimination of all these aliens. Even with such drastic measures to remove a thousand years of aliens, and to bring back the top predators, it is still not clear what the pre-human baseline to which all this aspires to revert would be, since it would need to get rid of most of the humans too. There were not many of us in the wild past. That is why it was wild.

Sheep and the uplands

Sheep cover all of the uplands, and are a key determinant of the resulting natural environment. There are around 23 million of them in Britain.

It is important to understand the incentives of sheep farmers. Maximising profits is best achieved by having as many sheep as possible on any given area. Shepherding is a hard life, on the margins of profitability, and the form of farming has evolved over centuries to exploit the natural environment to the maximum. From the early 1970s, the CAP subsidised farmers on a per-head basis, further increasing the incentives to overgraze. The 2005 CAP reforms weakened these headage payments, and numbers fell back somewhat. Agri-environment schemes have helped to reduce the stocking densities. The overall position nevertheless remains one of subsidy-driven excess stocks.

Nowhere is all this history more apparent than in the Lake District. In *The Shepherd's Life*, James Rebanks sets out beautifully how the sheep-farming business works on the fells, and how the sheep are 'hefted' to a particular location.[5] This is an uplands culture, and one that many feel ought to be preserved.[6] Why? Because it exists. It is a bit like the argument for keeping coal pits open in the mid-1980s – because they underpin a local mining community and its culture.

These cultural arguments are important and should not be ignored. Yet they are only part of the picture. The culture matters in itself to the local people and because it is sold to tourists, who are fascinated by 'how the locals live'. This is true too in the high Alps in Switzerland, and other beautiful rural locations. A tradition is valuable *because* it is a tradition, and because we can gape at it and imagine what it is to live like that, but then go home to our comfortable lives.

The argument about sheep on the uplands is not about whether there is sheep farming (expect for the rewilders), but rather how many and how they are managed. It is an argument about whether the current and recent sheep densities have done too much environmental damage, and whether the pressures should be lessened. Reducing the numbers reduces the sheep-related incomes of the farmers, but not necessarily their *overall* income. In the Lake District, most farmers farm the landscapes as well as the sheep, and the tourists come for the landscape the farmers manage but not for the densities of sheep. This is about balance, managing natural capital and searching for greater overall prosperity.

The deer problem

The deer problem is huge in the uplands, especially when it comes to red deer. These are the targets of stalkers, and have been the sport of kings and the aristocracy. Indeed, so much so that 'forests' were created as hunting parks, even if the word 'forest' did not have its current meaning.[7]

Deer stalking is big business, and it is a social prestige activity predominantly for the better off, even when it is not profitable. To get the best chance of shooting a deer, it helps if there are lots of them; shooting estates resist plans for substantial culls.[8] Their interest is in the deer herds, not the wider environment. The result is mass overgrazing of the uplands, and especially the highlands. So great are the resulting populations that it is a Malthusian solution that nature sometimes imposes on them: starvation in winter. Overpopulation leads to stress, and to weaker animals as there are no predators to kill the more vulnerable and smaller animals. In fact, stalking can induce the reverse, by killing the biggest and strongest stags with the largest antlers.

In the case of red deer, the answer is obvious: there should be a serious reduction in numbers, and then permanently managed lower numbers. This is active management to encourage the return of a lot of plants and animals, and insects too. The state of the uplands and its biodiversity is a public good that the private interests of estates should not trump for short-term profit. The current deer population is reducing the natural capital, not enhancing it, impoverishing the biodiversity and thereby reducing the prosperity of everyone else. Ironically, it will in the end seriously damage the estates too, for the ultimate victims of overpopulation are the deer themselves and those who profit from them. It is another example of the folly of assuming that those who own the land are the best guardians of nature and the public good, or indeed even of their own.

Game shooting

Grouse moors are also a part of the way uplands have been managed. To maximise the population of these tricky creatures with their very particular requirements, the moors are intensively managed for their benefit. Indeed, grouse moors are among the most intensively managed of all upland habitats.

The moorland management comes in various forms. There is the heather, which is treated as a crop for grouse, and takes over from the native boglands. Grouse need short heather with fresh growth. To achieve this outcome, the heather needs to be regularly burnt. This, like all such management techniques, is good for some things and bad for others. It creates a fairly uniform and drier sward.[9] Add sheep, and this is an overgrazed and over-managed habitat.

Grouse are not only fussy eaters but also vulnerable to predators, particularly as their numbers are kept artificially high. To the estates and their gamekeepers, anything that gets in the way of the game birds is vermin and should be killed. Gamekeepers are masters at this and over the last couple of centuries have got rid of lots of golden eagles, hen harriers and buzzards, as well as stoats, weasels and foxes. In the Cairngorms, the estates even shoot the relatively rare mountain hares for sport and because they might spread diseases from ticks, which might then infect the grouse.[10]

The case of the hen harriers is perhaps the best known. Hen harriers are well adapted to Britain's uplands and were once common. The gamekeepers have put paid to this abundance through poisoned bait and traps and by shooting them. There are only a few pairs left, and still some gamekeepers try to kill them. The hen harrier's problem is that the grouse chicks appear at a critical time in its breeding season, and hen harriers do what predators do – predate on them. The obvious incentive on the estates is to kill them. Indeed, to eradicate them. That is what they have done.[11]

At one level this is just criminal, and we are more prosperous if the criminals are deterred.[12] But the chances of getting caught, the unwillingness of the police and the courts to prosecute, and the paltry fines that are imposed, mean that criminal sanctions are pathetically weak. Add in the historical politics of landowner interests, and the tie-in with the local community from which gamekeepers come and for whom the estates represent jobs, and the hen harrier looks doomed. A serious criminal system would make the landowner and the gamekeeper criminally liable and the law would be enforced. When the Duke of Somewhere, the Laird of Somewhere Else, or a leading landowning financier is jailed, then the deterrence might work. The added advantage of the criminal route is that a very small number of people own most of the grouse moors, and hence a few individuals can turn this around. It is noticeable that as a result of estates becoming 'vicariously liable' in Scotland in 2012, the number of reported crimes has dropped.[13]

Responsibility for the consequences of grouse moor management lies with the owners. They are the 'polluters' imposing costs on the rest of us, and they should pay. A more prosperous uplands would start with the licensing of game shoots and then a levy to put right the damage caused. The result would be a more sustainable and, therefore, ultimately more prosperous game industry.

Other game and their consequences

Pheasant shoots have become a big economic activity in a number of upland areas (and lots of lowland areas too). In Exmoor, the place to go for high shoots, it is probably more economically significant than other forms of farming. Over Britain as a whole, at least 40 to 50 million (and perhaps as many as 80 million)[14] pheasants are let loose every year for shooting, and around 35 per cent of these get shot. Pheasant shoots employ more people than do grouse shoots, and they employ them in the winter months when other jobs in the uplands are scarce. The uplands shooters frequent the local pubs and hotels during these quieter periods. These activities therefore have a positive economic footprint, albeit narrowly measured, in the uplands where they occur.[15]

Pheasants are very vulnerable to predators. They are big birds, slow to take off, and they nest on the ground. In the old systems of rough shooting, local wild populations of pheasants, augmented by a few releases, comprised a niche. Now they are sometimes unleashed on an industrial scale. Feeding pheasants is relatively simple: they need grain, lots of grain. This is spread out in feeding stations, and is a bonus for woodpigeons and rats. It can be rather like free-range poultry-keeping.

In order to get the pheasants into shooting positions, special crops are sown in the middle of the year to provide pheasant cover in the winter. These are very good for some species, and particularly replace the stubble that seed-eaters once relied on in winter. They also provide roosts for starlings. Lots of pheasants are wounded rather than killed, providing abundant carrion for corvids (predominantly crows and magpies) and foxes. The higher populations of corvids predate in the summer on small birds' eggs and chicks (as do rats). The foxes are simply shot. Owls, buzzards and other birds of prey (largely) survive the pheasant interest because they are protected, and, unlike on the grouse moors, there are many more eyes to see what gamekeepers get up to.

Pheasant shooting, like grouse shooting and deer stalking, brings jobs to the uplands and provides habitats and food for wild birds and mammals. But there are minuses too: pheasants are avid omnivores, consumers of insects and small reptiles, and they eat plants too. Too many pheasants can have a big impact on biodiversity, largely of the sort not so obvious to the casual observer. Furthermore, killing this number of pheasants puts literally tonnes of lead shot onto the landscape, and from there into the water courses, and into the bodies of the birds and animals that eat wounded birds. The widely asserted claim of the shooting lobby that the pheasant shoots are on balance good for the environment and conservation is unproven, and depends on locality, and especially on the intensity and management techniques. On the large intensive shoots, it is probably wrong.

With red deer stalking and grouse and pheasant shooting, there is a considerable environmental difference between *some* and *a lot*. In the absence of proper economic incentives and licensing, it is easy to predict that there will be too much of all of these. Indeed, that is precisely the case, and the reason is that the game interests do not face the costs of the environmental damage they cause. The polluters don't pay. The results are economically inefficient, and economic prosperity is lower. Some deer, some grouse and some pheasants are, on balance, fine for nature; lots of them are bad.

The National Parks

The National Parks have a long history, motivated in part by the example of Yellowstone in the USA, and the story of John Muir.[16] In the USA, the concept was tied up with ideas about the frontier, the open lands of the west, the early settlers and the 'wilderness'. Much of this was of course romantic nonsense. The land had long been shaped by the indigenous populations, conveniently blotted out perhaps because they were thought to be 'wild' too, and removed to reservations.

Britain is a comparatively small country. There was no frontier, but rather a highly urban population and densely populated lowlands. The Hobhouse Report[17] led to the National Parks Act in

1949. It was part of the new planning framework that emerged in the late 1940s after World War II, largely within the ambit of local authorities. Green Belts would be the lungs of the cities; the planning framework would limit ribbon development and urban sprawl; and the National Parks would protect the uplands for the wider public's enjoyment. Britain's land has different purposes and should be divided up accordingly. It was a highly managed model.

That was the theory. In practice, landowning interests watered down the National Park plans in two ways. First, there were delays in implementation, taking a decade for the first batch to be designated. The New Forest was added only in 2005 and the South Downs in 2009. Others that would like to have joined from the ranks of the AONBs were blocked. Second, the powers of the National Parks were strictly limited and in practice they were largely planning authorities, governed by local government interests from the neighbouring towns. They were about stopping people doing things, rather than positively shaping their areas.

As a result, the National Parks are quite small, and the main impact has been in limiting developments by refusing planning permissions. This has been a big plus in that most of the Parks have survived the major housing and other development pushes in the 1960s and subsequently. It has been greatly to the credit of the National Parks that they have so far resisted growing pressures as the population has expanded. But there has been a minus too: the National Parks authorities have struggled to manage their environments in a proactive way, and indeed quite a lot has been left to the National Trust and other organisations. The reason is that they have neither the powers nor the money to do so. They should.

Notwithstanding these limitations, National Parks are popular, and they have potential to play a much bigger part in the enhancement of our natural environment. Not only do they represent a well-liked brand, they also cover distinct areas and now have the administrative systems in place. There are lots of options, and all will need to incorporate the 25 Year Environment Plan objectives in their statutory duties to enhance their natural capital.[18] The Glover review of the Parks launched in 2018 went some way towards this, but not far enough. It remains unfinished business.[19]

To do this properly in the uplands, the National Parks will need to have a relationship with, and a role in, the post-Brexit agricultural policies. If agricultural subsidies are for public goods only, and most of these are environmental, then the National Parks are the place for the development and implementation of public goods strategies. As part of the rolling planning cycle, the agricultural subsidies will need to be factored in.

It is a small step to give the National Parks a share of the monies for the subsidies as part of their financial allocations. There are two routes forward which are discussed in greater detail in chapter 11. The Parks could decide what the money is to be spent on and then contract for the required services; or they could invite farmers and others to bid for them on the basis of the greatest net environmental benefit. They could do both options in partnership with the river catchment system operators, discussed in chapter 3, and act on the system plans and operations of the uplands.

Public benefits in the uplands

The uplands, and especially the areas covered by the National Parks, lend themselves to landscape-wide projects. They are corridors for wildlife, and their high streams and rivers tend to carve out the valleys that make most of them so distinct. An upland plan will need to include catchment plans, pollution control and monitoring, and the protection of peat bogs and moorland. Each of these needs its own support and enhancement in this man-made landscape.

The starting point is the capital maintenance of what remains, to avoid any further deterioration. Measures include the reduction of sheep grazing as discussed above, the culling of deer, the special protection of peat bogs, and the maintenance of walls and hedges. Further encroachment onto moorlands will need to be stopped. These are the obvious first moves. Deer culling produces venison; peat bogs reduce flooding and improve the quality of water supplies; and the walls and hedges provide key public goods to the landscape that attract the tourists, who in turn spend within the Park boundaries. They all increase prosperity.

The hills themselves should not, however, be left without grazing altogether. Deer and sheep have roles to play in preventing the encroachment of scrub (to stop unplanned rewilding), but they are not necessarily always best at moorland management. Cattle play a part too, as do ponies because of the particular way in which they graze. Exmoor and Dartmoor have their respective pony herds on the moors, and many conservation bodies use ponies on specific areas of land.

The uplands have specific habitats that support rare plants and insects, and a number of these areas are recognised as SSSIs. To prevent further losses many of these require direct attention. Sometimes this is just protection from sheep, but there may be other requirements too. Reducing the use of artificial fertilisers to 'improve' grassland and going organic is more cost-effective where the value of the final product is low. Limiting the incursion of pheasants onto moorland helps protect both plants and invertebrates, and some reptiles too. Branding upland produce as organic and local can increase value-added.

When it comes to the upland birds, the main problems are persecution and pollution. The persecution is largely illegal. As noted, the problem is enforcement and credible punishments. There is a good case for tying landowner subsidies to full compliance with the spirit and the letter of the law, and in addition to

fines and prison sentences, withdrawing subsidies from criminals. Killing protected birds should be as socially unacceptable
as smoking in public buildings and drink-driving. Both were once
widespread and accepted, as was the persecution of wildlife, and
the change in attitude has come about with changes in the law,
education, science and social approbation. Better still, we can
encourage the birds of prey to return. Imagine hen harriers once
again skimming across the Exmoor hills, the Pennines and over
the Yorkshire Moors.

The upland landscape has value beyond its biodiversity. The
hedges and the fields, the stone walls and the copses and woods
all form a particular landscape with which people are familiar.
This upland infrastructure is worth maintaining, and worth
paying for. There is nothing purely natural about this, and it is
not always environmentally optimal, but this is what people have
come to identify with and what they find beautiful. There is
therefore merit in incrementally working with what we have,
rather than attempting substantive change. Cultural value stands
alongside environmental value.

The upland population

The uplands are low-population-density areas with farming as
the main land use. Farming, however, is not the main economic
activity and farmers now employ only a very small number of
people and ancillary trades. While it is true that the social and
cultural life of the uplands has been shaped by farmers, they are
no longer the main players. As the farming technologies march
on, as described in chapter 4, farm employment will fall back
further.

The uplands are now populated by the retired, the second-
homeowners and the tourist industry employees.[20] These range
from the traditional hotels, inns, guest houses and campsites to

outdoor pursuits such as guided walking, horse-riding, climbing, bike tracks, fishing, sea adventures and so on. The second-homeowners and retired bring the demand for services and property maintenance, and again these can outweigh the demands of farmers. Indeed, many of these categories benefit the farmers as sources of diversified income. Quite a lot of the incomers own the farms. To this population are added the visitors, and there are millions of visits each year.

The economic value of all this activity is considerable, and it is part of the economic output of the country. Increasing this value-added increases prosperity. Thought of as environmental businesses, the National Parks cover economic growth zones of the economy. Unlike other parts of the economy, this economic growth depends on keeping much of the fabric of the upland economy as it is, rather than building and development as elsewhere in the economy. It is easy to add new attractions and developments, each perhaps bringing in more business to the areas. But each individual investment can add to the eventual demise of what it is that makes the areas attractive in the first place.

One example is the proposal for a zip wire between Borrowdale and Buttermere, which the Lake District National Park has approved. The zip wire is an economic proposition and in itself would bring more and perhaps different people into the Park. It is a new business with new revenues and new spending. On its own it might not make much difference to the Park as a whole. But add lots of others of this type of project and it becomes gradually more of a public amusement park than an area of outstanding beauty.[21] Contrast this with the approach to Ennerdale, where the driving strategy is to make it quiet and peaceful on the west side of the Lake District.

For the farming community, the demographics point to a bleak future. Many upland farmers are ageing, and there is little evidence that the upland farming life appeals to the next generation. It is often hard, not least because the land is poor and steep, and the weather exposure considerable. The sheep are worth little, and losses can be considerable. The farming systems have evolved over a millennium, combining the higher fells with lowland transfers for fattening. They are now falling apart for a variety of reasons. There are few young farmers who are willing – or, if willing, able – to step in. It is literally a dying demographic.

The temptation is to buy off this trend with more and more subsidies. For those who remain, the 2018 Agriculture Bill proposed encouraging farmers to retire by rolling up future subsidies. The future of the upland farmers lies in a very different business model, and indeed it is one that some are already embracing. Upland farms do not make ends meet from pure farming, and diversification and second incomes are now the norm. This needs to go one stage further, to seeing farmers as managers of the uplands in the public interest and less as primary food producers. There will be food niches and there will be a demand for local produce, but this is never going to add up to enough of a business for most farmers. It is a fantasy to pretend otherwise.

Given that the upland farming industry exists on subsidies, the other side of the equation is that it would be better to spend the subsidies on long-term viable and sustainable activities, rather than propping up excess sheep production. There will always be a need for the grazing and maintenance of the landscape that sheep bring to the uplands, but it is better to recognise that that is what the subsidies are for, rather than pretend they are supporting a viable food production business.

Once this approach is taken, the public goods can be defined. The uplands are ecosystems, and each has its key assets. In the Lake District, it is about controlling pollution in the lakes themselves, and, in particular, agricultural run-off of nitrates; about the protection of the thin soils and reducing the grazing densities; and about protecting and enhancing the mountain tops and pathways from overuse and erosion. The dry-stone walls are integral parts of these landscapes just as they are in the Peak District, whereas it is the hedgerows that form the landscape of Exmoor.

Delivering these public goods is often labour-intensive, and the sort of labour that is often of greatest value is the sort farmers are familiar with. Maintaining walls and hedges, and managing grazing and maintenance of paths all require machinery and a knowledge of the landscape that is embedded in the farming communities. They are the obvious contractors to take on this work and benefit from the income and employment it brings.

Managing the land for people, wildlife and carbon

What would the uplands look like if their natural capital were properly managed, protected from further damage and enhanced to increase prosperity? Some of the metrics would be about species. The uplands would have many more hen harriers, and golden eagles would extend their ranges. Wading birds that nest on the high moors, like the golden plover, would return with their haunting sounds. The uplands would see increases in all these birds and this would be achieved through recovery programmes for the most at risk. This is renewable natural capital that nature gives us for free, provided we do not drive the populations below key thresholds of extinction. It is natural capital that delights and at the same time has economic value.

Next would be the moorlands themselves, and here the vegetation would be more varied. The rowan and the hawthorns would return to provide some cover on the landscapes. The bracken would be controlled.[22] Natural heathers would be protected through more appropriate grazing, in particular controlling the molinia grass (*Molinia caerulea*). This would not be full rewilding. It would deliberately create a more varied habitat.

The peat and the peat bogs would be protected and where possible enhanced. Heather moorland, once drained, would be rewetted. These are important carbon stores, and reservoirs for biodiversity. The grazing would be light. The bogs would retain water and hence manage the catchments more effectively, both improving water quality downstream and limiting flooding. Some new woodlands might be created on the lower slopes to act as natural flood defence shields. The wind farms would be kept out.[23]

The fields would be more colourful. There would be more wild flowers, and this in turn would require a return to more traditional hay-making rather than silage. Hay meadows support an enormous diversity of plants, insects and birds.[24] The hay itself is probably not economic to make, but if the public goods – in this case both the landscape and the biodiversity – are valuable enough, the practice can be maintained. The important point is that it would not be under the current subsidy regime.

Fertilisers, pesticides and herbicides will become consigned to the sadder parts of upland history. From a natural capital perspective, 'improved grasslands' are not improved: they are stripped of their colour and biodiversity. A really radical idea, and perhaps a step too far, would be to prohibit the use of pesticides and herbicides in the uplands, and reduce subsidies to those who use artificial fertilisers.

It is a similar concern with hedges and walls. Across many of the National Parks sheep have broken down the walls and the hedges. Barbed wire is cheaper and easier to manage than traditional hedge laying and wall repairs. But the hedging and walling are valuable in maintaining both the landscapes and the biodiversity. They have costs and benefits, and more benefits probably than the sheep that the barbed wire is intended to keep in. As with the hay meadows, this is an opportunity as well as a cost. There are urban visitors who enjoy these activities, and courses run by volunteers to make them happen. Money *plus* volunteers *plus* local farmers can add up to a resource to do the capital maintenance. The total costs are not that great, and in any event, it is the maintenance of some and not all of the hedges and walls.

Capturing the value of capital maintenance and enhancements is problematic precisely because they are public goods. The visitors go, for example, to Tarr Steps in Exmoor, expecting to be able to walk across. Yet they do not pay for the repair and maintenance of the stones, which are dislodged from time to time after river spates. The value exists, but it is not captured in any direct price that visitors pay.

There are several solutions, which are discussed more extensively in chapter 11. One is for a visitor charge. This could be collected from hotels, holiday lets, guest houses and campsites – essentially from anyone who takes a bed overnight. Many Swiss resorts levy such a charge, and this contributes to the maintenance of the general infrastructure, visitor information centres and other public services. Such a model could be applied to National Parks on a case-by-case basis. It could be described as a membership fee. In return for paying a levy, the visitor could be given a card, along the lines of that issued for National Trust membership. We could all join our National Parks.

The voluntary bodies, notably the Trusts, have a key part to play too. There are already 'friends' of all sorts in the uplands. There are National Trust projects, Wildlife Trust initiatives, and small local initiatives to protect and enhance specific natural capital assets. To these could be added the contributions from companies with specific interests. The Exmoor Mires Project is one example, where a combination of voluntary bodies, the Exmoor National Park and South West Water work together, and these can in turn attract funding from further afield. Initiatives of this sort require coordination, and it is here that the National Park strategic plans come into play.

The enhancement of the uplands will not, however, happen spontaneously, and there are controversial choices to be made and conflicting interests. Vested interests tend to shout loudest and get their way. Enhancement requires a plan, some coordination and money. Building on what is already in place, the National Parks are obvious leaders. What they need is an element of control over some of the agricultural subsidy monies, freed from the CAP. With a plan and the money, the Parks can coordinate, invite bids from farmers and others to deliver the public goods, and ensure that these projects are delivered. The result will be vibrant and local upland economies, an end to the decline of farming (and farmers), and a much-enhanced natural environment.

What is not to like about this?

6

THE COASTS

Nowhere in Britain is more than 50 miles direct from the sea. The sea has shaped not just Britain's military and political life, but also its natural environment. Although physically cut off only 8,000 years ago from Europe, and only by just over 20 miles, the closure of the land bridge with the continent, and the land bridge to Ireland, has already biologically marked us.

People's love of the coast has taken different forms throughout history. Once it was the source of fear – fear of invaders, from the Anglo-Saxons and Jutes, to the Vikings and the Normans and, most recently, the Germans. It has been a source of danger from flooding and to shipping. Our shores are littered with wrecks. It was only in the nineteenth century that the coast became a draw for holidaymakers, and the idea of the seaside holiday is very recent.[1]

Now, millions of people visit the coast, and many often repeatedly. Outside the cities, the coast is the destination of choice for tourists, so much so that in Cornwall the pressure was so great during the hot summer of 2018 that the tourist authorities suspended their promotion of certain beaches.

The reason that people get so much pleasure from our coasts is partly that they are so varied, and partly that the sea is warmer than the latitude would otherwise dictate. The Gulf Stream, and the shallowness of our seas, also explain why our coastal waters are rich fisheries – rich for people and for birds and other wildlife.

The long-running BBC series *Coast* testifies to the affection the public has for this special area, caught between the solid land and the uncertain seas.[2] Its history, the violence of its storms, its beaches and its cliffs have an obvious hold on the collective imagination of 'our island nation'.

When it comes to the state of this natural capital, some bits get much better protection than others. On the land side, access and use have gradually increased, and there has been a long slow process to opening up the coastal path around the whole of England, building on separate paths, like the South West Coast Path. On the beaches, plastic and associated rubbish pile up. In the coastal waters, it is sewage, agricultural chemicals and other pollution and overfishing that take their toll. In estuaries it is all of these, as well as the industrial and housing developments and sea walls that take up mudflats and salt marshes, and bring the shore to an abrupt halt. At least an astonishing 70 per cent of the seabed is harrowed for shellfish and trawled. Nobody would tolerate this on land where it could be seen.

In all these cases, the scope for enhancing nature is considerable, and especially valuable since it is these areas where people are likely to directly benefit most, and where there are lots of businesses that depend on coastal use, leisure and tourism. The scope for more damage is also considerable. Barrages, tidal lagoons, new ports and docks all press on the coastline, while the shallow coastal waters are ideal for wind turbines. Holding the line is not without its challenges.

The coastal fringe

The strip of land between the sea and the agricultural and built environment is an extraordinarily valuable bit of natural capital.

It is valuable because it comprises a set of special niches and habitats. Britain's seabirds nest here, and the gorse and coastal scrub provide good nesting sites and a refuge for insects and mammals. It is diverse too: some of our coast comprises high cliffs, such as those on the Exmoor coast, others the gradual blurred landscapes and habitats where the land slips gradually into the sea, such as the Essex coastal marshes.

This strip of land has other competing uses, and it is where lots of towns and cities touch the sea. The promenade is the subject of great novels and great scandals.[3] Towns create their own special coastal features. The coastal towns developed as ports, with harbours and the fishing and shipping trades. As the fishing has largely gone, and as shipping has concentrated on much larger boats and especially containers, Britain's coasts are littered with the relic villages and towns, and these tend to be among the most picturesque – history without modernisation and without the industry. The southwest coast is dotted with these.

Natural capital at the edge of the sea is a major attraction for walkers, and there has been a long history of battles for access, largely now finally won. The early coastal paths joined up local rights of way, but the continuity around the whole coast has come up against private property rights, in some cases including claims to own the beaches.

The project for a path around the whole of England's coast is due to be completed by 2020, making it at 2,795 miles the longest such managed path in the world. From a strictly natural capital perspective, filling in the last gaps is of limited value to nature. Yet its symbolism, and the idea that you could walk around the entire coast, captures people's imagination. As such it has a value, even if few actually walk the whole length.

Connectivity has a special value for nature as well as people. The coast is a series of wildlife corridors, a large-scale bit of joined-up nature that allows its inhabitants to move around.

Joining up the path for people raises a parallel challenge to joining it up for nature.

Imagine a joined-up nature pathway around the whole of England to complement the footpaths. This is already an aspiration of the Marine and Coastal Access Act 2009. As with the creation of the long-distance footpaths, quite a lot of it is already in place. There are nature reserves, SSSIs and land managed by the National Trust and other NGOs. There is also Ministry of Defence land.

Joining up the dots would be a big, ambitious project – big in the sense of the scale of the challenge, of greater natural capital value precisely because it is big, and of big value to the existing pathway users. Given that most children do visit the seaside, it would also be a great way of increasing their engagement with nature, and hence enhance the subsequent benefits they get throughout their lives from having a deeper appreciation of wildlife.

The land on the edges is often associated with active ports and industry. The coast is not always beautiful. It is punctuated with nuclear power stations, industrial works, and the hard landscapes of ports and housing. Yet even here there are surprising opportunities to make even the most concrete of waterfronts more nature-friendly. To many creatures, and especially to birds, ports are just particular kinds of cliffs. Legacy brownfield sites offer huge opportunities. Take West Thurrock Lagoons or West Canvey Marsh on Canvey Island. Next to the sea, with surprisingly varied habitats, they have lots of biodiversity. To these can be added the brownfield sites of most of our industrial ports. The coastal urban areas can also be greened.

To make this a joined-up nature corridor would require a great deal of coordination, and it would be a great British project. The pays-offs in terms of prosperity would be immense, and for two reasons. It would enhance the attractiveness of the coast itself to all the leisure and tourist businesses, and this would increase prosperity for many places which otherwise have little going for them. And it would also be applied to areas where there are typically few alternative uses and hence little cost of lost other outputs.

The beaches and marshes at the sea edges

The beach is what most children aspire to visit and it is where most people go when they visit coastal destinations. Yet many of the visitors are unaware of the natural wonders of the sand and the surf, and all the invertebrate life that inhabits these in-between zones. They might peer into the rock pools, but mostly it is about sun (or lack of it) and surf.

The main environmental issues people are aware of are those that threaten the 'cleanliness' of the beaches. There are good reasons for concern: many beaches experience the impacts of sewage discharged by pipes into the sea. Surfers Against Sewage is just one of the organisations trying to stop this. Sewage is obviously a health risk, but it is also a risk to marine life.

Plastic waste is both ugly and harmful: it is the antithesis of what people think of as 'the beach'.[4] Look at any beach holiday website: there is no rubbish in the photos. With the growing public awareness of the plastics problem, the sheer scale of the pollution of our coastline is becoming apparent. In Scotland, there is now a real-time map of the plastic rubbish left around the entire coastline.[5]

The Blue Flag system and the EU's Bathing Water Directives are major initiatives to tackle some of these issues, and the investment by the water industry to meet the 2006 Directive's requirements has had a significant impact on water bills.[6] The most notable area affected is the southwest, where shortly after the privatisation of the industry in 1990, an 11 per cent price increase was required to cover the necessary capital works. For much of the southwest, its narrow steep valleys and sparse population meant that sewerage pipes went straight to sea (augmented by agricultural run-off) – as sewage had once been dumped straight into the rivers. It was largely out of sight, and out of mind, until some of the least savoury bits appeared on the beaches.

Dog faeces is a major preoccupation for beach management, with dogs banned from many popular stretches of beach in summer. This is very much a human health issue, although dogs can also disrupt wildlife. A large dog running about in the dunes can be a disaster for ground-nesting birds. They can also be a danger to farmers' livestock. The cost of keeping dogs under control is small and the benefits large.

When it comes to marshes, the traditional approach has been to drain and protect the land from the sea with sea walls and hence reduce the marshlands to the fringes. Marshes have been treated as wastelands. The greatest example of this strategy is the Fenlands, drained by Dutch engineers in the seventeenth century and protected by sea walls and pumps. Along the east coast of Norfolk, Suffolk, Essex and Kent, this strategy has resulted in the loss of the great marshlands and their associated wildlife. Its great carbon store – the peat – continues to shrink and blow away.

The scale of the loss of wildlife will never be known because the records of what was there are sparse. Not many people lived in these areas and few, other than wildfowlers, recording their bags of ducks and geese, kept any tallies. We see now only a fragment of what was once there – the migratory ducks, geese and other waders – and those that remain are increasingly confined to nature reserves.

Holding back the tides proved impossible for King Canute, and it is proving increasingly expensive for the modern-day successors on the east coasts, as the land gradually sinks and the sea levels rise as a result of climate change. This creates the possibility of allowing the sea to take its natural path, flooding coastal land and re-creating the marshes and coastal mudflats that were once much more prevalent. Agricultural land, expensively protected by sea walls and drainage, is lost, but the offsetting gains are more than compensatory.

There are particular examples of deliberately doing this, notably at Wallasea Island on the Essex coast, created from 3 million tonnes of soil extracted to build Crossrail. Where breaches in sea defences occur during storms there are also examples of simply letting nature take its course, such as Porlock Marshes in Somerset, following a breach in the shingle ridge in 1996.

A natural capital approach to the sea defences would have lots of advantages if applied more generally. It would reduce the costs of coastal defences, add to the wildlife spectacles, especially for wintering birds, and bring a new dimension to the attraction of coasts. Salt marshes also store lots of carbon. They act as giant sponges and can ameliorate extreme coastal climate conditions.

The Minsmere RSPB reserve on the Suffolk coast is a good example, with 90,000 visits per year.[7] The avocet, the RSPB's mascot, returned to become an established breeding bird at Minsmere and is one of the success stories of the marshlands. Marsh harriers have been growing in numbers. Further up the coast, there are the Cley Marshes and a host of protected areas for wildlife. Elsewhere, in the southwest, Steart Marshes is a large-scale wetlands project, promoted by the Environment Agency and now managed by the Wildfowl & Wetlands Trust.[8]

For sustainable fishing, the marshes create a protected nursery for fish fry, adding another contribution to rebuilding fish stocks in the North Sea after decades of overfishing. As discussed below, areas like these, which are protected from fishing, are in the best economic interests of the fishing industry, even if it does not always see it this way.

The estuaries

Most of Britain's great rivers have estuaries, and all of them form substantial areas of mudflats rich in marine life.[9] The Thames, the Humber and the Solway Firth are on a very large scale, as is the Severn. These are some of the most important overwintering sites for birds because the mud is extraordinarily rich in invertebrates.

In addition to these major estuaries there are lots of smaller ones, from the Dovey in North Wales to the Camel in Cornwall, the Taw and the Torridge at Barnstable, the Stour and the Blackwater on the East Anglian coast.

Estuaries exaggerate the tides, and because of the meeting of fresh and salt waters offer up a remarkable variety of rich habitats. There are the permanent saltwater areas, the intertidal areas, and the brackish water as the rivers meet the sea. These are influenced by the geomorphology: some estuaries are outsized to reflect a drowned landscape. Others reflect more recent erosion. The rise in sea levels as the ice melted at the end of the last ice age submerged the land beneath what is now the Irish Sea and the estuaries on the west coasts, and these impacts can be seen at scale at Solway and the Severn, right along to small estuaries like the Fowey and the Dart. On the east coasts, the rise of the sea levels meeting low-lying coasts creates a much gentler effect as the land slips into the sea, modified by attempts to hold back the tides with sea walls and other coastal defences.

Most of these estuaries have significant ports and many have fishing activities too. They are all threatened by pollution, and most by major infrastructure projects. The muds collect the chemical pollutants. Just as ice cores record our past climate, estuary muds hold the history of our industrial past. The Thames Gateway project on the south bank of the Thames estuary required major dredging, disturbing ecosystems and the polluted sediments, which were then dumped elsewhere.[10]

A new threat to the estuaries comes from tidal lagoons and tidal power stations. The key idea here is to tap the tidal range and the result is to decrease the full intertidal range in the estuary, drowning the intertidal mudflats. The Tidal Lagoon project for the Severn Estuary off Cardiff is a case in point. In place of the natural estuary water flows of one of the largest tidal ranges in Europe, the Tidal Lagoon would require a large and long wall, with turbines capturing the energy in the flows for electricity generation.

The environmental impacts are hard to estimate because no one has done anything like this in the Severn Estuary before. The estuary is important for migrating fish, salmon, sea trout and shad, and for a host of creatures that follow the ebb and flow of the tides. It is yet another example of conflict between the environment and renewable energy, between the pursuit of the single climate change objective and wildlife and biodiversity.[11]

The coastal waters

For most people, the coastal waters of Britain fall very much into the 'out of sight, out of mind' category. Some people are aware of the depletion of the fish stocks, but less aware of the bottom trawling and scraping of the seabed. Even fewer notice the damage from centuries of fishing and from the use of the sea as a dumping ground for wastes.

The impacts of pollution are cumulative. The waters of much of what is now the very brown North Sea were once much clearer, filtered by large-scale oyster and mussel beds. These are all long gone, and with them the notion of oysters as the food of the poor. These filtering shellfish beds could be restored, both to yield food and to clean the water.[12]

The waters of our marine habitats are rich for several overlapping reasons. One is temperature and the impact of the Gulf Stream. One is the shallow nature of the coastal waters, and another is the juxtaposition of so much coast and intertidal zones.

The first big threat comes from pollution, and yet again agriculture is a major cause. The pollution plumes of the Rhine and the Thames can sometimes be clearly seen from space. The flows of nitrates and phosphates enrich the coastal waters and encourage algae to take out the oxygen. The pollution from the Industrial Revolution is in the sediments, spread out from the estuaries as noted above. Then there is the pollution from shipping, and from oil spills and the flushing of tanks. Add the flushing of leisure boats of their sewage and the water is in far from a fit state to support biodiversity.[13] Then there is the rubbish that flows down the rivers, that is thrown off boats and ends up accumulating in the great rubbish dumps that seas have become. Landfill requires a positive dumping of waste on land. Marine waste is more like fly-tipping and littering.

The plastics that now pervade our seas have only recently been recognised for the threat they pose, with every living creature likely to be polluted with plastic in one form or another. Plastics make up more than 75 per cent of marine litter. They are ubiquitous because they are so useful and because they take so long to biodegrade. Tonnes of plastic water bottles on the beaches are just the visible tip of the iceberg of microplastics in the natural food chains.[14]

The impacts of fishing are well researched, at least when it comes to the legal stuff and the recorded species for direct human consumption. Where once the impact of fishing was limited by sail, the coming of powered trawlers, and especially the diesel engine, meant that so much more could be caught. Add on recent information technologies and now the fish literally have no place to hide. Where once a skilled fisherman read the signs of the sea, such as the seabirds, and knew the nature of the seabed and the fishing grounds, now a sonar can detect the fish and they can be caught with surgical precision.

Since the seas are a form of 'commons' they are vulnerable to the tragedy of the commons – and they have been.[15] In a free-for-all there is always the incentive to catch the marginal fish, even if it pushes the stocks below the renewables thresholds, because everyone else has the same incentives. Nobody pays for the damage that repeated scouring of the seabed causes. The polluters, those who trash the sea floor, do not pay to restore it. Why is this allowed to happen?

This is the classic example of the vulnerability of renewable natural capital. The fish will carry on renewing themselves provided our human predation does not drive them below a threshold from which they become non-renewable, unable to maintain the stocks. What is lost is far more than the immediate catch. Think of herrings in the North Sea, a very abundant source of fish protein for generations. If the stock is protected, it can go on delivering that protein for centuries, indeed for ever or at least until evolution catches up with the species. Exterminate them now, which we nearly did, and not only is the catch lost now, but also for ever. This is a tragic loss of economic benefit for all future generations.

Yet this is what we have been doing for the last couple of centuries, both globally and in British waters. The well-known collapse of the Grand Banks cod fishery off the eastern seaboard of Newfoundland is one of the greatest examples of human folly.[16] But closer to home, the same very nearly happened to North Sea cod and for other species too. The cod's partial recovery shows what can be done if fishing is limited, but it and most other North Sea fish stocks remain vulnerable and too close to their thresholds for comfort. The blue-fin tuna catch collapsed in 1963 and has never fully recovered.[17] The partial recovery of cod should not be allowed to encourage further testing of the safe limits.

Fishing does not work as an unregulated activity unless the techniques are very primitive and inefficient. Except in special cases like bass, the angler on the seashore is unlikely to catch so many fish that there is a serious impact on fish stocks. But an angler on a riverbank can damage salmon stocks, and a poacher with a net in the estuary of a salmon river can do a great deal of damage.

It is not just wild fish stocks that are critical to our natural capital. Fish farming has been developing for several decades, and in the last decade has reached a new intensity. The primary fish farmed in Britain is salmon, although there are other examples.[18]

Salmon fish farming looks innocuous enough to the casual observer. A few fish cages in sea lochs, and some for the smolts in freshwater lochs, look tiny against the great expanses of the Scottish and Irish coasts. A closer look at the complete supply chain tells a different story. The fish need food, their concentration gives rise to diseases and pests, and their excrement goes out of sight below the fish pens. They escape too – surprisingly often – and disrupt the wild salmon.

The marine habitat is a food chain, like any other natural environment, and what matters most is what is at the bottom. This starts with the plankton, and moves up through the sand eels to the birds and the fish. Around Britain's coast there are several canaries in the mine whose song is falling silent. The seabirds have faced some catastrophic losses, and the wild salmon and sea trout populations have fallen sharply, despite the improvements in the rivers to which they migrate to spawn. The Tyne once again has a salmon run because the industrial pollution has been cleaned up, but it is a good news story set in the context of a general decline.

The data on the seabirds suggests something is going seriously wrong with their food supplies. Part of the answer is that these are being sucked up for other purposes, notably feeding on fish farms. They may literally be starving to death. Under the EU rules, Denmark has the UK sand eel quota to feed its fish farms.[19]

The islands

Britain's coasts are dotted with small islands. These include the Isles of Scilly, the Channel Islands, the Isle of Man, the Hebrides, the Orkneys and Shetland, and the Farne Islands, as well as a significant number of rocks and outcrops.

With a few notable exceptions, the economic value of these islands is almost entirely tied up with nature and tourism. There are few large industries on any of them,[20] and very few now have significant agriculture with a positive return net of subsidy. The exception is possibly salmon fish farming, although here the economics are questionable too. Rather, they are home to a number of niche industries, from knitwear and textiles (Harris Tweeds and Shetland woollens), to specialist plant and food products (Jersey Royal potatoes), and niche communities.

There are many reasons why being islands makes their economic prospects poor, but these reasons are also why their wildlife potential is high relative to the mainland. Their isolation makes it possible to limit some alien invasive species, and in some cases to eradicate them. This applies to many attempts to eliminate rats where they have been damaging seabird colonies (the Shiants, St Agnes), to the eradication of mink, and to at least control the hedgehogs that were foolishly introduced to the Outer Hebrides in order to control garden slugs.[21]

Crofting is the traditional form of agriculture on the Scottish islands, with long and sometimes bitter political histories. Many of these islands once had much bigger populations, but the Scottish Highland Clearances reduced them substantially, and where the process was allowed to follow market economics the populations declined anyway. The Isle of Skye had a peak of around 25,000 people in the first half of the nineteenth century; now it has around 10,000. Crofting is a hard life, and the young have many more opportunities elsewhere. It is often more a lifestyle choice than a serious economic proposition.

By accident, this crofting legacy has left some wonderful biodiversity, of which the machair of the Uists is notable for its flowers, invertebrates and nesting waders. As crofting declines further, this is rewilding by accident, and a good example of the costs to biodiversity. The corncrake, the great yellow bumblebee and the flowers of the machair have nowhere to go.

Returning the coast and the seas to good health – and increasing prosperity

The seas around our coast tell us what happens where natural capital is overexploited. We may claim to value its renewable natural capital, but we neglect to put a cost on the impacts of what has been going on, out of sight, out of mind, and without constraints. This renewable natural capital stops renewing itself. It happens gradually, and then there are sharp falls in bird and fish stocks. Weakened by decades of excessive exploitation, recovery becomes more challenging, and the *status quo ante* harder to claw back. One day we will wake up and find no puffins, Arctic skuas or kittiwakes left.

The necessary steps in a restoration of our marine environment include the following: controls on the fishing industry and hence a sustainable fishing policy; properly protected marine areas; regulation of fish farming; seabed habitat restoration to a good ecological standard; eradication of alien species from islands and biosecurity measures; and a sustainable approach to tourism, again with no net environmental losses. Let's take a closer look at some of these to see what could be achieved by 2050.

A fishing policy fit for purpose

As with agriculture and the CAP, it is not hard to come up with measures that improve on the EU's fishing policies. Indeed, it is easier because so little economic value is at stake and so few people are employed in the industry. There are now only about 12,000 people left in the fishing industry, and most of these fish for supplies to export. (To put this in perspective, this is roughly equivalent to the total staff of the Environment Agency.) All forms of fishing contribute only around 0.07 per cent GDP, and the narrower catch is less than 0.05 per cent.[22] If we stopped commercial fishing altogether, the brutal truth is that the economic impacts would be small and the environmental gains considerable. We would have greener and more prosperous seas. The reasons we don't simply ban most commercial fishing are cultural, and about a way of life and the political grip this has on fishing policies. Sea shanties, folk songs and films reflect and reinforce this cultural image. Fishers, like farmers, have a sympathetic press and emotional tug on our politics.[23]

There are several layers to a sustainable fishing policy. A key distinction is between inshore and offshore fishing. The inshore waters are where shellfish and fixed-net fishing are found. This is where lobsters, crabs, oysters, cockles, mussels and scallops are taken. Some of this is low-impact and relies on simple methods. Lobster and crab pots do only limited damage, as do hand-dived scallops, and much is about the supply to local markets. Innovative approaches, such as rope mussel farming and the lobster hatchery at Padstow, can help to maintain sustainable yields and hence renewable stocks.

It is pretty straightforward to define what level of fishing for shellfish is sustainable, and it is relatively easy to see what methods are sustainable too. It makes good economic sense to protect areas, such as those around the Isles of Man and Arran in a proactive way, and even the fishers themselves get to see that this is sensible if they want to have a future. Stopping fishing altogether in protected areas is likely to raise total fish catches.[24] This is a win–win outcome.

More difficult is the white fishing regime. Fish have the inconvenient (for regulation and policy) habit of swimming between different territorial waters. Some are more local than others. Bottom feeders like sole and plaice tend to stay put, whereas cod move around a lot. In each case, the task is not a new one. It is to define the relevant area and its sustainable catch, and then to make sure this is all that is taken.

Defining the sustainable catch is a scientific question that cannot be accurately answered. Because this is a case of renewable natural capital, the limit is the threshold below which the fish cannot reproduce and maintain their populations. It is what was breached on the Grand Banks with cod. The risk is asymmetrical: go over the limit and recovery is in doubt; err on the generous side and that leaves a few more fish to sustain the population (and allows seabirds and mammals to recover too). A safe limit above the threshold is required. Applying the precautionary principle is a sensible precaution to take.

Under the EU's Common Fisheries Policy (CFP)[25] these limits have been a game played between scientists and fishing interests (and politicians too). The fishers usually push for larger quotas. It is a game the fish have been losing for decades.

It is a game that is further complicated by the problems of enforcement. A fishing net does not perfectly distinguish between different types of fish, and fish have a habit of swimming into the danger of the nets even if they are outside the quotas or just too small. There are solutions: the number and type of boats can be limited through controlling the number of licences (a bit like black cabs in London); the number of fish caught for each species can be fixed in quotas, which may in turn be auctioned; there can be a minimum size; the number of days and hours fishing can be capped (as with lorry drivers' hours); and some prohibited areas can be declared. Enforcement and monitoring are required.

All of the above have been variously tried out, and often several of them simultaneously. The key regulatory tools are licences and quotas. A licence comes with conditions and these can be changed. A quota is a maximum that can be checked and, as technology gets smarter, checked more effectively. The 'discards' problem remains: what happens if you catch too many of the wrong sort of fish, or fish are below a minimum size?[26] Very little of the costs of regulation and enforcement are paid for by fishers, and it reduces even further the already trivial economic value of the fishing industry.

The inshore waters play a special role: they are not only a potential fishing area, but are also critical to the early life cycle of many fish. A fishing policy needs to have regard to the full life cycle of the fish, and therefore be a habitat policy too. Key spawning grounds and areas for fish fry to grow can be kept out of the allowed fishing zones. These can be Marine Protected Areas, although they are designed mainly for other purposes. New nurseries can be created. The breaching of the sea walls at Abbots Hall Farm and then Wallasea on the Essex coast are examples.

The Marine Protected Areas, gradually being extended around the coasts, add to these measures. They are meant to be the National Parks of the sea. Yet the roll-out has been dogged by delays, slowed by the lobbyists of vested interests, and the level of protection they offer has been insufficient to protect and enhance stocks. Inevitably they will require further limiting of fishing. The economic benefits are considerable: future shellfish and white fish populations will be greater, and seabirds and marine life generally will benefit. This in turn adds to biodiversity, and all of this contributes to the coastal economies.[27]

The regulation of fish farming

The issue for fish farming is less about the yields and more about the pursuit of sustainable practices. It is not necessary to deplete the seas to feed the salmon, and it is not necessary to pollute the sea lochs with sea lice. The wild salmon and the farmed salmon can be kept apart. Indeed, the latter can even be farmed in land-based tank systems, a nascent technology.[28]

These more sustainable practices may have *apparently* higher costs. However, what many of the current fish farms are doing is akin to slash-and-burn early agriculture. It leaves the degraded environment behind in its wake and moves on. It takes years for a seabed to recover, and the wild fish may never recover. The feedstocks may struggle to recover too, in turn leaving the breeding stock of seabirds vulnerable to starvation.

It is not a practice that its customers may ultimately tolerate. With the coming of greater scrutiny comes the need to meet standards and codes of practice, and these feed through into consumer demand, or lack of it. The fish farms lag behind the battery hen farms in public scrutiny, but the trend towards greater consumer requirements changes their economics. If the public knew what is really going on they might not be so keen on ever-cheaper salmon.

Addressing the environmental problem of fish farming is not difficult. It requires a sustainable regime, which means that the polluter should pay, and in this activity, as with many others, there should be no net environmental loss. This is just good economics: it is not efficient to ignore costs and focus only on the market value of the fish. A sensible licensing and planning framework would require proper economic and environmental assessments, a set of regulatory rules, reporting requirements that provide credible transparency and compliance with those rules, compensation for any expected damage, inspections, and serious penalties for 'accidental' damage such as escapes, chemical overdoses and so on. The licences would be time-limited, and require that the decommissioning of the fish pens returns the lochs and the associated seabeds to the *status quo ante*. Prepaid bonds would cover these decommissioning costs. Finally, the licences that are granted would be capable of being withdrawn in the event of compliance failures. Obviously this all needs a strong regulatory body.[29]

Habitat restoration

Habitat restoration involves getting the coastal fringes and the islands to a good ecological state. Every specific bit has its own specific ecology, and restoration requires tailored programmes. It might be the removal of invasive rhododendrons on the north Devon coast, the clearing of bracken on St Martin's on the Isles of Scilly, or the creation of a buffer zone between intensive agriculture and the sea walls and salt marshes on the Essex coast.

The first task is to make sure that everything that needs to be designated for protection is in fact designated. Quite a lot already has some protected status classification, from Marine Protected Areas to Marine Conservation Zones. But not all, and even where there is designation, the level of protection can be inadequate. One possibility is to create a new coastal category, and to set out minimum standards of protection, as well as access. The two go together economically: better habitats make the access more attractive to walkers and other users of the coastal paths; and more access brings more people who will value those enhanced habitats. There is an obvious link to the coastal footpath concepts, discussed below. This could be a Blue Belt of more Marine Protected Areas and Marine Conservation Zones (as currently being developed), and a coastal Green Belt on the shorelines.[30]

Given the specific nature of these habitats, the enhancements need to be made with a careful eye to the science, and with an engagement with those who access these habitats. For the islands, it is *island* projects and *island* initiatives that have the best chance of delivery, and it is local island populations who have the most to gain from the economic activity these projects generate. It is also local people who have the better understanding of the specific characteristics and who are likely to have the greatest personal enjoyment of enhanced habitats.

On the coast, again it is local communities that are the best drivers of habitat improvement. Local Wildlife Trusts and local natural history and community groups have attachments to specific bits of coasts, and are the immediate beneficiaries. Their involvement, as with the islanders, is also likely to bring direct health and educational benefits as they engage in what are outdoor physical activities.

The bigger players have the opportunities to facilitate these habitat restorations. The National Trust owns a lot of coast, and local authorities have planning and other powers. In partnership with the locals, these are possible vehicles to channel enhancement funding.[31]

Eradication of alien species from islands, and biosecurity measures

Getting rid of the aliens that humans have inflicted on islands is often a very practical proposition with the potential for speedy results. Getting rid of rats on the Shiants and St Agnes directly feeds through into better seabird survival. The elimination of rats from Lundy has brought back Manx shearwaters to breed successfully (and on St Agnes too). Beyond rats, there is much more that could be achieved. We could draw up a list of all the invasive vertebrate species on all the islands that it would be good to get rid of, and then set about the task over the next

25 years or so. Mink are already on most lists. Deer can be controlled.

Do these measures increase prosperity? Yes, and for a particular reason. What the eradication of, say, rats does is open up the habitats to the restoration of seabird colonies, and this is the critical bit, potentially for ever. There is an initial cost, and then there is a potentially infinite benefit given that the birds are then potentially with us for ever.

Often the costs of eradication are not costs at all if these tasks are done by volunteers. They will get a sense of personal satisfaction from doing something for nature, and the activity itself promotes their well-being and hence contributes further to prosperity.

What about invertebrates and plants?[32] A visit to the Isles of Scilly, and in particular Tresco, reveals an invasion of tropical plants that have escaped from the Tresco Abbey Gardens. Walking around the proximity quickly demonstrates what a huge task it would be to get rid of them. It is a phenomenon around our coasts – and the coast is a good place for many to get established because these areas are warmer, often sunnier and less cultivated. Invasive, alien plants leave seed banks, and pulling them up is a hugely intensive job. Chemicals are almost everywhere a bad idea, and not even appropriate for invaders like rhododendrons. Unlike vertebrates, eliminating alien plants is a hopeless task, given the scale of the gardening industry and the associated import of plants and their relentless self-seeding. As the great farce that is the war on ragwort has demonstrated, control is the best that might be achieved, and often at very high cost.

Invasive insects are all but impossible to control, unless nipped in the bud on arrival, and even trying to eliminate the Asian hornet is a very tough ask. Then there are marine crustaceans that have arrived on ships from around the world. Plants, insects and marine aliens are practically uncontrollable once they get here. Often, the best that can be done is to try to manage their impacts on local ecosystems.[33]

What we can do is introduce serious biosecurity measures to stop future aliens. It is not obvious why some species should be allowed to be deliberately imported. Why was Japanese knotweed allowed in? What are the next waves of plants coming our way? Why are ships allowed to take few if any measures to ensure that they are not carrying alien cargoes as a condition of entering a British port, given that we are controlling for illegal immigrants and drug-smuggling? There is great scope to limit the damage across all the environments with a properly funded biosecurity regulatory system, and it is economically efficient to make the polluters pay, and hence the horticultural and shipping industries in particular to contribute levies to ensure that security systems are adequately funded.[34] The costs of these biosecurity measures need to be weighed against the full economic impacts of established alien colonies throughout Britain.

A sustainable approach to tourism with no net environmental losses

In taking economic benefits and prosperity seriously, the main source of income for the coast and the associated islands comes from tourism and local leisure and recreation. It economically dwarfs farming, fishing and local small industries. Whereas farming is 0.7 per cent of GDP, and fishing 0.05 per cent of GDP, tourism is nearly 10 per cent of GDP (respectively around £9 billion, £0.7 billion and £260 billion). Whereas fishing employs around 12,000, tourism accounts for around 3.8 million jobs. Obviously not all of them are at the coast, and numbers are difficult to pin down and are of course seasonal, but around half the British population visits the coast annually, as do quite a lot of the 40 million overseas visitors to Britain each year.

There are two ways of thinking about how to maximise the economic benefits. The first is to see it from the perspective of the tourists; the second is to see it from the environmental side.

Tourists face a classic problem of the commons: they often want wild, isolated places where they can engage with nature, free from the hustle of everyday urban life. A tourist brochure typically has pretty cottages, open spaces and empty beaches. We want the access, but only for ourselves.

It is not a credible wish. The coast is a public good, in the classic economic sense, and turning it into a set of private cliffs, beaches and marshes is incredibly economically inefficient, since it excludes the benefits to all the others who could enjoy the natural capital already provided, up to the point where it is crowded. As a public good, there is an overwhelming economic case to make it publicly provided and publicly accessible, and then try to manage numbers.

The problem of overcrowding diminishing everyone's benefits arises only in hotspots. The challenge is to get visitors to go further and enhance their health and well-being further. Where there is crowding, there are several positive steps that can be taken. The first is to price tourism, to put a local tourist levy in place to help manage footpath access and information, and help to offset the damage of lots of cars and walking boots. As noted, this is what many tourist areas around the world do. These levies should be set to ensure that there is net environmental gain, and can be linked to the habitat restoration projects discussed above. People find paying more acceptable if there is a direct link between the charge and the environmental enhancements.

The second approach is regulation and in some cases prohibitions. People are kept off Tean and St Helen's in the Isles of Scilly in the bird-breeding seasons, and areas for little terns on Chesil Beach are roped off and monitored by volunteers round the clock in the breeding season. The large numbers who go to see the seals and seal pups on the North Norfolk coast follow roped pathways, managed by the local Friends of the Seals. Environmental purists may want many more 'Keep Out' signs, but they need to recognise two things: in doing so they reduce the benefits to people; and if people are excluded they may not be willing to pay so much to protect them. People are part of nature.

The coastal prize in 2050

Imagine the coast of Britain mid-century. This is what it could look like. The seabird colonies could not just still be with us, but expanding. There could be more puffins, Manx shearwaters, petrels, guillemots and skuas, nesting on cliffs and in the rocks, free from rats. The coastal fringes could be fully open to access, and their habitats better managed to enhance their beauty and their biodiversity. There could be a wildlife corridor all along the coastline – a coastal Green Belt. Visitors would get much more nature, be better informed, and they would know and appreciate nature all the more. Their prosperity would grow.

Coastal communities could have thriving economies based around natural capital. They would have more and better natural capital for people to enjoy. The introduction of a tourist environmental charge would make sure there was no net environmental loss from the tourists, and indeed help to enhance the natural capital on which this industry depends.

Local volunteers would protect and enhance their communities. The huge number of specific locality projects would be better funded and there would be greater engagement. The locals would get more nature and more exercise, and they may even come to see that volunteering to enhance their local environment is as important to the community as volunteering to serve on the lifeboats. They could get rid of the plastic rubbish.

The inshore waters would all form part of a continuous Marine Protected Area (a Blue Belt) wrapping around Britain, complementing the coastal Green Belt. All the coastal waters would be covered, meeting minimum conditions, as the existing Marine Protected Areas and more conservation areas are gradually expanded. There would be a thriving shellfish industry, sustainably managed. The seabeds would no longer be scraped and the wonders of the biodiversity of the shallow waters would return. Fishing would be banned from specific areas, thereby increasing fish stocks, and ultimately the sustainable catch.

Fish farming would be in much better shape. The slash-and-burn approach to the location and management of fish farms would give way to sustainable aquaculture. Depleting natural capital would prove self-defeating.

Further offshore, fish stocks would be managed sustainably, with the fishers directly involved in this management in the context of agreed principles. This would be a fair fishing system, and one that can go on for ever.

All of these bring connectivity on a grand scale. This would include managed retreats along low-lying areas, bringing back salt marshes as sea levels rise. These would save money on sea walls, and would bring great environmental benefits and much better protection from coastal flooding.

What is not to like about this?

7

NATURE IN THE TOWNS AND CITIES

Developed land might comprise around only 12 per cent of Britain, yet its influence extends throughout. More than 80 per cent of the population live in towns and cities, and most of the rest of the countryside is there to serve them in one form or another – for food, leisure and water, to filter the air, and to take away the urban waste. Cities might look like they can do without nature. In fact, they are utterly dependent on natural capital and extremely vulnerable to its decline. Cities and nature are inextricably tied together.

Urban environments matter for all these people. They are where they get to interface with nature more often than anywhere else. It is also where nature has sought refuge from the relentless intensification of agriculture. It seeks to escape the arable deserts and bright green nitrate-fed grasslands, in favour of the urban jungle and its niche habitats. If we are to have a green and prosperous land, we have to have greener towns and cities. Green urban infrastructure is both achievable and has high economic returns, because it is right next to people who can benefit from it.

Urban environments that neglect their natural capital impose a heavy price on their populations. The costs come from the health consequences of air pollution, from the mental and physical impacts of a lack of green spaces, and from the hard concrete approaches to the challenges of flooding, water quality, transport and energy supplies.

Clean air

Air quality is perhaps the most obvious and immediate urban challenge, and the one with the largest economic costs. Poor air quality literally kills people. It reduces the life expectancy of everyone in the urban environment, and it reduces quality of life as the toxins impact on the heart and lungs. It may even increase the chances of suffering from dementia. London's air quality ranks with that of Beijing, Delhi and Paris as among the worst in the world, with Marble Arch recording levels over five times that set by the EU upper limit.

The good news is that most cities in Britain are seeing improving overall air quality, albeit from a low base. There are no pea soup fogs anymore. These improvements have come from driving out domestic coal fires and more generally the closure of large-scale coal-powered industries from the surrounding areas. The coming of natural gas, gas central heating, and deindustrialisation have together made a big difference. The phasing-out of coal-fired electricity generation, which contributed nearly 80 per cent of generation as recently as the 1980s, should be completed by around 2025, representing another step change.

Yet just because it has been improving does not mean that it is good enough. The bad news comes from the newer forms of pollution that have crept in. These include diesel vehicles and ammonia from agriculture, as well as the very localised household pollution that comes with household chemicals. Energy efficiency policies have had the effect of increasing internal pollution in buildings by preventing airflows. Modern carpets, air and fabric 'fresheners', and central heating systems have been associated with rising levels of asthma and respiratory conditions and diseases.

The use of diesel has been promoted as a way to reduce carbon emissions, without proper regard to emissions from particulates and nitrogen dioxide. The costs are considerable. How many extra deaths? The answer is that we do not and cannot know with any precision because it depends on all the other contributors to poor health, and the counterfactual. Lots of urban features in addition to air pollution damage people's health and well-being, and it is this *combination* that can be fatal. The state of the world without these various pollutions is not going to be perfect either. Lots of apparently rural areas suffer from local pollution too.

Notwithstanding these obvious difficulties, the numbers are still likely to be large. The estimates for Britain as a whole are in the range of 40,000 to 50,000 extra deaths per annum as a result of outdoor air pollution.[1]

The conventional approach to addressing air quality is focused on technologies and regulation. These are important and they work. Applying producer responsibility to the many household products, as well as pollution charges, would make a significant difference, as would tighter regulation of heating systems, including wood-burning stoves, and the phasing-out from cities of diesel vehicles, and indeed fossil fuels more generally. These all address the causes of the pollution.

Natural capital solutions

It is not just about limiting the pollution getting into city air. It is also about mopping it up afterwards, and it is here that natural capital methods have a big role to play. Better still, natural capital methods typically have multiple benefits, tackling not just air quality but mental and physical well-being too, as well as increasing biodiversity.

Proactively trying to improve urban environmental systems was something the Victorians started, and primarily for economic reasons. They got serious about green spaces within towns and cities. Our cities would be much greyer but for these pioneering efforts. Following the rapid industrialisation and urbanisation in the nineteenth century, the plight of the poor industrial classes attracted attention from the capitalists, the reformers and the revolutionary socialists. The capitalists could see that it was in their interests to have a workforce that was fit for work, and many in the dense housing and slums obviously were not. It was in their interest to alleviate some of the worst of the conditions they had created, and in the process to limit the risks of urban diseases, just as it is in parts of China and India today. The reformers could see that the poor air quality, the polluted water supplies, and the stench of the sewage were core priorities if the lot of the poor was to be improved. Both capitalists and reformers knew that if they didn't act, revolutionary elements would step in. It is a threat to the autocratic Chinese regime today.

The air quality concerns motivated major changes to urban natural capital. In the late nineteenth century, the need for workers to have access to cleaner air gave rise to the great movement for parks and gardens. Instead of concreting over all the greener bits of the inheritance of the past, especially on what had been the fringes of then much smaller urban environments, many of these survived. Around 46 per cent of the Greater London area is still 'green', although with enormous scope for improvement, as we will see.[2]

Most British cities still have parks and public green spaces. In London there are the great parks, including St James's, Richmond Park, Hyde Park and Regents Park. There are numerous squares built around gardens, although many are still private. A walk through any of these reveals that they could be much better for people and nature.[3] Most are mown grass, heavily trampled and with large specimen trees. The water areas have great scope to be wildlife habitats of much greater vibrancy. St James's Park has its water birds, but not much else, and the water is often caked in thick green algae. There are few aquatic plants.

Urban parks face the sheer pressure of numbers and commercial interests, and it is remarkable that so many or indeed any have survived. The value of the land for development is great, and for municipal authorities strapped for cash to pay for other services, including social care, the temptation to surrender a bit here and a bit there of the green spaces they own or manage is massive. So, indeed, it is proving.

When it comes to management, large organised events in parks and green spaces can be lucrative in the search for revenues. Hyde Park is a regular venue for big events including concerts and the Christmas fairs. The ground is covered over at just the time of the year when nature needs it most. Encroachments are particularly attractive if they can be presented as 'temporary', and then the temporary shades into the permanent. They shift from green parks to amusement parks. Urban parks survive only by deliberately leaning into the wind of development pressures.

The route to their erosion is often simply neglect. Local authorities spend less and less on their upkeep and the capital maintenance simply falls away. Many parks are in a sorry state as a result.[4] And yet it is also remarkably cheap to reverse these declines, through a combination of regulatory protection, spending on maintenance and the engagement of the voluntary sector.

Set against this the benefits to health, notably for the old and the young, which come from fresher air and exercise. Consider the overall filtering of the air that parks provide. Just on health grounds, the repair and further greening of the urban parks is a no-brainer. Sometimes it actually involves spending less, through managed neglect. Walk away from Hyde Park's tightly mown areas into the few areas which are not cut, and you will find all sorts of wonderful wild flowers, including yellow rattle.

Greener streets and greener roofs

The parks are linked by streets. Planting trees is an obvious option to absorb the air pollution. Every street could be planted, with the right sort of trees. Why aren't they? The main reason – beyond a lack of imagination – is that trees add at least two extra costs. Tree roots can interfere with infrastructure, pipes and cables; and fallen leaves clog the streets and storm drains. Neither argument is especially convincing. The infrastructure network problems arise as a result of short-termist measures such as simply burying the infrastructure, leaving it directly exposed to soils and hence roots. Utility tunnels and broader-gauge pipes would be one solution. The leaves can be composted, and if left in 'untidy' heaps, can be a valuable resource for wildlife too. Such costs as these pale into insignificance against the benefits to air quality (and hence to the people breathing this air), as well as to wildlife. There is also the benefit of reduced noise pollution. Trees make streets quieter, reducing stress. The recent tree-felling in Sheffield has attracted justified criticism. Sadly, it is but one example among many.[5]

The buildings in the streets have roofs, many of which could be greened. This is about design and planning, and it is easier to incorporate greenness into new developments than to retrofit existing ones. The opportunities are plentiful and diverse. Some cities, like Tokyo, have a significant number of green roofs and benefit from the cooling effect, greater biodiversity and better air quality. Green roofs, by making urban areas more wildlife-friendly, would provide large additional green resources, especially where these are developed alongside greener streets.

Green roofs can also help minimise the impact of flash-flooding by reducing run-off and, better still, can even help to tackle climate change.[6]

Urban water quality and sewerage

The Victorians approached the water problem through hard capital projects – the sewerage systems. The famous Great Stink of London in 1858 led to the creation of the sewers that still serve London today. Elsewhere in the other great inland urban conurbations, notably in Manchester and Birmingham, municipal utilities began to emerge as conscious local government interventions. In others, proximity to the coastline meant that sewage could be more easily dumped at sea.

In getting new supplies of clean drinking water, the municipalities turned to new reservoirs. The Victorians developed the Lake District for supplies to Manchester, and built the Thelwall Viaduct. Birmingham turned to mid-Wales and the Elan Valley, and the Derbyshire Peak District provided supplies to the northern conurbations. Not since the Romans had such grand countrywide water systems been put in place, and they remain today the backbone of supplies.[7]

With drinking water coming from new reservoirs, the urban rivers could be left polluted, and they were. The Thames might not stink anymore, but it – and the Mersey – remained close to biologically dead. It would take until the late twentieth century to see significant improvements. The new sewers were good for rats, but the cleaner streets were less good for scavengers.

Nature in the city

Urban parks are sanctuaries for wildlife. Towns and cities are home to a remarkable number of invertebrates, plants, birds and mammals. This is partly a reflection of the fact that the country-side to which they are compared is much more barren. Indeed, lots of brownfield sites can be much richer in biodiversity than 'green' sites. As noted, two brownfield examples are Canvey Wick on Canvey Island, on a disused oil platform site, and West Thurrock Lagoons, on an old coal power station site. These are now hotspots for biodiversity. Then there are the reclaimed brownfield sites. Gravel extraction has created the Walthamstow and Springhead wetland opportunities in London. The London Wetland Centre opened in 2000, and was created from four disused Thames Water reservoirs.

Nature has proved remarkably good at adapting to the multiple niches that urban environments can offer. The urban fox is now endemic. Its presence is a response to the opportunities that cities provide. There is abundant food, from the takeaways and other food waste that literally litters the streets. In the modern city, people can afford not only to buy junk food, but to throw it away too. There is warmth and shelter: winter is a lot milder in cities than in the countryside. The risks of crossing busy streets are worth the extra protein on offer. Sometimes people step in and feed them too, for the sheer pleasure of watching them.

Waste has enticed others to trade the country for the city. Gulls are attracted by the ready availability of food, especially as the coasts have become culinary deserts for them with the seas being purged of their natural foods. Herring gulls are more likely to be spotted on landfill sites than at many coastal locations now. So much so that they are beginning to be regarded as pests in some areas.

Of all the urban birds, the most spectacularly successful has been the pigeon. It has made the city its home in great numbers. The buildings are the cliffs with abundant nesting sites and warm roosts. The pavements are littered with the waste of cast-off food. They have few predators to make any serious inroads into their numbers, and attempts to organise large-scale culls come up against the biophilia of the urban populations. Peregrine falcons have started to colonise the cathedrals and skyscrapers. In the City of London, you can watch them dive at up to 200 miles per hour from office towers onto an unsuspecting pigeon. Given the sheer delight these birds bring, more of them would add a twist to the engagement of the urban dweller with nature 'red in tooth and claw'. A greener urban world would have many more peregrines, and possibly kestrels too. Maybe one day even the goshawk will see the dense skyscrapers and streets as hunting corridors, just as it sees the trees and woodlands of the Forest of Dean. A dream probably, but it does whet the appetite and beg the question of what we would need to do to make this happen.

Cities witness rapid change, and as a result they are hotbeds for evolution.[8] This change was spectacular in the nineteenth century, and though urban growth rates for the largest cities have slowed down, technology is now transforming in the twenty-first century what the Industrial Revolution created. Gone are the horses and their droppings and the oats and cereals that fed them. In 1900 there were around 50,000 horses in London. Now there are a few at the army barracks and a few horse-riding specialists, offering lessons in places like Hyde Park. Gone are the insects that fed on the dung and excrement. Gone too are the uninsulated roofs with gaps and nooks and crannies for roosting and nesting birds.

The modern city is increasingly a sealed world of glass, and the streets are full of cars, buses and lorries. In a Victorian city the streets would have been very general feeding grounds for nature. Now they are for the scavengers of modern waste – the pigeons and gulls. Cities have become cleaner, less messy places, except for the food litter. The Victorians would never have wasted food like we do.

The most obvious casualty is the house sparrow. It was once

a common urban bird. Now in central London you will struggle to see one, and perhaps even record it for its rarity. The red kites – the urban scavengers – have gone too. There are few starlings roosting in the cities. Swifts have fewer places to nest. These are the absences that older people will notice, but may mean nothing to you if you are young, since probably you have never seen them in an urban setting.[9]

Much time is spent on considering reintroductions in the countryside and the return of rural birds and animals. The osprey, the cranes, the bittern, the sea eagle and avocet are all great success stories. But what about returns and reintroductions to the cities? As noted, the peregrine is one making this transition from cliffs to skyscrapers. They were once killed on military grounds because they preyed on messenger pigeons. But now there is great scope to make the inner high cliffs of the city the basis of a big population expansion. What about bringing back the house sparrow, by carefully focusing on both building design to create nesting sites and also their food supplies? There are many more people in cities so there are many more people to join in and benefit from a great resurrection of key species, and in the process the return of habitats.[10] We mandate all sorts of requirements for buildings, from energy efficiency to smart meters and aesthetics, but fail to do so for nature. Indeed, many building regulations damage natural capital.

The new green spaces

Part of this return of nature to our towns and cities is about public spaces and public initiatives. But much of the wildlife potential is in the hands of private companies and individuals. In the peregrine case, every major skyscraper could have built-in nesting sites and roosts for birds. It could be a very low-cost opportunity to improve their space. While the boss might worry about office workers being distracted by the magnificent sight of a peregrine swooping past their window, it would do wonders for the workers' sense of well-being, and productivity would go up as a result. It could add a little to the soul in what is often a soulless workspace.

Offices, office blocks and skyscrapers have lots of other ways of adding nature back to their buildings. Green walls are one option, and they not only benefit wildlife but they purify the air. Green plants are good for health as well as for a sense of well-being. They can soak up pollutants. This is true for inside as well as outside spaces. Studies suggest that houseplants not only improve office air quality, but also the general sense of well-being.[11]

Some environmentalists may see these as literally window dressing, but they are not. They are first small steps to get people to re-engage with nature, even if it is to look at the beauty of a flower on a pot plant. The next step is the window box; a remarkable number of urban dwellers in flats and tower blocks, and without gardens, grow stuff in window boxes. The benefits are considerable: they start to create new greener spaces, and the flowers can be important sources of nectar. It is hard to overestimate the health benefits. Studies show that physical and mental health outcomes are linked to exposure to 'green'. Although there is as yet little evidence of the size of the economic gains, they are likely to be significant. Mental health problems have high costs.[12]

Moving on from the inside to the outside, and into the gardens, these constitute a remarkable reservoir for wildlife. There are the obvious beneficiaries: the garden birds like robins and blackbirds; the small mammals like hedgehogs; the plants and trees and nectar and the insects.

There are some wonderful urban gardens and there are gardens which are, from a wildlife perspective, more barren and sometimes deadly. Wonderful wildlife gardens are not what the typical glossy magazine or garden TV programme shows. A wonderful garden for nature is typically quite messy. Gardening for nature is not the same as gardening for the Chelsea Flower Show. Immaculate lawns are usually the product of fertilisers and weed- and moss-killing chemicals. Unblemished foliage is usually the result of slug pellets. Garish colours are usually exotics rather than native plants.[13]

Many gardens are deathtraps for wildlife. The slug pellets harm the thrushes and the hedgehogs that feed on the poisoned slugs and snails, both because there are fewer of them and because the poisons accumulate. They go into the food chain. The weed-killers are every bit as dangerous and damaging here as they are applied to agricultural fields. Often the high doses gardeners apply and the lack of controls on their applications make them even worse for nature. For urban gardens to yield their wildlife potential there needs to be a very different gardening culture. As with the use of peat, this is an area that cries out for more controls, and one that programmes like the BBC's *Gardeners' World* and organisations like the Royal Horticultural Society already tackle, but could do more about. If the true costs of peat extraction were reflected in the price of horticultural peat, few would buy it.

Urban gardeners do not have to maximise yield, even if, as noted, their soils can be better than those of the agricultural fields. The 'damage' from 'pests' needs to be inverted. It is a chance for predators to gain a niche. Untidiness needs to become the new normal for urban gardeners. Instead of the perfectly manicured lawn and immaculate borders, the new objects of desire in garden design should be the pile of logs for hedgehogs to hibernate under, the heap of rotting wood blooming with fungi and full of beetles, and the longer grass areas for wild flowers. There is no need to use chemicals at all.

Every garden needs a pond, however small. Ponds not only

encourage frogs, newts and toads, but lots and lots of invertebrates, and they provide water for mammals and birds. Imagine showing your children frogspawn in the spring, and watching it turn into tadpoles and then little frogs, and in the process provide a meal for predators too. You might even get a heron to turn up, and larger ponds sometimes might get an occasional grass snake and kingfisher. But even a shallow water container helps.

These are all steps that would turn a potential wildlife resource into something altogether more exciting. The steps are simple and cheap: stay away from chemicals; leave aside areas for wild flowers; let some of the grass grow longer; stop using peat; create a compost heap; add a pond. Imagine showing your friends a hedgehog, or having a family of young thrushes on the lawn. Even better, share this experience with your children. Imagine setting the urban challenge to increase the number of species to include some major additions, and explaining to people how to achieve this.

Urban green corridors – connecting networks of green highways

So far we have looked at all the things that can be done inside each urban garden, and what can be done to individual buildings and tower blocks too. Wildlife does not, however, live in neat and separate garden islands. It is not my nature or your nature. It is our *shared* nature. Nature needs a connected world. Connecting up urban gardens and urban green spaces is what turns a resource into a cornucopia. Instead of 'dig for victory' we could have 'garden for nature'. The result is that we will all benefit from more nature.

This can happen at several levels. Simply making a hole in a wire-netting fence can let hedgehogs get from one garden to the next, and allow the establishment of bigger territories. It is the holes and gaps that create the links that turn one garden on its own into a network of habitats. Brick walls do not lend themselves to mobility for the smaller mammals and amphibians. Holes in the wall allow the network of garden ponds to form a whole ecosystem.

Even better, each garden could be managed with a view to the diversity of habitats in their neighbours' gardens, and a street might be considered as a unified ecosystem. Each garden then contributes to the greater portfolio of natural capital.

The connection of gardens releases much greater potential. Nature does less well in isolation. To this can be added the concept of urban wildlife corridors on an altogether bigger scale. This can be on a street, an estate, a water course or a town level, and new developments and new towns can build in linkages from the start. Take a look at the RSPB's project at Kingsbrook to see just how much nature can be engineered into new housing developments.[14]

For most urban settings, corridors are provided by rivers and canals. Many towns and cities are located on waterways. Birmingham has more canals than Amsterdam. Think of the opportunities these present to create natural water corridors. Their banks can also provide connectivity for nature. The obstacles are typically properties that have no waterfront margin, but are right on riverbanks and concrete paths and roads. Small changes in the engineering and the introduction of green pathways (and even green vertical pathways) can make a big difference. Green infrastructure needs to be infrastructure for nature, designed with this purpose in mind, not an add-on afterwards.

The outer rings – the Green Belt and what it could be

The central urban areas abut the countryside, and they can do this in a variety of ways. Left to normal market forces, ribbon development and urban sprawl would result. Every builder loves a greenfield site. That is what happened in the 1930s and still happens across the USA. The problems with sprawl are not just the ugliness that John Betjeman wrote poems about.[15] It is also that by stretching out the city, the access to the countryside is made much weaker for the people in the middle. The countryside as the lungs of the city becomes ever further away, and ribbon developments as opposed to urban hubs lend themselves to the car, and hence major roads. None of this is good for wildlife or for people's access to nature.

For these and other reasons, after World War II, and when much redevelopment was necessary in any event as a result of the bombing, planning became central to the design of the countryside, and the Green Belt was an explicit attempt to surround urban areas with a circle of green. The idea was to provide a sharp discontinuity, with housing concentrated inside.[16]

The Green Belt areas have largely survived the 70 years since (and indeed some have been expanded), but they are now under immense pressure. House-building targets, as a result of decreased occupancy rates and population growth noted in chapter 2, have made many areas of land vulnerable, and developers know that they will make maximum gains if they can get permission to build on Green Belt land. This has led to a sustained attempt to undermine it and build on it. Ministers have swallowed the lobbying.[17] The powerful house-builders' lobby is reinforced by the NFU and the Country Land and Business Association (CLA): the builders want to build on the land; the landowners want to bid the development land value up; and both want to minimise any compensation for the environmental damages.

The central argument advanced, in addition to the economic benefits of the houses themselves, is that the Green Belt is not really green. Much of it is covered by intensive agriculture, there are few access rights, and golf courses and horses are argued to add little. It has been pointed out by developers that there is often more biodiversity in the gardens of the houses they build than in the actual Green Belt.

Sadly, this is all largely true. Belt it may be; Green much of it isn't. A lot of it is very brown. There are many more biodiversity-rich brownfield sites. Yet the case for building on the Green Belt does not rest only on a comparison with what is there now. The Green Belt should be green, not brown. The challenge is to compare two options with the status quo: covering it in houses; or making it truly green.

The reason why the Green Belt is so coveted is its location: it is right next to people. People are in easy range: they could enjoy a green Green Belt. The benefits of green spaces near urban locations are likely to be reaped by many more people. This is potentially not just prime land for developers, but also prime land for enhancing the natural environment.[18]

This land is well placed to clean the air of the city, complementing the inner green spaces, and thereby providing the lungs for the city dwellers. It is well placed for children to play, and for outdoor exercise and recreation. It is well placed to join up the natural wildlife corridors between the city and the countryside. Green Belts are good in principle for absorbing water and helping to manage flooding. To the west of Oxford, Port Meadow and the surrounding areas help to mop up heavy rainfall, and flooded fields protect the city centre.

To make the Green Belt green a number of steps are necessary, and all economically beneficial. The first relates to the agricultural land. In the Green Belt, the potential public goods of health, education and well-being are greatest, and these need to be supported by an agricultural policy that subsidises only public goods. It is not just the uplands that matter for nature. The lowlands around cities are key public good areas. Just as monies should go to maintaining hedges and dry-stone walls, they should also go to nature-friendly farming in the Green Belt. A wild flower meadow right on the edge of the city is likely not only to benefit insects, but also to delight lots of people close by.

There is no longer any reason for concentrating intensive agriculture close to cities. The old agricultural necessity, in a world of limited transport and refrigeration, of the land around the cities feeding these cities, is long gone. There is little link now between agricultural production in the Green Belt and the consumption of this production in the neighbouring cities. Perhaps there should be, but that is simply not how the modern food supply chains work.

A further farming-related reform is to tax the capital uplift from selling land for development. Planning permission is a public, not a private, good, a function of a society-driven property right. By allowing private landowners to capture the rent from a public decision, land prices are obviously higher near to cities, and the landowners have a great incentive to encourage the developments. This was once captured by the state, and it could be again. Lower land prices make the incentives of public good subsidies more attractive than they would otherwise have been.

The capital uplift, when combined with the net environmental gain principle discussed at greater length in chapter 9, creates a perverse incentive. The landowners have an incentive to minimise the environmental value of their land, to minimise the net gain payments, and hence to increase the capital uplift of their land. In the extreme this is an incitement to trash. The old solution to this problem was to treat the uplift in value as a public and not private gain. It should be again.[19]

Part of the funding for greening the Green Belt can come from the requirement for net environmental gain placed on developers once this perverse incentive has been tackled. An obvious place for the gains to be accrued is in the Green Belt next to the developments in cities. This is, in effect, a green infrastructure

requirement, alongside transport and schools and other infrastructure requirements that are rightly placed on developers.[20]
Where there are permissions to build on the Green Belt, these
should require further and considerable net environmental gains,
and against the backdrop of the better, greener Green Belt that
could be in place instead.

For the leisure uses of the Green Belt for private benefit, such
as golf courses and horses, there is no reason why these cannot
be required to meet more demanding Green Belt standards. A
development on the Green Belt for *any* purpose might be given
a special regulatory context. This is somewhat akin to National
Parks, and indeed the Green Belt could be turned into one or
more Green Belt National Parks, with their own planning regime
and special Green Belt environmental standards that could be
added. Such a coherent overarching body might make sure it was
environmentally joined up.

Green Belts are not much use to people if there is no access.
This is partly about footpaths, but it is also about access from
the city. It needs transport links, cycle ways and footpaths from
the city centres. Instead of the highly polluting model of our
commuting, cycle ways and footpaths through 'green' Green Belt
have multiple economic benefits – less pollution, more exercise,
mental health benefits from the green expanses of nature and
much more biodiversity. In parallel with regulation and technology to reduce the causes of air pollution, transport policy
needs to integrate access to the green spaces within and around
cities as part of urban planning.

A broad Green Belt plan would include provision for woodlands, access to rivers and streams, wildlife corridors, flower
meadows and the regeneration of substantial hedgerows. Specific
trails and exercise areas, as well as opportunities, especially for
children, to experience and study nature would have a high
priority, and links to schools would play an important part in a

rejuvenated Green Belt strategy. This is a big idea, on a big scale, with big multiple benefits.

A biodiverse and green urban environment

So here is what our towns and cities could look like. There would be a genuinely green Green Belt and for all of them. Every major town and city would have its own Green Belt, as part of a network of Green Belt National Parks. The green Green Belt would have open access with cycling and footpaths. The city would have a network of green parks and green gardens within its boundaries, with open access. Wildlife corridors would deliberately link the Green Belt and the green parks and green gardens.

The green wildlife corridors would explicitly plan in greener canals and canal paths and green railway corridors. Every street would be greened with trees, as required green infrastructure, horizontally and vertically. Every brownfield site would be greened with wild flowers and niche habitats.

Every commercial building would add wildlife-friendly features including gaps and spaces for birds to roost and nest, and holes for insects. Every roof would be greened, and there would be incentives for green walls. Building regulations for offices, factories and houses would be revised and greened. New housing developments would be required to demonstrate how they would increase biodiversity.

There would be a campaign to green private gardens. Chemical regulation would be tightened. Garden centres would be required, like food retailers, to explicitly label their products, as with 'Smoking Kills' labels on tobacco. Slug pellets would be required to state 'these chemicals kill wildlife', and weedkillers would state 'chemicals kill wild flowers and harm bees and other insects'. There would be pictures of ruined peat bogs, dead thrushes and hedgehogs and dead bees on the packaging. The costs of these causes of pollution would be reflected in their prices.

Schools would be required to engage their children with nature. Outdoor experiences of nature would be a compulsory part of the curriculum. They would engage in school projects, to include every school's buildings and grounds. All schools would take part in a natural capital census, a modern green version of the Domesday Book.[21] The children would be physically and mentally healthier; they would experience the wonders of nature; and they would play their part in creating a better future for themselves.

The extraordinary thing about the above list is that it would not cost very much, and would cost less than business-as-usual even in the narrowest sense. It would save the money now spent on intensive park management, reduce the health costs of lung disease, heart failure, diabetes and other illnesses resulting from poor air and obesity, and improve mental health. We would be much healthier and more prosperous.

What is not to like about this?

PART THREE

Principles, Paying
and the Plan

8

PUBLIC GOODS

Natural capital is the ultimate public good. It is provided for everyone for free. Its use by each person and each business should not reduce the enjoyment for everyone else, provided nature is not overexploited. It can go on and on delivering its bounty, provided it is not reduced below its thresholds.

The attempt to privatise nature has been the history of agriculture, forestry and fishing. By asserting property rights over nature, private individuals have sought to keep the bounty of nature for themselves. Economists sometimes argue that if something is not owned it will be misused, and they point to the tragedy of the commons. Overgrazing, overfishing and overhunting will be the inevitable result. What we need to do to protect and enhance nature, according to this view, is to put a fence around it and exclude others.

Most recently this idea has been extended to the atmosphere. The creation and trading of private property rights in carbon, the subject of chapter 10, makes carbon a private good, to be bought and sold. Some economists would like to see this principle extended to the oceans, and in particular to the Arctic and Antarctic.[1]

The privatisation route does not, however, remove the public elements, and it is just bad economics to assert this. The public bit is inherent in nature, and it is for this reason that private ownership (and private companies) will not, of itself, necessarily deliver a better environment. On the contrary, without the provision of the public goods there is little chance of bequeathing an enhanced set of environmental assets for future generations. Private goods and private services depend on public goods being provided.

Private companies can help *deliver* public goods, but they cannot be left to decide how much of them to *provide*. These are the basic building blocks of an economy and a society. Without them the economy would collapse. They include such things as law and order, the institutions (including markets themselves), and the core infrastructures too. Of these, the provision of natural capital is the most important. Economists should start with public goods, not the other way around.

What is a public good?

We need to get a bit technical to define public goods.[2] Economists classify goods according to a two-dimensional matrix. The dimensions are *excludability* and *rivalry*. Property rights mean that the owner can exclude others from the enjoyment of the good. It is mine, not yours. I own it, so you can't have it without my permission, and without paying me. What's more it is rival: if I consume it, you can't. It can only be used once. Think of buying something in a supermarket, say, a leg of lamb. You have to pay for it – until you do it is not yours. The supermarket owns it. Once you buy it you take it home and eat it. No one else can eat it at the same time. It is a pure private good.

When economists talk about a private decentralised market economy, it is things like this leg of lamb they have in mind. Contrast this with a pure public good. Think of the BBC and broadcasting. If you watch *Planet Earth II*, I can too. Indeed, over

13 million people did, 40 per cent of the viewing public. Your enjoyment does not have any impact on mine. Everyone in Britain could watch without reducing the enjoyment of anyone else. Indeed, everyone in the world could and, in principle, for ever in endless repeats. It gets better: my enjoyment might actually be increased if you also watch, since we can then share the experience. Anything on the internet has these public good, non-excludable and non-rivalry properties.

But you may have smelt a rat already. You and I can't enjoy the BBC without a licence. We have to pay by law. The licence fee creates excludability. The reason it does so is that if it is non-rival and non-excludable, there is no way to recover the costs. Someone has to pay. By creating excludability, we, the licence-fee payers, underwrite the costs of the BBC. Technically it becomes a club: you have to belong to the club to use the facilities, even if your doing so imposes no costs on anyone else's enjoyment.[3] In theory it is still a public good. It is just that in this example we have chosen a club model to pay for it. This is what many charities and environmental bodies do. You pay a membership fee, which contributes to the costs of the organisation, augmented by other donations and subsidies. The National Trust, the RSPB and the Wildlife Trusts are all examples of the club approach. Nature might be free, and it may cost nothing for another person to enjoy it, but protecting and enhancing it costs money. Someone has to pay.

It works, after a fashion, in all these examples. But it is only after a fashion: it is technically inefficient and many natural capital (and other) public goods cannot be provided in this way. The inefficiencies arise from the combination of non-rivalry and trying to impose excludability. If something is genuinely non-rival, the marginal cost of another person using it is zero. Price should equal marginal cost, a cost of zero, and therefore price should be zero. If it is not, some people are excluded from getting benefits that would have no costs for others. These are people who can't afford to pay, and when it comes to natural capital assets like urban green spaces and National Parks, this matters.

In many cases, the better, more economically efficient answer is to provide the public goods for free, as nature is provided for free, and then to recover the fixed costs through taxation. The deal is that the state ensures that the public goods are there for all to enjoy, and that the state takes money from the citizens to pay for them. Again, you may smell a rat. In the example of the BBC, perhaps the government should pay for it from taxation, not the licence fee. The obvious objection is that this might jeopardise its independence: the government might use the BBC for its own narrow political ends, like getting re-elected.

This is a general and big problem. We might want public goods provided for free, but we don't trust government to do the right thing about the level and content of their provision. Governments have lots of other pressing demands, like health, education and offering lower taxes. They might not provide enough of the natural capital public goods, or they might simply fail to do the necessary capital maintenance. This turns out to be all too true when we look at the state of some of our urban green spaces: local authorities are pressed to meet social care requirements as a higher priority. What we want here is an institutional structure which carves out the particular natural capital niche from the general pressures on government spending. The subsequent chapters offer some solutions to this critical problem.

What cannot be escaped in trying to design environmental institutions is that the wrong answer is to try to turn pure public goods into pure private ones. We should not privatise the forests, and we should make public the rights of access to the great open spaces. The private interests (and whims) of companies and the wealthy should not determine our use of the natural environment. That is what went wrong with the attempt in 2011 to privatise the forests, and why there was such an outcry, and why government had to abandon its ill-thought-out plans.[4]

Before moving on to consider what the most important natural capital public goods are, we also need to bring in another bit of technical economics – externalities. These are goods that are rival, but non-excludable, and, as with public goods, economists try to solve the problems externalities throw up with private solutions. In this case, the approach has much greater potential.

A classic externality is the emission of ammonia from farm manures, slurry and other wastes. Ammonia from farms is a major contributor to air pollution, and air pollution affects people's health and well-being, and can even kill them. The ammonia is a by-product of pigs, poultry, cattle and other livestock. Standing in Trafalgar Square, breathing in the ammonia alongside the diesel particulates and the pollution from biomass burning is a rival activity. If you breathe it in, it is in your lungs. It is a cost you bear, without the producer paying for it. The obvious answer is to make sure the farmer pays, and when the farmer does pay, these external costs will be taken into account on the farm. There is now a clear incentive to cover up the slurry pit.

The polluter, the farmer in this case, pays. This can be via a pollution tax, by having to pay compensation for the external damage done, or by regulation imposing the costs of remedial action (such as putting a cover over the slurry pit). In the next chapter we will look in detail at this polluter-pays mechanism to internalise the costs of externalities through charges and taxes, regulation and enforced compensation (the net gain principle).

Public goods, ecosystems and coordination

The reason why the public good concept is so relevant to natural capital is that it comes in ecosystems. An ecosystem is a set of interrelated species, intimately linked together in their physical environment. Although it is possible to knock off some of the bits and still retain most of the whole, in practice there are many keystone species, and the ecosystem is nested in habitats that are self-reinforcing and bound in with their biodiversity. Put simply, the best way to think about an ecosystem is that it is a public good. Everything depends on everything else, and hence there are mass externalities between the different components, and they all depend on the habitat as a system. There is nothing conceptually private about the river catchments, the forests, the mountains and the moors. They may end up being privately owned, but these private property rights have to be attenuated to make sure the private owners have the incentives to provide the public good elements and also internalise the externalities their ownership creates.

In the mix of private ownership with public good dimensions, the easy bits are where there are specific and easily identifiable public goods. Take, for example, the maintenance of a stone wall or a hedgerow, creating the public goods of beauty and biodiversity. Although they fit into a system of walls and hedges and landscapes, it is clear what a good hedge and a good wall look like. We can pay the private owner to provide and maintain these public goods, which we can all benefit from.

These sorts of examples are the ones that usually get referred to. But they are the easy ones, and actually not very typical. The bigger problems come with the landscapes, the wildlife corridors and the rivers – indeed all the main areas discussed in part two.

Take a river catchment. The key public good is defined at the catchment level. It is how all the bits fit together to create a river which is in good ecological condition, and this in turn means internalising the externalities (like slurry spills and sewage effluents), and ensuring that the riverbanks and the woodlands are well maintained and open to access for the general public benefits of health, exercise and well-being.

What matters here is coordination – of all the different kinds of natural capital so that the public good *of the whole* is best provided. It involves the integration of the multiple decisions by all the catchment parties: the farmers, the water companies, the providers of flood defences, the protectors of SSSIs and nature reserves, the timber interests and the tourist industry. The key non-excludable and non-rival function is the *coordination* of these to provide the overall catchment plan. Although theoretically possible to construct a complete set of prices to allow markets to optimise the outcomes, in practice the key incentives are weak and, in some cases, nonexistent. It needs a plan within which markets and prices can play their roles.

It is this plan that matters. The plan is designed to provide a set of catchment assets that not only produce the outputs, like clean water and protection from flooding, but also the potential to produce these outputs for ever. Some of this is spatial, such as limiting the sorts of crops planted near riverbanks. Some of it is for specific public goods within the system, like river paths and access. Some of it is to ensure that natural capital flood defences are created upstream, and some is to allow for estuaries and salt marshes to protect and enhance a host of species that depend on them.

Every ecosystem is different, and yet they all have generic properties. They all need an overarching plan, and they all need coordination between the various public and private bodies. This is what the 25 Year Environment Plan is for: a plan to comprehensively provide the public goods.

What are the most important public goods?

When the 25 Year Environment Plan and the proposals for reforming agricultural policy were contextualised by the principle of 'public money for public goods', farmers and others scrambled to claim that the things that were in their private interests were public goods. Most blatantly, the chairman of the Environment, Food and Rural Affairs Select Committee, Neil Parish (a farmer and an NFU member), asked the Prime Minister in the House of Commons whether she agreed that 'supporting food production in this country is a public good'. The Prime Minister rightly gave a non-committal answer.[5] The Secretary of State for Environment, Food and Rural Affairs added to the confusion, stating at the NFU Farming Conference in March 2018 that, 'I also believe investing in higher animal welfare standards and in improved training and education for those in agriculture and food production are clear public goods', and swiftly added broadband to this list.[6]

Part of this is explained as a failure to understand the concept of a public good. Parish confused the public interest with public goods, although quite what the public interest in food actually is remains far from clear. Parish may not have separated out the private interests of farmers like himself in the subsidies from the public interest. Food is a quintessential private good. Think back to the leg of lamb example above. There is nothing non-excludable or non-rival about this bit of meat (although its production might include some externalities, such as the overgrazing of the uplands discussed previously).

Next up, some in the NFU argue that food *security* is a public good, and deliberately hark back to the days of the shortages in World War II. This argument superficially has a bit more merit, although with radical implications that the NFU members might not like. Eating food is rival, so if, during the war, I eat more, you would have less of the fixed amount. People all starved together, or they survived if food was rationed and centrally allocated, although even here the black market indicated that food itself remained a private good.

It is not clear that there are any food security problems for *really?*

Britain today, but just for a moment suppose there are. What policies would result? As noted, the answer is that food exports would stop, and land would not be used to produce biofuels, game shooting or the many non-basic food-production activities it is currently used for. There would probably be little or no oilseed rape, sheep and pig exports would stop, and emphasis would be placed on domestic chemical production. With the control of net immigration, we would on this argument want to stop another 10 million being added to the population to prevent the creation of yet more demand. As a national agricultural plan, it is nonsense, and it is not hard to imagine that this is what the NFU really wants. If it is looking for arguments that it can marshal in defence of subsidies, it should think carefully about what it is wishing for.

So what do they mean? Do they mean *some* measure of self-sufficiency? Again, think what this requires. We would divert food production from export, and curtail imports. We would disrupt the global food supply chains. There would of course be some environmental benefits, like reduced carbon emissions, and animal suffering would probably be reduced. Local and smaller-scale production has many environmental and ethical benefits. It might also mean more local mixed farming too. These are all steps with considerable merit. But the reasons are to do with the externalities, the pollution, and the loss of biodiversity caused by intensive global farming and the trade that goes with it. The degree of self-sufficiency that goes with this is a by-product. It should also be remembered that the 'dig for victory' rallying cry for national self-sufficiency during the war came with very considerable environmental costs, including the ploughing-up of much marginal land, from the Brecklands to the moorland fringes. On balance, self-sufficiency would probably be an environmental disaster.

We can therefore rule out food, food security and self-sufficiency as serious candidates for the public goods that might be appropriate priorities for subsidies and the 25 Year Environment Plan.

What then are the key public goods? One answer is provided by the goals listed in the 25 Year Environment Plan, and the set of underlying required assets to produce them now and in the future. The key overarching public good is a better natural environment for future generations. Its components are clean air, water, beaches and good marine habitats, flood defences, carbon-rich soils and biodiversity. While there will be much debate about the relative merits of these, none can be excluded from the core list, and all of them depend on each other – and hence on the overall natural environment.

Which should we spend what on?

Resources are scarce. So is money. Allocating them is about working out the relative merits of the practical options and their cost–benefit ratios. We want to spend our limited funds where we are going to get the most natural capital benefits relative to the costs.

The starting point is to make sure that we stop the declines, that we do sufficient capital maintenance to stop us sliding further backwards. The baseline today is not generally a good one, but it is a first priority to stop the public goods getting worse.

To do this, the baseline has to be fully understood. We need to know what we have got so we can make sure it will not be lost. The basic requirement is an asset register of the existing public goods. This is a physical list in the first instance. It is not about assigning monetary values. The aim is to hang on to what we have, not to question whether we should have these assets. The only valuation exercise is a cost one: what does the capital maintenance cost to prevent deterioration? It may be that some costs could be lower, and others will have to be higher since we are currently going backwards in lots of areas.

What is on the asset register? Some items are easy to agree. They include: the urban parks, the National Parks and the uplands generally. They also include river catchments, the Green Belts, the nature reserves, the SSSIs and much of the coastline, and the long-distance paths. For some of these, capital maintenance is already well provided. Those natural capital assets on the register that are managed by the National Trust, the RSPB and the Wildlife Trusts are probably in safe hands. The SSSIs in private hands and the Natural England nature reserves are more at risk.

Within these broad public goods there are some more specific items that fall into a special category on the asset register: those that are renewable, but are at risk of falling below the threshold from which they can renew themselves. We lose these at our peril: of losing them for ever, and hence foregoing all the benefits they yield for now and in the future. This includes endangered species, and it is why particular attention is paid to red lists and species in rapid decline. Sadly, this now includes not just hen harriers and redstarts, but also once-common birds like the curlew and even the lapwing. Soon we might add swallows, swifts and spotted flycatchers, and even house sparrows too.

Making these asset registers practical, we can look at each of the areas described in part two, and write down the list of the renewable natural capital at risk, and then more generally the natural capital public goods, and allocate monies to ensure that the declines are stopped. We can cost out the expenditures required for each of the great natural public goods.

There will sadly still be damage to these critical natural assets. There is a lot of housing and infrastructure development coming. This will damage natural capital public goods. HS2 will bulldoze its way through ancient woodlands. In these cases, and only after all the other alternatives have been exhausted, compensation will be required so the overall baseline does not slip backwards. There must be net environmental gain.

Once, and only once, the baseline has been held, and capital maintenance properly provided, we move on to enhancing public goods. Here is where valuation comes in, because it is here that we have choices. Should we spend public monies on breaching a sea wall and creating a new wetland? Should we plant new woodlands? Should we take out weirs and other river obstructions? Should we clean up the toxic chemicals in the sediments of the Thames estuary? Should we develop a green corridor around the coastal paths? Should we open up new living-landscape corridors? How do we decide which are the priorities?

There is a case for saying we should do all of them. Indeed, every one of the above list is being actively pursued by someone. Why should we do them all? In economic terms the answer is simple – at least in theory. It is that all of them have positive net present values. The benefits exceed the costs, even on a conventional discounted basis. If we don't discount future benefits (and arguably as stewards of the assets for future generations we should not), then it is not difficult for all of the above to pass the cost–benefit test. Anything with a positive net economic return enhances economic growth, even conventionally measured.

Many of the above have much more attractive cost–benefit ratios than other things we are spending very large sums on. It is hard to see how HS2, the Hinkley nuclear power station and Heathrow Airport could yield as much as, say, a new wetland or a coastal green corridor. Rather than shy away from this resource allocation test, it would be better both in principle and pragmatically for environmentalists to realise that this is an argument that they can and should win, and in many cases very convincingly. Contrary to repeated assertions that economics undermines the environment, the opposite is the case.

The more nuanced objection to using a cost–benefit test for

public goods is that it is very tricky to value many of the sorts of natural capital we might worry most about. How can we put a value on a landscape, a scenic view or a dragonfly? This is a serious objection, but it is a category mistake. Few, except the most inward-looking economists, could seriously argue that it makes sense to put a price on a dragonfly. But that is not what is going on. Rather, the question is: how much should we spend on enhancing the habitat of dragonflies to have more of them? This is not about holding onto the baseline: that is all about capital maintenance. We do not need any valuations for this. But we do have to choose between enhancement options, and we will in fact make choices. We do it all the time. Those choices involve spending money. And money comes as a number.

So where should this number come from? In conventional cost–benefit analysis this is based on a series of practical empirical tools. The analyst asks questions like: how much are people willing to pay for the public good? How much would they be willing to accept for its loss? How is its value capitalised in asset prices, like house prices? How much do people spend on enjoying the public good, in time and travel costs? What actual risks do they take?[7]

All of these questions are relevant and all provide information. They are, in effect, snapshots from different angles of the same object – the public good. But there is a difference between doing this sort of exercise as helpful input into decisions, and deciding what to do on the basis of a cost–benefit analysis. It is the difference between useful economic input and dangerous economic determinism. Recall that I have students who could not identify what a swallow is. Recall that knowledge of natural history is now very low, and recall that there are large numbers of the urban populations, and especially children, who have little or no experience of the countryside, and who do not know what some of the animals that they eat look like – the meat having been bought in plastic packaging from the supermarket. The degree of ignorance is frighteningly large.

It does nevertheless matter what current people are prepared to pay for. They vote for the politicians who decide how much money will be spent on public goods. They in turn might choose between more money for the National Health Service versus maintaining the £3 billion subsidies going into agriculture, reflected in the battles between the Treasury and DEFRA.

Is there a better way of working out which public goods to prioritise? Cost–benefit analysis leaves out future generations, and recall that there is a distinction between focusing on the assets and focusing on the outputs. Instead of ranking projects only by their cost–benefit analysis values, based on current preferences imperfectly valued, we could ask a different question: what is the option value? In other words, how much might future generations regret not having the natural asset?

This might at first glance look like 'willing to accept' in the standard cost–benefit analysis toolkit, but it isn't. It is rather about thinking through the set of natural capital assets that we should bequeath to the next generation to ensure that they can live good lives and choose how they want to do this. This question leads to defining the enhancements to public goods in terms of what the river catchments, the farmland and countryside, the uplands, the coasts and the urban environments should look like in, say, 2050. In other words, we should bequeath them the list of assets described in each of the chapters in part two, and (imperfectly) listed in the 25 Year Environment Plan.

The argument is simple: to deprive future generations of an enhanced natural environment would be to fail in our duties to them, and fail in our specific duty as stewards of natural capital. They should get an enhanced environment because the current one is not sustainable. If we don't do our duty by them, they will be subjected to further effects of climate change and have a lot less biodiversity, and they are likely to experience a deterioration in mental health and general well-being. We owe it to them to make good on the damage we have done, as well as to make sure it does not get any worse. This is something a democracy should be able to decide on.

The answer to the question put this way starts with the high-level public goods. It focuses on the enhancements of river catchments to ensure that not only water quality improves, but so does the biodiversity, the flood resilience and the access. It focuses on enhancing the soils, the peats, the fungi, and the insects and birds and mammals that live on our farmland. It focuses on developing and enhancing the uplands. It focuses on creating and sustaining genuinely protected marine areas and enhancing the coastal paths and associated hinterlands, and it focuses on giving every child access within a short distance to green spaces which are genuinely green. These are the high-level objectives, and they can be informed in the details by cost–benefit analysis, but since they are public goods, these are non-marginal decisions, which cost–benefit analysis cannot dictate. They are about the whole natural environment, which is much more than the sums of lots of disaggregate parts.

Filling in the details

In the great agricultural debate about public money for public goods, farming interests often claim that landowners are the best stewards of the land since they have a vested interest in maintaining and enhancing it. What we should do, some claim, is give them the money and they will spend it wisely. Farmers, it is argued, rely on the soil and the ecosystems that support it, and they can be relied on to look after it.[8]

There is something in this. It should not be dismissed out of hand. But it is also less than it seems. There are great family estates where the owners treat their land as assets-in-perpetuity, and focus on passing on their estates to their children and their children in turn. But this is not how farming works generally, and even on the estates it is not clear that their interests are exactly in line with those of the public and the public goods required, rather than those of their families. Many estates run managed game shoots. The maintenance of grouse moors, excessive deer populations and the growing pheasant industry are not without their problems, and these estates have not historically encouraged access by the public. Indeed, historically, quite the opposite. When someone says that the public interest is the same as their private interests, and seeks to blend them seamlessly together, a degree of scepticism may be warranted.

This should not rule out a central role for private parties. There is a deep asymmetry of information: farmers and landowners, water companies, tourist companies and leisure interests tend to know a lot more about the specifics than any bureaucrat. While the overall public goods should be defined at the national and regional level, top down, the details typically can't be. This is where auctions and markets (discussed in more detail in chapter 10), as well as local community initiatives, come in, and have a big role to play.

Think back to the river catchments and the idea of a catchment system plan and a catchment system operator. We know what the public goods are – enhanced water quality, better diversity, flood protection and resilience. What we don't know is what crops should be planted where; how many of what sort of trees should be planted upriver; and how many sheep should graze the headwater area. We do not know what sort of slurry pit works best without knowing the soils and the rainfall. And so on.

The water company does know a lot about what comes down the river, and how much it costs to get rid of the metaldehyde, for example. The farmer knows the cost of planting different crops and at which times of the year. The Environment Agency knows a lot about the river flows and how flooding works in each catchment.

The task is to allocate the public monies to best leverage this information, to get the best outcome for the least cost. An obvious way forward is to ask all the parties to bid the public goods they can offer and the associated costs. Take the CAP subsidies that may now be allocated on the principle of public money for public goods. Instead of getting Natural England to go around each farm and tell the farmers what they have to do for the subsidies, we could start the other way around. We could ask the farmers what they could offer by way of public goods and the associated costs. They would also need to offer up assurances that they would actually deliver these benefits, and there would need to be a compliance and penalties regime.

In the case of the rivers, farmers could offer to hold back floodwaters on the farmland, to plant new hedgerows and to create wildlife corridors. Better still, adjoining farms could work together and offer a larger wildlife corridor. They could offer to open new footpaths and improve access, and to keep the ground covered in winter to avoid soil erosion. Payment could be by result: if biodiversity goes up, if soil erosion goes down, and if more people access the land.

The public monies can come indirectly too. Water customers pay for a lot of public goods in their water bills, and often inefficiently so. A water company could instead offer to pay farmers not to put certain chemicals on specific bits of land and to retain ground cover. This is, in effect, a partial auction among farmers to offer up the public goods associated with less-polluted water. As noted in chapter 3, this is what Wessex Water is doing in Poole Harbour.

For the auctioning of public money, someone still has to fix the amount. One way of doing this would be to set public budgets for each catchment, for each upland area, and for each city and marine area. The total subsidy could be parcelled out accordingly, all within the context of the top-down broad public goods that form the content of delivering the objective of enhancing the natural environment. We could, for example, have a budget for the Thames, and then auction this out among the various interested parties, all competing (and cooperating) to provide the best public good outcomes. The bidders on the Thames might include the farmers in the catchment, the local authorities, the flood defence providers, leisure interests, and the National Trust and Wildlife Trusts.

Note that this auction approach leaves it open as to whether the providers will be private water companies, trusts, private landowners or public bodies like the Environment Agency and flood defence installations. The auctioning of the public money is where the public interest comes in; the delivery against the bids can then be left to whoever offers the best value for money – provided there are credible mechanisms for checking that the public goods are actually delivered and credible penalties for failures.

This does not mean that ownership and the great nationalisation versus privatisation arguments are irrelevant. There are particular circumstances where the choice affects the efficiency of the delivery of the public goods. It does not, for example, make sense for a body charged with regulation, licensing, enforcement and prosecution to also be involved in the necessary works. The former is a public function where public duties and requirements should apply. Flood defence is an operational and capital works activity, and best left to the private sector or, if not, to standalone trusts charged with this function. The canals, for example, are not run by the Environment Agency but by the Canal and River Trust.[9] Trusts tend to have two big advantages over private companies: they do not have to pay dividends; and they have the assets-in-perpetuity and the interests of the next generation in their core legal objectives. The disadvantage is that specific groups can capture them and they do not necessarily have sharp cost-efficiency constraints. In the bidding world of catchment system operators, everyone and anyone can bid to deliver the public goods.

There is little evidence that nationalisation in itself would improve environmental outcomes, and indeed there is quite a lot of evidence that public ownership can make matters worse through the mixed incentives that public sector managers face. Private owners can face much harsher scrutiny, for the simple reason that they are assumed to maximise profits, while state-owned companies are assumed to pursue the public interest and so are often subject to lighter-touch scrutiny. The great attraction of the catchment system operator is that we do not have to decide which is best. We can simply leave it to bidding to determine who can offer the best public goods outcomes.

Richer and greener public spaces

To summarise, natural capital is all about public goods, and the 25 Year Environment Plan is in essence a public goods plan. Public goods are defined as non-rival and non-excludable, and it is nonsense to pretend that anything that suits private vested interests can automatically be called a public good. Food, in particular, is not a public good. A policy based on the principle of public money for public goods is radically different from one that provides public money for private goods and hence private vested interests. The CAP, and especially the basic farm payment, is one of the worst examples of the latter: paying farmers to own land, with few credible and enforced commitments.

By focusing on the public goods, the scope for considerable efficiency benefits becomes apparent. Private markets will not provide public goods, but an efficient economy will provide them. It is good economics, and proper provision of public goods will be reflected in greater prosperity.

Because they are public, there needs to be a public way of deciding how much of these goods should be provided. Economists offer up cost–benefit analysis, but this is at best only a partial answer, because it is marginal, whereas the environment comes in systems, and because cost–benefit analysis is narrowly based on the utility of the current generation, as interpreted through their (lack of) information. That doesn't stop hard choices having to be made, and these can be made by thinking seriously about what the interests of the next generation might be and what natural capital they are going to need. Auctions, markets and private farmers and companies have a big role to play, competing to provide these public goods.

Two things remain to be determined: what the private parties are required to do *before* we decide about the public goods and the auctions start; and where the money comes from. It is of little value to graft public goods auctions and prices onto a flawed and distorted market system. From the natural capital perspective, the big gap is the externalities. Before we get to the auctions of public goods, we need to make sure that polluters pay, and that those who damage the natural environment have to pay compensation in pollution charges and in net environmental gain payments. There needs to be net *gain*, because of the risks and safe limits, and hence the payments need to respect the precautionary principle.

9

PAYING FOR POLLUTION

The provision of public goods is a public matter. So too is the prevention of harm. The polluter-pays principle says several things: that all costs should be taken into account in an efficient economy; and that those who do damage by their actions should pay those costs. There should be compensation, offsetting any damage. The net gain principle goes further: it states that we should be risk-averse and err on the side of overcompensation. It incorporates the precautionary principle, especially where renewable natural capital is involved and we don't know precisely where the safe limits lie.

These principles should guide who pays what and where the money goes. But they don't. When we think about what actually happens, two things come to mind. The first is farmers demanding subsidies in order not to pollute, to be paid to limit the destruction of nature; and the second is the appeals from the wildlife charities to save the barn owl, the swallows, and species of butterfly from the consequences of intensive agriculture, loss of habitats, and development. This is exactly the wrong way around, and if this is what it takes to enhance the natural environment then we are done for. Neither is going to hold back the tide of destruction.

The polluter-pays principle

Pollution is inefficient: it reduces economic value, by not taking into account the damage some production causes to others. It is also unfair in a very basic sense: most people assume – rightly – that, as citizens, they have a right to clean air, water and to the enjoyment of the countryside, and a right not to have pollution from others thrust upon them against their will.

The polluter-pays principle is the common-sense way to tackle this. In an efficient and fair economy, polluters should and would pay.[1] So far, so good. Except that it is not always obvious who the polluter is; sometimes they cannot be identified at all, and often they are dead or the company responsible has long gone. Even if they can be identified, they may not be able to pay.

Think very long term. When our ancestors long ago started cutting down the native forests, did they know they were adding to carbon emissions? Did the Victorians realise that the heavy metals in some of their new heavy industries would still be dangerous in the sediments of our rivers and especially our estuaries today? Even when the polluters are still with us, much pollution is diffuse, so who is responsible for what is far from obvious.

This all implies that the polluter-pays principle is going to be rough and ready, applied only where it is practical to do so. Yet not to make polluters pay is to be exactly wrong: better to be roughly right.

Imagine what would happen if the pollution from modern agriculture, from sewage-treatment works and from factories and the plastic wastes were all treated as part of the full costs of production. The cost of fertilisers would now be the price charged by the manufacturer *plus* the delivery charge to the farm *plus* the costs of applying it *plus* the costs to the rivers of the run-offs (and the subsequent eutrophication and algae blooms and the loss of oxygen in the water) *plus* the costs of the carbon emissions in the production of the fertilisers. Extend this to pesticides and herbicides too. The economics of agriculture would be transformed. These would be the right – efficient – prices for these chemicals. Modern agrichemical farming is anything but efficient.

The results would be dramatic. Higher costs mean lower demand. Less fertiliser and fewer pesticides and herbicides would be applied. The apparent overwhelming economic advantage to intensive agriculture over organic and less-intensive schemes would be reduced. What are claimed to be efficient farms may turn out not to be so. The sheer costs of their pollution might outweigh other cost advantages of scale and intensity. On marginal farmland with marginal profitability, the more conventional farming systems may be rendered uneconomic. That is effectively what happened at Knepp Castle Estate, even before these costs are added in (see chapter 5). Conventional farming turned a loss, even before it paid its full costs.[2]

A further extension is to antibiotics and their widespread and potentially dangerous use in animals. It has become routine to rely on antibiotics for the raising of meat, and especially poultry, to such an extent that bacterial resistance is inevitable. The consequences could be catastrophic: 'cheap' meat could come at an enormous cost. The reason for this unsustainable use is that farmers do not face the consequences. They pass on the costs to society. If antibiotics were to price in this risk, not only would their use be reduced, but a number of highly intensive animal factories would no longer be sustainable. Not making the polluters pay will not make the risk go away.[3]

Our lands would be much greener and more prosperous if all these costs were internalised. This would be good economics. There would be direct beneficiaries from making polluters pay. The gainers would include water- and sewage-treatment companies and hence water customers, since water quality in the rivers and the aquifers would be less polluted and therefore less costly to treat. Anglers and a host of other river users would be better off, and biodiversity would improve. People might not die from bacterial infections, as they are now from MRSA.[4] These would be the winners.

The costs would be passed through into food, and although water companies would gain from the less-intensive agriculture, there would also be a cost to the phosphates that water-treatment works discharge. Every one of the ten goals set for the 25 Year Environment Plan would be advanced. Once land prices had adjusted, farmers would be no worse off, and their natural capital – especially their soils – would be in better shape. Some crops, like oilseed rape, would decline, and others would take their place. Changing the price of the inputs would change the composition of crops and land use. Intensive factory farming could be challenged. This is all radical, environmentally benign and economically efficient.

Putting a price on pollution

How would the polluter-pays principle be applied? How much would the polluters pay? The conventional economic answer is that the pollution should be charged by putting a price on the estimated damage.[5] Some environmentalists object to this approach, as of course do farming and agrichemical interests. The environmentalists sometimes argue that the problem with pricing pollution is that it allows it to go on happening, even if at a reduced and more costly way by the polluters. They argue that it should simply be stopped.

This might be intuitively appealing, but it runs into a huge brick wall. The optimal level of pollution is rarely zero. Very dangerous chemicals can and should be banned, but if we were to ban rather than charge and regulate most pollutants, the results would be catastrophic to our way of life. Why? Because zero pollution really means zero humans, or close to. We are always impacting on our environment, changing it for our own purposes. There is a world of difference between treading lightly on our planet and not treading at all. We could erase all human-induced carbon emissions immediately, and stop all pollution to land, water and air. But this would require us to stop too. Zero pollution is not prosperous, and the green that resulted would be very, very different. If the purpose of making our land green and prosperous is to benefit us humans, it is not a good way to go. Leaving us out of nature would leave nature to its own devices. But we should not think that nature cares.

Farmers and agrichemical industries object to the polluter-pays principle because it increases their costs and hits their profits. In the list of *Farmers Weekly* six big breakthroughs of recent decades (see chapter 4), seeing off pesticide and herbicide taxes is presented as one of their big wins.[6] They claim that food will be more expensive as a result. They would be right about food produced by chemically intensive methods. They would be wrong when it comes to the alternatives, and here the prices might fall as the market expanded and less-polluting farming methods were able to gain the advantages of a bigger market share. But even if food prices go up, this is still the right thing to do. It is us consumers – who buy these pollution-inducing agricultural products and are therefore really the polluters – who should pay for the damage our consumption habits cause. It is ultimately our fault, not that of the farmers who respond rationally to the incentives they face. Cheap food cannot be an objective without regard to the consequences. Otherwise why not simply lower – or even abandon – environmental standards?

How to calculate the pollution charges? Contrary to what many economists claim, there is no right answer that we can know in advance. If we were perfectly informed, we could simply fix the problem and not bother with the niceties of the polluter-pays principle and the charges that result.

There are two ways of handling this uncertainty. We can try to use the best economic techniques to make an educated guess at the right answer. Alternatively, we can set an initial pollution charge and see what happens. Take the example of the 5 pence plastic bag tax. Who would have guessed that it would lead to an 85 per cent fall in use? The reason nobody guessed the effect would be so dramatic is that the psychological and social and media dynamics could not be easily gauged in advance. It suddenly became rather shameful to have to pay the 5 pence for a new bag when everyone else was re-using theirs.

There have been other examples. The tax differential on leaded versus unleaded petrol produced a sharp switch. The land-fill levy, which makes dumping an expensive practice, has worked well.[7] Thinking ahead, getting people to re-use plastic cups at coffee shops, and getting rid of the ubiquitous plastic water bottles, might work well too if only a small extra charge is added to the purchase cost. When asked whether you would like to pay to have the plastic to then throw away, it prompts you to think about what the impact of your choices might be. It can, as in the case of plastic bags, work miracles. In doing so, it means that the pollution charge people pay can turn out to be very small in total. If nobody buys the plastic bags, then there is no charge to pay. An ideal environmental charge is one that abolishes itself.

Not all pollution lends itself to charges, and in some cases identifying the polluter is so difficult that it is better to just regulate. There are cases where the impacts are so bad that outright bans are appropriate. In any event, all charges work in a regulatory context.

The pragmatic approach is to start with those cases where charges have obvious advantages, where the polluters can be identified, and where the impacts are expected to be considerable. The best candidates to start with are carbon, fertilisers, pesticides, herbicides, plastic bags and plastic cups and bottles.

The carbon price already exists, as does the plastic bag charge. In the case of carbon it really does matter how high the carbon price actually is, and to whom it is applied. In the electricity sector, it has been an effective way of driving out coal.

But it has not yet been extended to agriculture, and hence leaves carbon emissions from agriculture free from paying for their consequences. As set out in my 2017 'Cost of Energy Review' for the government, given that agriculture's economic significance to the economy is so low, this is a serious mistake, raising the cost of meeting the carbon targets and budgets more than necessary.[8] It should also be extended to peat – and urgently.

As with carbon, fertilisers, pesticides and herbicides are readily identifiable charging targets, and all of these can be levied on producers. Although producers do their producing ultimately for us consumers, the principle of producer responsibility helps to nail the pollution at source. The alternative consumer responsibility principle is typically harder to apply, and in any event consumers will always pay the economic incidence of the charges in their shopping baskets as the higher costs are passed through.

Pragmatism is important here: it is easier to charge an electricity generation company or a fertiliser company per unit of input than try to work out how much fertiliser and pesticides went into producing the loaf of bread. What is lost in producer responsibility is perhaps the halo effect of doing good, as in the plastic bag charge example, although again companies now compete to project the best environmental image to their customers. It is also politically expedient to charge producers: most voters seem to believe that if companies are charged, they themselves are not ultimately paying. This is an illusion as the pollution is caused in producing goods and services for us, but it nevertheless helps to get an efficient answer in place, and it has been politics rather than economics that has been the barrier to increasing efficiency, and, therefore, prosperity through properly pricing pollution.

Pricing pollution and the money

Putting a price on pollution corrects otherwise distorted prices and hence is a good thing. But in addition to this substitution away from more-polluting to less-polluting production, there is also an income effect. Pollution charges raise money and, in the case of carbon, lots of money. From a government perspective, it is much better to raise money by taxing 'bads' like pollution, tobacco and alcohol than it is to tax 'goods' like labour through income tax. As governments find it increasingly challenging to raise taxes generally, taxing pollution rather than labour has a double advantage: it makes the economy more efficient, and hence more prosperous; and it raises much-needed money for public expenditures generally. This is a double dividend.

An economic strategy to enhance prosperity is therefore one that goes with the grain of environmental enhancement. It taxes bad things like pollution, and in the process raises money for good things, on which governments can spend the money. Some environmentalists want to go further: they want the money raised from these pollution charges to be spent only on green things. Chapter 11 explains how a Nature Fund could be the conduit for such monies.

There is a case to be made for this sort of hypothecation or earmarking of the revenues to specific green expenditure purposes, especially where there is a close connection between the pollution and the enhancements. This is where net *environmental* gain, as opposed to net *general* gain, comes in. But to argue that it is sometimes (even often) a good idea to hypothecate does not mean that it is always so. The pollution charge in itself leads to a better environmental outcome. Governments do need to raise general revenue: there are few that argue that the taxes on tobacco or alcohol should be spent exclusively on addressing lung cancer and liver cirrhosis. When we come to the Nature

Fund, some rules to best strike this balance between hypothecation and general spending will be set out.

Fines for pollution

Economic incentives are not limited to charges and taxes. In most
cases we use regulation. Indeed, regulation is pervasive: what you
can build, where, what chemicals you can and cannot use on farmland, what sorts of land are protected, what a water company can
discharge into a river, and what emissions to air can come from
power stations and industrial facilities are all governed by regulations. All pollution charges are set in a broader regulatory context.

Having regulations begs questions about what levels they
should be set at, and on what. They also raise questions about
the consequences of breaking the rules. What are the punishments? In some cases, the impacts demand jail sentences, but
in general environmental crimes are treated much more leniently
than many other sorts of offences.

Take the stealing of birds' eggs and the poisoning or shooting
of predators like the golden eagle and hen harrier, discussed in
chapter 5. Individuals get fined, and very occasionally jailed. But
the shooting estates that employ the gamekeepers are liable only
in Scotland, and even here the fines are very small. Wildlife crime
is a risk activity, with costs (fines) and benefits (no hen harriers
eating grouse chicks). As already noted, when the first great landowner goes to jail for the consequences of the actions of the
estate's employees, or the estate faces serious fines, persecution
is likely to stop pretty quickly.

On the corporate side, there are numerous incidents of water
companies breaking discharge consents and polluting rivers, and
lots of examples of farmers failing to properly manage slurry. The
fines are just 'business expenses' to be set against the costs of
ensuring full compliance. Thames Water, for example, was fined

a record £20 million for pumping 1.9 billion litres of untreated sewage into the Thames. This represents an insignificant amount against turnover, and no shareholder has felt any noticeable effect on their wealth. In the case of slurry releases, *Farmers Weekly* reported that a dairy farm was fined just £14,000 for repeated offences. This is a paltry sum in comparison to the damage caused. It is likely to be less than the CAP subsidies received.[9]

Compare this to abuse of market power and anti-competitive behaviour. This can result in a fine of up to 10 per cent of turnover. If the Thames pollution case had had this penalty, the fine could have been £200 million. Why should we regard gross acts of pollution as less serious than anti-competitive behaviour?

It is not just about the size of the fine. It is also about the chances of getting caught. Gamekeepers have been killing birds of prey illegally for a long time, but they know the chances of proving their guilt on the wide expanses of grouse moors are slim. They know too that the cost of trying to prove it saps police resources, which could be deployed elsewhere. Similarly, ships wash their tanks off the British coast. Rubbish is dumped. Fly-tipping is widespread.

There are two ways to improve outcomes: the fines can be increased; and the probability of getting caught can be increased. Take speed limits as an example. Here there is considerable enforcement, with a whole panoply of detection mechanisms including speed cameras. Because the chances of getting caught are high, the penalties do not have to be that great to have an impact. But imagine a radically different approach. Suppose speeding resulted in a fine proportional to your income and a jail term. There would not need to be many speed cameras: the chance of getting caught would be lower, but the consequences draconian.

Since the objective is compliance, and since compliance is good for the economy, fines and other penalties are an important part of the regulatory armoury. The aim, as with pollution charges, is ultimately to render payments negligible because the crime is deterred. There can be little doubt that this area needs urgent attention. Being caught stealing birds' eggs and killing hen harriers ought to be so painful for the criminals that they desist, since detection is so difficult. A further twist might include extra penalties where there is a renewable bit of natural capital close to the threshold of becoming non-renewable. Killing or otherwise interfering with endangered species, locally, nationally or globally, demands a much higher disincentive, for it destroys all the benefits of that species for ever, a really big loss of economic prosperity. If the estate on which the crime was committed ceases to be able to carry out shooting then there would be less persecution. If game shoots were licensed, the licence could be withdrawn. If ships that wash their tanks at sea are confiscated, and if farmers who let slurry escape into rivers forfeited their subsidies, then the level of compliance with the law would be much higher. The problem can be readily solved: it is having the will to do so that is missing.

Waste crime and fly-tipping are examples where the focus should be on detection, since licensing already exists and most of the criminals are outside the licence framework. New technologies could make detection potentially much easier since waste can be tagged and followed. All waste items come from somewhere and lots have barcodes and other identifiers. Technology, along with the Internet of Things, brings lots of new and exciting ways of fixing what have often seemed intractable problems. We can be a lot smarter about detection, but for this we need a proper Environment Protection Agency, as will be explained in chapter 12.

Net environmental gain and developers

What about the cases where developments lead to environmental damage? Here there is a loss of 'green', and however much conservationists might lament the losses, there are cases where they can be justified. It is perfectly possible to build a lot of new houses on already urbanised sites and thereby increase housing density, but it is pretty unlikely that this can be achieved only here when the aim is to build more than 200,000 houses a year. Similarly, it is possible to cram in more and more passengers on existing rail lines, but there comes a point where new railways are needed. Even in the brownfield and urban contexts, the land that houses are built on could instead be turned into urban green spaces, and some brownfield sites are biodiversity-rich already. The fact is that there will be damage from development. And there will be development.

The way to think about this damage is to regard it as a form of pollution, and to apply the polluter-pays principle. Compensation is the way the polluter in this case pays. As with the pollution charges, there is rarely if ever a right answer to the question of how much. The reason is that we don't know the full environmental consequences, and especially where a renewable natural capital asset is involved. Recall that a renewable goes on delivering its bounty for free for ever, provided it is not depleted below a critical threshold from which it can't recover. Recall that because of the uncertainty as to precisely where this lies, and because the risk of getting it too low is asymmetrically much worse than getting it too high, we apply the concept of a safe limit, a sort of buffer of insurance. This means that we do not apply our best guess of the exact threshold, but go for a higher number.

Compensation for damage should result in net environmental gain, not net neutrality. Compensating green improvements elsewhere should leave the aggregate natural capital higher, and hence the natural capital we bequeath to the next generation goes up, even if we lose some bits in the process.

Can this be done? In theory the answer must be yes. There are a host of ways in which the land, rivers, coasts and cities can be made more green. The list is enormous, and includes many of the projects noted in part two. But it is not the theory that is the problem: it is the practical application, measurements and enforcement regimes that cause serious difficulties. What looks like a sensible approach can easily slip into a 'licence to trash'.

Let's start with the simplest of examples. A developer proposes to build on a bit of Green Belt. Let's say that this bit of land is currently under intensive agricultural cultivation for oilseed rape. The soil is compacted by heavy farm machinery, and there is a lot of chemical run-off and silt going into the local river, which also happens to be a water supply for the local town. It is a poor piece of land, badly managed, with little or no biodiversity, and no access. Indeed, since the farmer might well have been hanging on for planning permission, there is every incentive to make sure it has no environmental value. The lower the environmental value of the land, the more likely planning permission will be granted and the lower the compensation payments.

There are lots of bits of the Green Belt like this. East of Oxford is just one example. The developer might have plans not only to build the houses, but also to improve the biodiversity per hectare developed, with gardens, walkways and the odd pond. Trees, hedges and access rights can be added. The mock-up model of the development presented to the planners looks very green, with pretty illustrations of happy butterflies and birds.

It is all very familiar, and can be very convincing to planning authorities. The developer says there will be little or no net environmental loss. In its own terms and in the context of current planning laws this is a very credible story. Indeed, the main concerns might be about infrastructure, schools and transport rather than biodiversity and the countryside. Yet it is also very suspect, and for a simple reason. There are *other* uses to which the land could be put, and the housing is probably irreversible. As set out in chapter 7 on the urban environment, this land could really be *green* Green Belt. Once under concrete there is no way back, and we will be limited to trying to make the newly urban environment as green as possible.

The question is: what is the baseline against which net environmental gain should be set? Is it to be determined relative to the *current* land use, or relative to other, possibly much better, uses?

The only way of cracking this problem is to have a more general plan, on a national and systems basis, which creates things like Green Belts – in other words, just what was intended back in the 1947 Planning Act. Net environmental gain will not solve this problem. At best it stops further declines, but not much more. It does not on its own deal with the opportunity to protect and enhance the public goods. It should.

The next problem is measurement. How exactly do you measure the cost of the lost environment? How do you calculate the value of what is replacing the damage done by the development?

This is where both economists and conservationists get into a mess. It is a mess of misunderstandings about what exactly is being measured. The first point – aimed at the economics – is that it is not the *value* that is actually being measured but the *cost*. It is about how much resources – how much money – should be spent to compensate. As pointed out in the previous chapter, decisions involve allocating resources. They have to. Spending on one thing precludes spending on others. There are choices to be made, and economics helps in calculating the costs. It does not tell you the value of anything. The second point – aimed at conservationists – is that damage is going to be done, and, in the absence of measurement, the compensation can easily end up as trivial or even zero. Look around at the big developments in recent decades. In the case of the M3 and Twyford Down in the 1980s, there was scant compensation for the scale of the damage done to the great chalk downland, which was bisected.[10] Look then in comparison at Crossrail, and the ways in which the spillage from tunnelling has gone towards helping to create new marshland. Look at the Thames Gateway and the consequent spending on the marshes and habitats of the Thames Estuary.

Compare these with the encroachments on the Green Belt, where little compensation has been paid.

Of course, any development should face the tests of avoiding damage in the first place, and there are lots of places where there simply should not be development. But if, after the proper assessments and due processes of planning have been exhausted, the development is to take place, we then need some way of working out what this compensation should be.

This runs into exactly the same problem we met above when considering alternative baselines. It is easy to take one small bit of land and say that the impacts of this specific bit being developed are typically small. They almost always are. But lots of individual developments add up to the loss of a habitat with more general consequences. Think of each case over the last 1,000 years of adding a few more houses in London. The result was eventually to incorporate all the villages surrounding London, and to concrete over lots of the green meadows and pastures nearby. Similarly, each new wharf and dock and port facility along the Mersey made little individual difference to the mudflats, but added together they certainly have. Think of Cardiff's marine area, and the Tidal Lagoon proposal. What happens when the next tidal lagoon is added, and then another? Almost inevitably the ecosystem of the Severn Estuary will be altered.

Damage therefore needs to be seen on a *system basis*, and again planning is essential. Each incremental incursion into the Green Belt causes little damage, but lots of them do and then the Green Belt is gone. The correct way to assess the damage is to start with the damage to the system, not the damage to the specific plot of land. Compensation should be determined in terms of the system impacts, as well as those affecting the specific site.

It applies too to the benefits side. We can swap one plot of land for another somewhere else, but the value of the enhancement is again a systems question. This is where the Nature Fund comes in.

Subsidies

A subsidy is simply the converse of a charge or tax. Good subsidies make it possible to produce public goods and to increase outputs which might otherwise not be produced at all, or produced in insufficient quantities. Hence, public money for public goods and subsidies for positive externalities. Bad, perverse subsidies encourage higher production of already polluting activities.

Agricultural subsidies have been notoriously perverse, and not just in Britain. British agricultural subsidies prior to joining the EEC paid farmers to do a lot of environmental damage, including drainage, the removal of hedgerows, and digging up marginal land, including moorland, as noted in chapter 4.

The form of the perverse subsidies in the CAP has varied over time. In the name of maximising food production, farmers were paid for the outputs they produced. They were given a fixed and guaranteed price for each unit of their production – for corn, milk, butter, wine, sheep and so on. The reasoning was that farmers faced a special problem: prices fluctuated. Never mind that this is the point of prices and markets, and almost all prices vary in order to allocate resources efficiently. This was seen as too much of a threat to farmers and they had to be protected. It is something they argue they should be protected from again now.

Were the bureaucrats to set the prices correctly so that they averaged out the economic fundamentals of supply and demand, this policy might have had limited environmentally damaging outcomes, although it would still have undermined mixed farms and crop rotations – the traditional way in which farmers reduced the risk of price fluctuations. But the bureaucrats went one stage further, fixing prices *higher* than the average. They did this in part because they were captured by powerful farming interests, in part because they thought excess production would improve food security, and in part to raise farm incomes.

The results of these subsidies were awful, and awfully predict-able. Europe ended up with the notorious butter mountains and wine lakes. It was economically stupid, full stop. But what was less noticed was the wider impact on the environment. Guaranteeing above-market prices induced the maximisation of production in excess of the optimal level. As noted, it led to very high stocking rates, and hence intensive overgrazing in the uplands. The extra subsidised sheep literally ate the uplands, and denuded their plants and habitats. The lowlands intensified too. At higher prices, marginal land was worth ploughing and lots of chemical applications were affordable because the higher prices increased profits per unit of output. The fields got bigger, the machinery got bigger, and the inconvenient hedgerows that got in the way were grubbed up.

The perverse subsidies did their jobs. Farmers, like any other business, responded to incentives, and the incentives were to maximise production. Good stewardship of the land, careful management of habitats and the ecology of farms, and especially their soils, the maintenance of ponds and hedgerows, all stood in the way of profits. And profit-maximisation was what they did, with a corresponding minimisation of the farmland biodiversity.

After the 2000 CAP reforms, things got a little less bad, but as described in chapter 4 the economics of agriculture remain pretty crazy. The CAP was taking up the bulk of the total EU budget (it still takes up around 40 per cent), and the butter mountains and wine lakes had reached an absurd scale, and even the most farmer-friendly politicians and media understood that it just could not go on. It did not stop the NFU and its sister organisations across Europe fighting a very powerful rearguard action.

The solution to the CAP excesses was to replace one set of perverse incentives with slightly less perverse ones. Instead of payments per unit of output, the link between subsidies and production was broken (except that it wasn't entirely, as we shall see). Out went production subsidies and in came subsidies for simply owning the farmed land.

In the CAP that runs to 2020, farmers receive a basic farm payment, worked out on the basis of the number of hectares they own, as long as the land is actually farmed (loosely defined). The result is entirely predictable and is described in chapter 4: the price of land rises to reflect the basic farm payment *plus* the value of the production on that land. Land prices neatly capitalise the subsidy. Other things also influence land prices and generally lead to their even greater inflation.

The basic farm payment is not, however, completely independent of production, and for two reasons. First, it requires farmers to farm the land. It cannot, for example, be left to nature or even planted with trees. So the uplands have to be grazed as the only farming option. Second, it keeps marginal farms going because the subsidy gives enough money to deliver a level of income just sufficient to keep them in business. Upland farmers hang on where they would otherwise go bust and cease farming. The result is doubly perverse: it yields more than would be justified in output on land which is not otherwise viable, and would be better managed as a natural resource.

The money could be spent much more effectively, as chapter 11 explains. It could be spent making the marginal farms produce valuable public goods, instead of focusing on uneconomic private ones. As perverse subsidies go, the CAP has been in a league of its own.

Not all the CAP goes into subsidising land. There are green elements in the so-called pillar 2 payments for agri-environmental schemes. These are often poorly targeted. By abolishing the perverse subsidies of pillar 1, and by replacing pillar 2 with a new public-goods-driven subsidy regime, we can move from perverse and inefficient subsidies to good subsidies for the things the market would not otherwise provide. Given that the amount of money involved here is currently around £3 billion, this is a very big chance to enhance the natural environment and our prosperity at the same time. Farmers could continue to receive money, but for good things rather than bad. Their livelihoods would consequently be more sustainable. Europe could make the switch too in subsequent reforms of the CAP, with or without the UK.

Other perverse farming subsidies – inheritance tax, fuel duties and rates

As if the perverse subsidies in the CAP were not bad enough, British governments have made them even worse by piling additional perverse subsidies on top. As explained in chapter 4, farmers are exempt from inheritance tax, they get lower taxation on fuel, and they are exempt from business rates. Planning restrictions are weaker, and there is compensation when livestock is affected by certain diseases. Farmers also benefit from a range of agricultural research and development support and advice. In the event of drought and flooding they demand more help from governments, and often get it. Almost everything that could be subsidised is subsidised.

Inheritance tax exemption was designed to allow farmers to pass on the family farm to the next generation. But if this was the rationale it is not what has happened. Many farms are now treated as a business asset like any other, and some of the land is owned by corporates, pension funds, charities and trusts. The result is again perverse: the exemption makes agricultural land a more valuable asset than other property from an inheritance tax perspective, and therefore land prices rise to capitalise the effects. Even worse, there is less incentive to retire from farming, which there would be under the general inheritance tax rules, whereby gifts are exempt if given away at least seven years before death. Instead of farmers passing on their farms to the next generation with the seven-year rule in mind, the tax exemption means they can hang on until they die. It is therefore no surprise that land is even more expensive and the average age of farmers is higher. The size of the impact depends on the alternative reliefs, such as business inheritance tax, but the fact remains that these are special provisions for landownership.

The lower fuel duty means that, at the margin, the incentive to reduce fuel use is lower than it would otherwise have been, potentially making farming more fuel-intensive. It is the opposite of a carbon tax. Relative to industry, it is a carbon subsidy. It artificially reduces the costs of production, and therefore increases farming activities at the margin. Where very marginal land might be ploughed up, having cheaper fuel may make this more likely. Applying a carbon price to agriculture would start by abolishing the red diesel subsidy.

Exemption from business rates reduces costs, and hence increases output, and at the same time makes land a more attractive commercial property asset from this perspective. Again this distorts the relative price of land.

The combination of all these perverse subsidies is a huge wasted opportunity, and an economically damaging policy, with lots of collateral damage to the environment. Looking at it more positively, there is here a considerable chance to improve the natural environment and do it at no net extra cost to the economy. Just taking away the subsidies and special tax treatments frees up a big sum of money to then spend much more wisely on farming and other environmental improvements. This is a double dividend: a more prosperous *and* a greener economy. For farmers in aggregate it can be neutral-to-positive. Some intensive farmers would lose their perverse subsidies, and others (for example, in the uplands) have a lot to gain. It is just that they will be producing better and sometimes different things.

Perverse subsidies in industrial policy and infrastructure

Sadly, agriculture is not the only perversely subsidised industry from an environmental perspective. There is a whole host of other subsidies to industry and infrastructure that encourage environmental damage beyond the efficient level.

Some of these are the result of direct grants and subsidies to industry for specific projects, which would otherwise not be economic. Historically, there have been a number of developments in poorer regions to build infrastructure and factories, reclaiming land, which subsequently have not matched up to the promoters' and the politicians' expectations. Estuaries and port areas have been particularly prone to these sorts of schemes, reclaiming marshlands that are deemed to be 'wasted lands'.

There are subsidies and tax examples applied to specific areas that are environmentally sensitive. Household electricity and gas are subject to lower rates of VAT. Then there are more subtle examples of subsidies that have serious environmental consequences. Roads are subsidised much more than, say, broadband, which encourages more people to travel more and leads to more road building and poorer air quality, rather than working from home.

The great infrastructures that are closest to natural capital, like water, are regulated in specific ways. Water companies have regulated asset bases, but the assets included are only hard physical capital. There is no natural capital in their regulated asset bases. Since it is these regulated asset bases that pension funds and other investors are most interested in, hard concrete is preferred to natural capital investments, so that water companies trying to do the right thing from an economic and environmental perspective are undermined by this distorting and implicit perverse subsidy.

The great improvements that come from proper economics

Imagine what the natural environment would look like if polluters paid for the damage they cause; if developers were required to fully meet the net environmental gain requirement; and if perverse subsidies were removed.

There would be immediate and dramatic environmental improvements. The use of fertilisers, pesticides, herbicides and antibiotics in agriculture would be reduced. This would be the most immediate and biggest gain. Artificial fertilisers would be much more expensive. Their price would now reflect the carbon produced in making them, a very energy-intensive process. It would reflect the damage caused to rivers and lakes, and it would reflect the damage done to the flora and fauna, including the soils.

Farmers would look more closely at substitutes, and at ways of managing the fertility of their soils rather than treating them as blotting paper. They would take natural processes much more seriously into account in their business plans, and in the process they would halt the decline of the carbon in the soils. They would have to think much more about how to work with rather than against nature. Crop rotation, mixed-farming approaches, which produce manure for the fields, and greater efforts to prevent the loss of the now much more valuable soils would all feature more strongly. There would be less-intensive factory farms. This would be an enormous win for the natural environment and all of it increasing economic prosperity.

The rivers would be in a better state, and in some cases a *much* better state. The algae blooms, which depend on the run-off of nitrates, would be reduced. Pollution would not be zero as a result. Recall that the optimal level of pollution is rarely zero. But it would be better, and a new equilibrium would be found in the balance of fertilisers, pesticides, herbicides and antibiotics, on the one hand, and natural approaches on the other. A lot less would be used, and that means more insects and soil invertebrates, and therefore more birds and mammals and more wild flowers with more seed for the birds and mammals. Best of all, this would all happen at *no net cost* because pollution would now be priced.

What is not to like about all this? But this is just the beginning of an efficient economy in which economic incentives are efficiently set. The pollutants should be charged. Out would go the tax reliefs, and out would go the basic farm payments.

At this point some farmers will be screaming, and others will be cheering. The shock to mainstream intensive farming will be profound. Some land prices will fall, some farmers will go out of business, and some marginal land will be taken out of production. The sheep on the hills will be scarcer. These farmers will be joined in their protests by the agrichemical industry, which stands to suffer most as a result. A lot of the glyphosate will go the way of the neonicotinoids. Demand for chemicals will go down and hence profits will fall.

Of all these effects the land price impact is the one that will be most immediately painful. Farmers in debt, with mortgages against the collateral of their farm land values, will be exposed. There will be some capital losses. There already have been – before leaving the EU and before the withdrawal from the CAP.[11]

Before we conclude that this is all just an awful violence to our farmers, we need to bear in mind the corollary. For all the losers, there will be offsetting gainers. Young farmers may actually be able to enter the industry, and the value of land might actually begin to reflect the true economics of the crops, for the high land prices are a massive barrier to entry.

To these specific beneficiaries will be added many others. Money not spent on perverse subsidies could be spent instead on the benign sort, in providing public money for public goods. All those hill farmers struggling on marginal land trying to eke out a living from lots of sheep may be eligible for subsidies to do good things instead, to maintain and enhance the landscape and its biodiversity in harmony with rather than against nature. They may protest that 'this is not farming', but then neither are the sorts of activities relying on the life-support system of the perverse subsidies and exemptions from paying the costs of pollution. There is nothing 'normal' about farming under the CAP: it has become a branch of the welfare state, paying money to farmers to do things, many of which are inconsistent with the public good.

This is the opportunity in front of us, and the wonder is that it is all without net new and additional costs. This is not just a bonus: it is a necessity, for it is always going to be a tall order to expect the Treasury to cough up more public expenditure for the private benefit of farmers producing private goods. Instead, we can get a lot more from the current spending, and in the process enhance economic prosperity.

The task then is to gather together all the various revenue streams from the current subsidies and from new charges on pollution, as well as the developers' net environmental gain payments, and see how these could be better spent to deliver a much improved economic and environmental outcome. The public money for public goods, the polluter-pays principle, the net environmental gain principle and the precautionary principle together provide the foundations for a green and prosperous land.

To deliver the most natural capital for all this money, to do it efficiently, and especially in the context of net zero, we need to develop new natural capital markets, using auctions where possible, so that farmers can play a key and positive part in offering up the least-cost options.

10

NATURAL CAPITAL MARKETS, AUCTIONS AND THE NET ZERO EXAMPLE

Getting the best natural capital for a fixed budget is what markets are usually very good at. Net zero, the new legal requirement that net emissions must be reduced by 100 per cent by 2050, adds a whole new dimension to how the natural environment is managed. Having spent the last 30 years focusing almost exclusively on electricity generation, and in particular on wind farms and solar panels, finally the penny has dropped: decarbonisation is as much about sequestration as it is about the emissions side.

Natural capital has been mopping up carbon for much of earth's history, and long before humans came along and started polluting the atmosphere. The oceans, the soils, forests and peat bogs have kept a check on carbon, and have been our natural climate regulators. The scale and urgency of climate change, and the imperatives of net zero, now add a great new opportunity to help green our land, and a further boost to the economic prosperity that comes from responsibly managing our land.

Better still, natural sequestration is not only cheap in comparison to some of the other options like industrial carbon capture and storage, but it is also best effected by applying the polluter-pays principle and insisting that carbon should be taxed and that sequestration should be the result of the net gain principle – compensation for the pollution. It is our economic principles in action.

To achieve the latter – to get landowners and farmers paid for natural sequestration – there is one further economic dimension that needs to be added to our three principles of public goods, polluter pays and net environmental gain: markets for carbon and other types of natural capital.

What net zero really means

Markets work best when there is a clear and well-defined objective to go for. So, before we get into the detail of how to do natural carbon sequestration, we need to start with a proper understanding of the nature and scale of the problem. What exactly does net zero mean?

The Committee on Climate Change, in its persuasive advocacy of net zero, makes the claim that once we get there in 2050 we will no longer be causing global warming.[1] Since we will not be producing net carbon emissions, the Committee claims that we will not be adding to the stock of carbon in the atmosphere. It sounds obvious, but it is not. It is wrong, and a dangerous illusion too.

It all comes back to the causes of pollution across the natural environment. When farmers apply fertilisers and pesticides, when water companies discharge phosphorus into rivers, they are doing it *for us*. We, the consumers, are the cause of the pollution. This applies to carbon too. All the petrol and diesel, all the steel, cement, fertilisers, petrochemicals and aluminium that indirectly go into making the things in our shopping baskets are *for us*. It is our carbon *consumption* that matters.

The way to think about this is to write yourself a carbon diary. Write down all the consuming you do over a typical day, and then take a guess at how much carbon is embodied in each and every choice you make. There is carbon in providing you with a water supply, treating it and pumping it to you through metal and plastic pipes. This is all needed when you go to the toilet first thing. Then there is toilet paper and the detergents you pour into the toilet bowl. Your central heating may have come on and you will want hot water for your shower. Most likely this is all from your gas boiler. Your breakfast is packed with carbon. It involves tractors and combines and fertilisers and pesticides, and lots of packaging and transport to get it to your cereal bowl. If you have a full English breakfast, including bacon, eggs and sausages, it is a whole new carbon story. Next, getting to work is pretty carbon-intensive, unless you walk, cycle or work from home. You might use biofuels, but then much of these come from palm oil, from plantations grown on cleared rainforests. Your laptop, smartphone and tablets are made in a carbon-rich way, use lots of metals and plastics to manufacture, and are shipped to you – before you even start charging the batteries. If you have children, they are carbon factories, from nappies onwards.

Try completing this, and then imagine how you would write a carbon diary in 2050, with the constraint that it must contain no carbon other than that which has been offset through sequestration. There would be some radical changes. You may already buy organic, have turned down the thermostat, and taken up walking or cycling to work, but even then there will be a lot of carbon still down to you. This is so much more than decarbonising electricity generation and your heating system. Indeed, these are the easy bits.

How does your carbon diary square with the new net zero 2050 target? The answer is not that well. For much of what you consume comes from imports. The steel that goes into the factories that make your stuff is probably made in China. Even the cement in all those new houses might come from there as well. The aluminium, the fertilisers and almost all the petrochemicals will have been imported. Your strawberries and French beans at Christmas might have come from Kenya and Peru. Britain is a deindustrialised country: service industries make up 80 per cent of the economy. We do not make much stuff anymore. We rely on other countries to make a lot of it for us.

You may now have realised why the Committee on Climate Change's claim about not causing any more climate change in 2050 if we are net zero in our own territorial emissions is such a dangerous illusion. If we bear down on emissions here by closing down the rest of British energy-intensive industry and agriculture, we will make great progress towards our domestic carbon emissions target, while actually making climate change worse. Think of the recent threat of closure to British Steel. Close it down and it is a big tick in the net zero box. But this conveniently ignores the unpleasant truth: we will then import the steel from China instead, and that steel will be coal-intensive in its production, as well as being shipped around the world in heavily polluting ships. Not such a smart move in combating climate change.

The key difference between many of the natural environmental concerns considered in this book and climate change is that it does not matter at all where the carbon is emitted, whereas location matters a great deal when it comes to biodiversity, air quality and the pollution of rivers, estuaries and our coast. Reducing British carbon emissions *unilaterally* works only if it is based on carbon consumption, and not merely carbon production. To do this we need to go back to our principles: we need a carbon price which is applied to imports as well as to domestic goods.

This sounds simple, and it actually is quite simple to apply in a rough-and-ready way, so that we are roughly right rather than precisely wrong.[2] But it has a nasty sting. Any illusion that the Committee on Climate Change and others might like to cultivate, that the consequences for our standard of living will be small, is just that. Once you try to substitute away to non-carbon alternatives in your carbon diary it is going to hurt. We are living beyond our means, our carbon consumption is unsustainable, and we will need to change our ways. It is not just about wind turbines and solar panels: this is a complete revolution to our economy. This is what is necessary for sustainable economic growth. And sustainable economic growth is efficient growth. Carbon-intensive GDP, without polluters paying, is not.

The natural way

Given the scale of the challenge, it is imperative not only that the transition to net zero carbon consumption is done at minimum cost, but also that the maximum co-benefits are delivered. Here is where natural carbon sequestration comes into play. Planting the right sort of trees in the right places will soak up carbon *and* offer the chance of improving biodiversity and physical and mental health, providing lots more space for recreation, and improving water quality and flood management. Putting carbon back into the soil transforms the biodiversity in those soils. Capping the peat bogs and limiting grazing to encourage their regeneration with sphagnum moss is good for biodiversity and great for water quality and flood management. It also makes agricultural sense: the sheep on the hills are uneconomic.

The Committee on Climate Change suggests that perhaps 20 per cent of farmland should be reforested. Trees are natural carbon sinks. But different trees have different absorption capacities and take different amounts of time to do the sequestration job. The worry here is that, in the single-minded pursuit of net

but only temporary

zero, fast-growing trees in dense forests are the approach of choice. Plant spruce plantations or eucalyptus and the job gets done faster and more intensively.

This would be a disaster for all the other benefits we get from natural capital. Take a look at some of the Scottish conifer plantations, with their impenetrability, lack of light and the acidification they cause to the land around them and to the upland water courses. They are green deserts, largely devoid of life. They do not offer much scope for people, their health and their recreation. They do not do much for flooding, and damage water quality. Planted on peat, as they often are, they can actually be carbon-negative too.

Take soils. British farmland has been losing soil for decades. It is the logical consequence of intensive agrichemical farming. An extreme example is the Fens, regarded as among the most productive farmland. But it is not, once the loss of soils and their high carbon content is taken into account. Arguably, at any modest carbon price, farming would cease. The pollution just from carbon alone is a greater cost than the revenues of all of the crops. Add in the other chemical pollutants, and the conventional assumption about its richness is turned on its head.

Take peat and peat bogs. Britain has a globally significant level of peat carbon storage, especially in Scotland. These peat bogs have suffered serious erosion, primarily from overgrazing by sheep and deer. Yet, as we have seen, sheep in the uplands are profoundly uneconomic. They cost more in subsidies than the value of their meat (not much wool is harvested now because it is not worth the cost of shearing). If the number of sheep grazing in the uplands were reduced, we would be better off anyway – even before the carbon sequestration element is considered.

Paying for carbon sequestration

A common carbon price across the economy is the most efficient way to go about net zero carbon, and it should also apply to imports at the border so we go for net zero carbon consumption. The natural sequestration bit comes in because there would be a payment for any and all carbon sequestrated in the soils, trees and peat bogs.

Think about it this way. A renewable electricity generation technology, like a wind farm, escapes the carbon price, whereas a coal- or gas-fired power station pays. The corollary is that a new forest gets paid for the carbon it takes out of the atmosphere. It is a negative emission. Since location does not matter, the same price should be paid wherever this service is provided.

In theory, the current carbon markets should converge to create a single unified platform. Polluters pay, but the natural sequestration gets paid. The various natural sequestration options bid in their costs and volumes into a reverse auction, and the lowest offer clears the market.

In practice this is a long way off and it is likely that the natural carbon sequestration will develop its own market first. Like any market, there are two sides: buyers and sellers. The buyers are the polluters who want to offset their emissions. This is another example of net environmental gain: the polluters aim to be net zero by buying up offsets, with an excess margin to take a precautionary approach to how well the natural sequestration works out.

Who is likely to step forward first? There are two main categories of early buyers. The first are companies in the hard-to-mitigate class. These include oil and gas companies and airlines and airports. Oil and gas companies are in the fossil fuel business. That is what they do. Shell has launched a global forestry initiative to provide large-scale natural sequestration.[3] Others will follow. Airlines already offer voluntary offsets to passengers, although so far take-up is very low.

The second category includes companies and institutions that want to demonstrate their ethical credentials, take ESG (Environmental, Social and Governance) issues seriously, and regard the purpose of their businesses as more than just short-term profit-maximisation. Investor pressures and the wider corporate social responsibility agenda lead them to ask: how can my company be net zero?

This is a much bigger category, and already contains pension and life funds, as well as lots of professional services businesses. As the numbers build up, the question may shift from the willingness of the few to take this path to: why hasn't your company done it? Pension and other investment funds turn to the companies in their portfolios, demanding carbon audits, carbon reporting and carbon mitigation. Since ownership is very concentrated in large funds, the pressure may snowball.

This build-up of voluntary demand for carbon offsets will chase suppliers of natural sequestration. While all landowners can play a part, and make offers into the carbon offset market, there are several obvious constraints. Big landowners can offer large-scale forestation and the conversion from cereals to pasture for soil carbonisation. Large estates often hold the really big peat bogs.

Smaller farmers may be able to provide only a coppice, more hedges and a small plantation. They cannot do bilateral deals with large polluters. To make economic sense to them, they need intermediaries who can aggregate their offers. The obvious way for this to develop is through new trading platforms, allowing anyone to buy and sell small or large amounts of sequestration. Such platforms have a further advantage: they can provide multiple benefits that come from natural capital, including the water and flood services. They can and should be *general natural capital platforms*, of which carbon is just one dimension.

Trading platforms will have to be sophisticated, taking account of the fact that some natural capital services are location-specific, whereas carbon is not. Modern digital platforms are very capable of handling multiple dimensions. All they have to do is match buyers and sellers; some of these will be highly specific, and others, like carbon, completely general.

Multiple trading platforms have a further advantage. By offering landowners a range of prices for the benefits that specific investments provide, they get round the carbon silo problem – the risk that only the carbon sequestration gets taken seriously, and that other natural capital dimensions may not only lose out on remuneration, but be actively damaged. As noted, fast-growing spruce and eucalyptus monoculture forests will maximise carbon uptake, but be seriously damaging to other forms of natural capital. Having seen the damage done by palm oil plantations for biofuel, burning word pellets as biomass, and the dash for diesel – all carbon-silo policies – it is imperative not to repeat these gross errors.

Timescales

The point of a 25-year environment plan, of which natural sequestration should form a key part, is that most enhancements take time. Trees do not sequestrate carbon immediately. It takes a least a decade to get going, and several decades to get the maximum effect. How should this be dealt with in the carbon auctions, when the polluters want instant gratification of their desire to be net zero?

The way economists think about this is through discount rates. Future benefits are treated as less valuable than current ones. They are discounted. The more the present dominates over the future, the less value is attached to these carbon savings a decade or so out. For trees, discounting can be deadly: at, say, 7 per cent per annum after just 10 years the value is halved, and over 20 it is reduced to 25 per cent. By three decades it is close to zero. Even at 5 per cent nobody cares much about what happens in 2050.[4]

This is a potential showstopper for some forms of natural carbon sequestration, and those that survive will be very quick fixes, like replacing cereals with grass, and biocrops. Yet before we rule out trees and longer-term natural sequestration, a couple of countervailing economic considerations need to be taken into account. The first is that the carbon price might rise as the net zero target gets closer, before falling back if and when we get to net zero. Although the discount rate bites, it bites against a steadily rising value. If the carbon price rises at the same rate as the discount rate, there is a balance of impacts (although note that the forest does not therefore benefit from the price uplift as the discount rate claws it back).

The second caveat comes from the discount rate itself. For discounting cuts right across the 25-year plan objective of leaving the natural environment in a better shape for future generations, preventing a decline in natural assets. Discounting has the radical implication that we should not care much about the future, and therefore not worry about the state of natural capital that future generations inherit. Why? Because it is assumed that they will be better off than we are. They will have more GDP to compensate for the loss of the natural environment.

This is where discounting breaks down. Suppose we are doing so much damage to the atmosphere and biodiversity as to render future people worse off. If they will have less, the discount rate should be negative, not positive. Yet there remains a problem: companies do have costs of capital, and they do discount. The way to deal with this is to legislate. Companies should not be allowed to escape the polluter-pays principle. They should have to recognise their carbon liabilities on their balance sheets. The emissions should be paid up, and future emissions should be listed as a liability, against which provisions are required. This, in turn, means that the companies' balance sheets will have to recognise the future costs and provide against them. They cannot simply discount them away. Entering the carbon auctions will then be on a low or even negative discount rate.

End of life of the trees – storing the carbon

Trees and soils sequestrate until they reach saturation, at which point they cannot absorb any more carbon, and they have nothing else to offer. They have become stores of carbon, and the problem now is how to prevent that carbon leaking back into the atmosphere. Similarly, industrial sequestration stops when the carbon storage well is full and corked. Where biocrops are grown, they are burnt to generate electricity and provide a fuel substitute for transport. The carbon that they have captured is re-released to the atmosphere.

Biofuels and biomass should pay the carbon tax when burnt. They are in an equivalent position to fossil fuels at the combustion point. The difference is that they will have received offset payments while growing, before being released. This means that they are *temporary* sequestration, not permanent. Think of all that wood 'imported' from the USA and burnt in Drax power station, and then referred to as a 'renewable' source of electricity. The carbon pollution from the energy used to dry the pellets *and* the trucking *and* the shipping should be charged. The carbon sequestration arises before this transformation takes place: that is, the carbon sequestration which should be paid for its offsetting. But Drax should pay the carbon price for its biomass burning, as it does already for its coal-burn.

What all this illustrates is how critical the question is as to what happens at the end of life. Trees can become timber and then be used for building. The timber carries on storing the carbon. The trees can simply be left to stand, eventually blow down and then rot over very long periods, with the soil taking up much of their carbon, and boosting biodiversity too. When a builder considers using steel, concrete or wood, only the wood should escape the carbon price.

The critical point here is that the common carbon price, and the pricing of emissions whenever and wherever they occur, is what leads to the best climate change outcomes. All the sources of pollution should be on a level playing field, without any exclusions, to create the right incentives, avoid Drax-type problems, and incentivise the sequestration and the subsequent storage of the carbon. Fail to do this properly, and it is easy to see how perverse incentives might kick in, as has been the case for Drax.

Establishing natural capital baselines

The tricky challenge for natural carbon sequestration is working out how much carbon there is already in the trees, soils and peat before working out the possible enhancements and then their valuation.

For this we need a fairly precise baseline, as we do for all natural capital assessments of progress and opportunities. A few years ago this would have been impossible, except in roundabout ways, like considering what might be the best practices and making some heroic guesses. Broad categories could be used, such as the average carbon in, say, intensive cereal production land, improved rye grass pastures, and the uplands. It would have been confined to general changes in farming practice.

That knowledge is still useful, but we can now do so much better. With satellite data the natural capital on the land can be mapped with ever greater precision. We can get from general knowledge to site-specific information about multiple natural capital opportunities. It is a revolution in the making. What happens on every few square metres of the land can now be seen. It is transparent. A farmer will no longer be able to get away with agreeing to do one thing, and in fact doing another for public subsidy. Field margins, protected habitats and SSSIs can be checked without a farm visit and all the costs and expenses involved. Cross-compliance for the basic farm payment will no longer be a fig leaf. It can be made to bite.

This matters because investors buying offsets for carbon, and governments paying farmers to produce public goods, are increasingly going to want proof that what they pay for will actually be delivered. This is about carbon and understanding the natural carbon sequestration processes. But it is also about the other natural capital benefits. Satellite mapping tells us so much more than simply what the soil and vegetation look like. It tells us a lot about the land's water systems, leisure and recreational use. To the mapping can be added data from photography-sharing platforms and a host of other data derived from social media. How much benefit is derived from, say, Tarr Steps in Exmoor? Take a look at how many photos are taken and, even better, by whom. There are of course privacy issues, but the point here is that the sources of precision information data have mushroomed and provide the potential to understand our natural capital in ever-greater detail. This in turn means we can achieve much better outcomes for less cost, making the land greener, but also more prosperous.

Satellite data gets us a long way to our baseline. It is a good start. Yet it is not the only way of establishing the baseline. The breakthrough comes when more detailed information can be spliced with the satellite mapping. First, there can be increasingly detailed resolution from the air. The Ordnance Survey has been flying around doing detailed mapping for decades. Now there are drones which can get even closer and be used for multiple purposes. Drone surveys can identify problems with train tracks and points along the railway line in real time. They can also identify specific soils and trees and give a lot more fine-grained information. To this can be added the on-the-ground data. New agricultural machinery reads the soil at every point that it passes along the field, from the drilling to the harvesting. Precision spraying of individual weeds is already working, radically moving farming from general chemical applications to exact targeting for fertilisers and pesticides. A by-product of that information could be very precise soil carbon measurements.

Taking data from satellite imaging, drone surveys and precision agricultural machinery offers a huge potential gain in our ability to understand what is there, and hence the starting point to work out which enhancements are best where. While it is true that some of this data is private, where farmers and other landowners want to get paid for enhancing carbon sequestration or the provision of public goods, it is reasonable to expect the availability of such data to be a condition for payments. The carrot of public money and carbon payments will be a powerful incentive to comply.

Working out enhancements

With a detailed baseline in place, the scene is set to review the land and see where enhancements might be made. The trick here is not to begin by working up a specific detailed proposal, but rather to come up with a list of possible improvements and investments. Why? Because with the baseline, possible enhancements can be compared to see how big the benefits are. The new enhancement-plus baselines can then be assessed for not only carbon but all the various natural capital benefits.

Consider a large land estate that needs to know the implications of responding to the new net zero targets by offering to plant more trees. It wants to know where to plant the trees to yield the maximum carbon sequestration. But it will also want to know what happens if it plants different types of trees for not only carbon but also water quality and flows, flooding and biodiversity. It will want to know whether changing grassland habitats, or encouraging sphagnum moss to grow on over-grazed peat bogs would be better, or whether all of these options would be beneficial. By looking at a series of hypothetical enhanced baselines, the best outcomes in terms of the multiple natural capital benefits can be established, and a supply curve drawn to identify the most desirable results in descending order.

Remember, however, that the aim is to be not only greener, but also more prosperous. For this there is one final and very controversial element. The value of the investment options needs to be estimated, and that is where numbers come in. While we could plan the landscape and tell farmers and landowners what to do, our difficulty is that we want to find the most cost-effective outcomes, for the very good reason that taxpayers and customers of companies that are going to need the offsets will ultimately be paying. There is nothing green about paying over the odds for these benefits. Many people struggle to live within their means now, and expecting them to pay more for net zero is going to be a stretch anyway. Some environmentalists might like to just assume that people are willing and able to pay; the reality is that there are limits to household budgets. The less well-off should expect their money to be spent wisely, going for the lowest-hanging fruit first, rather than trying to pick the whole tree immediately.

In the case of carbon, the task is simplified by the polluter-pays principle. There should be a price of carbon, and indeed there already are several. In the energy markets there is a price in the EU Emissions Trading Scheme, and there is a unilateral price in the UK, the Carbon Price Floor.

Rather than trying to get the carbon price exactly right, the initial task is to get in roughly the right ballpark. In land use, the current price is zero, and that is precisely wrong. Given the baselines and the enhancement modelling, why not try out several possible prices? The beauty of this approach is that if certain land use changes pass the test of being economically investible at several different carbon prices, then these are going to be more robust bets. If a land use change is dependent on a very high carbon price, it is probably not a good place to start. At a Carbon Price Floor of, say, £18 per tonne, a first sweep of the enhancement captures the low-hanging fruit and this is where it is probably best to start.

Once these first-best options have been identified for carbon, there is still the question about the other natural capital benefits, and in some cases detriments. Planting the wrong kinds of trees in the wrong places can lead to acidification of the soil and the streams and rivers, for example. If this is the outcome against the baseline, the polluter-pays and net environmental principles again kick in. There is a penalty for doing damage in one area in the name of gains elsewhere.

This is not a trivial point, as the example of the Scottish conifer plantations above illustrates. A one-track obsession with carbon as the overwhelming priority could ultimately lead to a browner and less prosperous land.

This is why it is imperative that the other natural capital benefits are valued too. Unlike carbon they are very location-specific, and require detailed local data mapping. The costs also need to be quantified: if they are not accounted for they will probably end up being treated as zero value, and the pure carbon-only approach will win out.

How could the non-carbon benefits be valued? The cost–benefit analysis approach that many economists favour is pretty hopeless and sometimes dangerous for the environment. Why? Because, as noted, the environment comes in systems and not just discrete pieces. A new woodland affects the whole river catchment and is part of the wildlife corridors (or not) around it. The benefits of a wood depend as much on what happens on its margins and the surrounding land, and where species can migrate between it and these other areas, as on the woodland itself.

With imagination and a sufficiently large research budget, some of this might get answered, although, in practice, homing in on the carbon is the easy bit and will probably take centre stage. Is there another way? Yes. Instead of getting experts to look at each enhancement and come up with numbers (and probably numbers that best suit whoever is paying for the studies), we could instead ask landowners to bid improvements. Instead of going from farm to farm and negotiating bilateral planned agreements, the farmers are asked to bid in the measures they are willing to undertake.

Notice how the incentives have changed. The farmers no longer negotiate and lobby for more money for the preferred scheme. Instead the onus is on them to work out their costs and options and to compete with others for a limited amount of public money (which the taxpayer is providing), or in the EnTrade example discussed previously for the water company money (and hence ultimately paid for through the water customers' bills). This is the exciting route of using auctions and markets to find the best enhancements of natural capital. What matters is that the benefits are costed and ranked, and this is done for all the benefits simultaneously to prevent a carbon silo-based approach.

There is an obvious hitch: some aspects of natural capital are very hard to measure, of which biodiversity is the obvious example. Valuing particular species is very difficult in practice.

It easily lends itself to ridicule and scepticism. But before biodiversity is parked in the 'too difficult' box, recall two things: that the market approach is about costs rather than values; and that 'too difficult' can easily end up with zero. However hard some environmentalists try to claim that nature cannot be valued (and they are broadly right on this), they cannot escape the observation that money is not in infinite supply, and that choices have to be made. Some aspects of nature might be priceless, but to preserve and enhance them, few are costless. In the real world, there are hard and unavoidable choices; there is cost and there is prioritisation. Even with very high taxation and redistribution the constraint will still bite, and it is worth observing that there is no evidence to suggest that more socialistic economies are more nature-friendly than capitalistic ones. It is part of our human condition. Not to take cost into account results in neglect.

The biodiversity problem remains. The costing is difficult, and the species are rarely location-specific, depending on complex ecosystems and habitats, and often these span several landowners and several countries. Think of migrating birds, mammals and butterflies. The pragmatic solution is to address the biodiversity enhancements through the more general farm subsidy schemes, of which the proposed Environmental Land Management Scheme (ELMS) is the latest incarnation. Subsidies need to take account of the multiple benefits, but should home in on those which cannot be paid for by third parties, through offset payments, payments for flood reduction, and payments for enhanced water quality.

To bring together the costs of all the various natural capital benefits of specific enhancements, the way forward should be (and indeed increasingly is) to create natural capital platforms for all the elements that can be traded, and then design the agricultural environmental subsidies (the public money for public goods) to complement – and not substitute – the bits that will inevitably be missing. The aim is to be comprehensive about all the benefits and pragmatic about the use of auctions and markets in order to achieve an integrated outcome.

Credibility, bankability and finance

Using a carbon price, auctioning water and other land use benefits, and tailoring the ELMS-type schemes to deal with the public goods not captured in these markets not only gets us more environmental gains for our money, but also opens up a host of additional opportunities. Once enhancements are properly costed, and there are potential trades between the supply and demand sides, the investments become 'normal', like any other investment opportunity across company and financial markets. They can be debt- and equity-financed and often by third parties. Your pension fund can invest in green bonds and buy into new green companies delivering these enhancements. Natural capital takes its place in financial markets in the way that it should alongside man-made capital and human capital in the workplace.

While it is easy to get excited about the 'green' bit in green finance, and imagine unleashing billions in funding for net zero and other environmental projects, the green element is not the important bit. The challenge – and the opportunity – is to make environmental investments 'normal', just like any other investment, to bring the environment into the economy and into finance, rather than maintain a special and separate status. The former offers up the chance to consider the environment as a serious contributor of sustainable economic growth. The latter leads to an isolated ghetto, full of environmental altruists willing to sacrifice returns in pursuit of their moral values. These are worthy people, but sadly there are not many of them. The reality is that most people are focused on their immediate needs and the value of their pensions, and less willing to give up their future income to do good. Altruism alone will not solve the environmental challenges: hard-headed markets offer a much better (and complementary) way forward, and since the better green investments help increase sustainable economic growth, they should actually work.

Markets are all about property rights and the trading of these. Natural capital markets are no different. Most of the opportunities to enhance natural capital lie with private owners and trusts. In the case of carbon, the property right is the carbon and, in particular, the carbon reduction. Offsetting polluters offer to pay for a property right – the reduction of a given number of tonnes of carbon at specific dates. They can then trade this with others, as in the EU Emissions Trading Scheme for emissions.

An obvious question emerges: how can an investor know that the carbon will in fact be saved, and by the exact amount specified in the contract between the landowner and the offset buyer? What happens if the landowner reneges, fails to do the proper capital maintenance, the trees become diseased or the farmer goes bust?

These are very real difficulties, and they cannot easily be solved within the current legal structures. They need institutions and third parties who can be trusted. Furthermore, there need to be penalties for failure to deliver. If you go on holiday and your airline goes bust, how do you get home? When the British travel firm Thomas Cook Group imploded in 2019, holidaymakers got home, and this was largely paid for through the airline industry scheme which requires all the operators to pay into a fund to deal with precisely this scenario. It worked.

So too with carbon, water enhancements and public-good ELMS-type schemes. In the case of trees, there may need to be some sort of a bond and a prior claim on bankruptcy to make good any detriments. It is something that could be dealt with like the travel example above, but there are alternative options. One is to administer these sorts of schemes through a Nature Fund, separate from the parties to the contracts, and not sheltered by limited liability. This is one option discussed in the next chapter. It is of course not the only one. There are lots of trusts, notably the National Trust, the Woodland Trust and the Wildlife Trusts, which have open-ended public interest commitments. The problem most of these have (perhaps with the exception of the National Trust) is that they may not be big enough to carry the scale of liabilities on their balance sheets. Hence the advantage of a broader-based and much larger Nature Fund. This would have the additional benefit of being able to run a really big portfolio, much more akin to the position the airlines find themselves in. Scale matters, and the Nature Fund would have this.

11

A NATURE FUND

A lot of money is already spent on the environment. There are agricultural subsidies, flood defence expenditures, water company bills to clean up the pollution of our drinking water, air pollution measures and climate change policies, on top of the host of local interventions by the numerous voluntary sector trusts and groups. Each falls under different departments and institutions, from DEFRA to the Department for Business, Energy and Industrial Strategy (BEIS), to the Ministry of Housing, Communities and Local Government, the Department of Health & Social Care, the Department for Education and the Treasury.

The trouble is that much of it is spent very badly: we can do much better with just spending this money in an efficient way. We could have a much-enhanced environment without spending any more, especially if we had the polluter-pays and net environmental gain principles already in place.

There are three main building blocks to the financing of a much greener and more prosperous land: using this existing spending more efficiently; using the money from green charges; and bringing in the net environmental gain compensation payments. These revenues can be brought together into a Nature Fund, which could also include the economic rents for depleting non-renewable natural capital assets such as oil, gas and minerals.

Redirecting current spending

There has been no audit of the current very inefficient total spending. There should be. In its absence, let us hazard a guess at the dimensions by looking at the five areas set out in part two – the river catchments, the land, the uplands, the marine environment and the urban areas.

The river catchment category receives a lot of spending. Take a river catchment like the Thames. The Environment Agency spends on flood defences. The water companies spend on cleaning up the pollution in the water they abstract to deliver clean drinking water and from the waste we put down our sinks and toilets. Trusts spend on cleaning up the consequences of river pollution. If the CAP was redirected, if polluters paid, and if river catchments were run as integrated whole systems, imagine what could be achieved on a whole-catchment basis. The floods budget could be partially redirected from concrete barriers towards natural flood management. In the Thames case, the Oxford concrete bypass channel referred to in chapter 1 might not even need to be built, or, if it is, at a much-reduced scale.

The land area is the most obvious place to start since its character and use is already all about subsidies. The starting point is the £3 billion CAP subsidies. Imagine you had £3 billion to spend on environmental improvements to agricultural land. Admittedly, the Treasury is very unlikely to allow the full £3 billion to survive a Brexit in the medium term (and in Europe, the value of the CAP will fall too), but whatever the final number, it will probably remain large for some considerable time to come.

In the uplands we have National Park budgets, significant National Trust spending, RSPB and Wildlife Trust spending, flood-prevention spending and considerable agri-environmental subsidies. In total, the uplands are where a lot of our natural capital still survives. Redirecting the CAP monies would reduce the overgrazing, thus reducing spending and improving the environment.

On the coasts, the spending on marine protection is minimal, but there are lots of implicit subsidies to fishing that can be perverse. As with farming, but on a much smaller scale, the fishing lobby has received concession after concession, and it does not pay for all the scientific, monitoring and enforcement mechanisms that add to the costs of fishing.

In the urban areas, city and town councils pay for the upkeep of the parks and a lot of money is spent on trying to clean up the air and water pollution. Imagine if this spending was directed to joining up the green spaces across the cities, with the parks and gardens as an integral place. Imagine if monies were spent on planting trees on all the streets, instead of vanity projects like the now abandoned Garden Bridge in London. Just the wasted monies here would have paid for a major environmental upgrade of several of London's parks. Then there is the budget for the air quality strategy, some of which could go to trees and green walls and enlarging green spaces.

If we add the CAP monies and other farming subsidies to the flood defence monies, add in a share of the water company spending and then add in the direct payments for National Parks, the total is more than £10 billion per annum under even the most pessimistic assumptions.

The alternative way of getting an estimate is to add up the spending by DEFRA on agriculture and water, the budgets of the Environment Agency and Natural England, together with the turnover of the National Trust, RSPB and Wildlife Trusts. Add to these the significant spending by local government on waste and local environmental facilities, as well as on air and other forms of local pollution. There will be some items that should not be included, but we will have left out a host of other spending by water companies and by private companies and individuals. This comes to an even bigger number.

Finally, we could look at how much we as individuals spend to enjoy the countryside and the natural environment, and all the jobs and economic activity that these support. The tourist industry has a turnover of £260 billion, of which a proportion is related to the natural environment. There are a host of outdoor clothing, camping and other businesses catering to the 'outdoor life' market, including walking, cycling, running, climbing, swimming, shooting, birdwatching, plant and insect hunting, horse-riding and fishing. The turnover of these businesses is much more significant than those of farmers and agriculture. These are, however, private spending on private goods.

What these various ways of looking at spending on the natural environment indicate is not only that there are many different revenue streams, but also that they are in silos. The value of the aggregate spent in an overall planned way would be significantly greater than the parts. Put another way, the immediate problem is to spend more wisely, before thinking about more money on top. We could do much better on any of these snapshots of current spending, and we could enhance the natural environment. The result would be more economically efficient and hence raise prosperity too. The gap is in coordinating all these budgets, and one reason that they are not coordinated is that there is no overall plan. That is where a 25-year plan comes in, the subject of the next chapter.

Adding in the value of pollution taxes

Charging for pollution is economically efficient. As noted, it sets the right relative prices and hence the right incentives. The results would be a dramatic change in farming practice and resource efficiency. But it gets better: we need to add a further benefit from pollution charges. The charges would also raise a lot of money, some of which could be spent on adding to the environmental improvements, making up the double dividend.

How much? That depends on how businesses and individuals react, whether as in the plastic bags case they simply switch, or whether, as in the Carbon Price Floor case, they largely pay the price, at least in the short term, for the lack of immediate alternatives.

Setting pollution taxes and charges is more an art than a science, and is a matter of learning-by-taxing. Economists think of this problem as one of the elasticity or responsiveness of demand to the tax, and in terms of the short and the long run.[1] The more inelastic (unresponsive) people are, the greater the revenue raised. Think of the yield from the taxes that make up most of the cost of petrol and diesel in cars. As hybrids and electric cars develop, switching becomes easier and the revenue yield is likely to fall, potentially a lot. This is a case of a short-run inelastic demand and a long-run elastic one. It is an example of a successful green charge: it gradually withers away with the polluting fuel demand.

Generalising a carbon tax across the whole economy would lead to some short-term changes of behaviours, but perhaps not much.[2] Farmers cannot easily instantaneously change their farming practices. Trees take time to sequestrate carbon. Faced with a charge, taxed ammonia emissions similarly would be hard to do much about in the short run. Adding pollution charges to fertilisers, pesticides and herbicides could have a much more immediate effect: decisions to buy and apply these, and the quantity applied, are made on a continuous basis. The incentive to increase the precision of applications through robotics and new GPS-targeted technologies would be strengthened, as would organic methods.

There are two conflicting objectives in play here when it comes to the money. For the Treasury, the objective is to raise money, to pay for health, education, defence and welfare payments. It wants to tax things that are inelastic in demand in the short and preferably the long run too. But from an environmental perspective the very point of the pollution taxes is to cut pollution, and hence they are best targeted at those areas that are elastic in demand. Where it takes polluters time to change their practices, it would be better to start with a low charge in the short run, but credibly commit to raising the tax in the medium to longer term, to give time and incentives to polluters to change their behaviours. That is how we should set the carbon tax.

The point here is to recognise that new green charges will not necessarily raise much money, and where they do it is because their impacts on pollution levels will be smallest. The hope of a great new source of funding for conservation from pollution taxes and charges is probably illusory, except in the short run. If and when we reach net zero, the carbon price will be close to zero too, limited to paying for the sequestration of residual carbon emissions.

This brings us to a further twist. We want pollution to be reduced. We want polluters to change their practices. We want them to pay lower pollution charges. This would be a mark of success. This takes time, involves changing the way farming is organised, and may require investments. Putting in new slurry tanks, creating grass strips to limit soil and chemical run-off into rivers, and changing harvesting practices all have short-run costs for the wider long-run benefits. If the objective of the tax is to change behaviours, an obvious way to do this is to use the revenues from pollution charges to help in this process. Grants might be provided for conversions to less-polluting farming methods, such as covering slurry pits to limit ammonia emissions, and measures to reduce the risk of spillages.

This is called *hypothecation* and cuts across the Treasury's interest in raising general revenues to finance general expenditures. Hypothecation involves a deliberate ring-fencing of the money for specific tasks. The tax (and it is a tax) you pay for the BBC licence fee goes to the BBC (and a few other things too). But the BBC example is clear-cut compared with most environmental considerations. Who exactly should the pollution tax revenues be hypothecated to? All farmers? On the basis of specific schemes? To the water companies, to offset the costs of cleaning up the pollution of the rivers and lakes? To the RSPB and the Wildlife Trusts for remedial actions?

The answers to these questions are unlikely to be efficient ones if it is all ad hoc on a case-by-case basis. What is needed is a clear separation of the charges and taxes to reduce the pollution, and their careful targeting on the pollutants themselves on the one hand, and the spending of the revenues on the environment on the other. Below we will see that one way of doing this is by setting up a Nature Fund to allocate the spending.

Adding in the net environmental gain compensation payments

To ensure that developers do not reduce the value of the environment in aggregate, but recognising that they will do damage in specific cases, they should be forced to pay compensation, and compensation that is credible and sufficiently in excess of the damage to avoid the risk that in fact there is a deterioration.

As we have already seen, this (as a version of the polluter-pays principle) is a very radical change of direction. We have been pursing net environmental *damage* rather than net environmental gain for a very long time. Indeed, we have been doing this for all of human existence.

How much money would the net environmental gain requirement raise? Since each development has its own location and therefore its own unique impacts, it is very hard to aggregate. There is also the question of the baseline discussed in the previous chapter. One way of gauging this is to look at the total number of houses to be built and to hazard a guess at the average payment. If it were £1,000 per new house, and 3 million are to be built, that makes £3 billion. If it were £10,000 per house (a more realistic guess against an average house price of, say, £250,000), it would be £30 billion. In the total price of £200,000, the £10,000 would hardly be noted against the fluctuations in the market.[3]

Next there are the compensation payments from big infrastructure projects such as HS2, the Thames Gateway and road building. HS2 is likely to cost far more than £56 billion. Against this total, and bearing in mind the amount of land taken out along the way, the specific damages could be calculated. Indeed, some are already included in the £56 billion. An alternative, cruder, measure would be a cost per unit of land taken out. For either approach it should be more than £1 billion. It would be hard to value just the ancient woodlands at less.

Most of these are one-off payments for compensation, but since the developments are continuous, there would be a continuous annual flow of revenues from the aggregate developments. There would also be the need to provide for the capital maintenance of the sustainable compensating assets that are created.

Adding in the avoided perverse subsidies beyond the CAP

Although abolishing the other perverse subsidies is technically a cost saving rather than a source of revenue, it could be argued that these savings reduce the need for the Treasury to raise other sources of revenue, and hence from a fiscally neutral perspective this could be added to the revenue streams identified above.

The value of the non-CAP perverse subsidies can be calculated from this revenue foregone, but in practice it is a complicated calculation, since the perverse subsidies typically have complex consequences and multiple rationales. Not all the impacts are environmental; nor are they typically intended to be so. For this reason, it is best to leave them out of the revenue flows for the moment, even if the amounts involved are likely to be in the hundreds of millions.

Separating spending from revenues

All of the above revenue lines, potential and actual, are currently dealt with and variously spent by multiple agencies, in their own particular institutional contexts. The result is seriously suboptimal. Instead of starting with a top-down view of the most environmentally important projects, and then working down the list, spending on those with the biggest net benefits first, the monies are instead scattered over a range of projects. The result is that a great deal of potential environmental gain is lost, and we are, as a result, less prosperous. Worse, the benefits are often captured by particular vested interests.

The alternative approach is to separate out environmental spending from environmental revenues, a bit like the Treasury separates out general tax from general expenditure. Who pays what amount tells us nothing at all about which spending is going to deliver the best environmental bucks for our money. By separating out the environmental revenues from the environmental spending, we have the best chance of getting as much gain as possible, and hence as much prosperity.

This is not just a neat academic point: every bit of suboptimal spending means that there is less nature for us to enjoy. It might mean that we lose an endangered habitat and instead get a local marginal improvement.

The organisation of the separation of revenue and spending requires a focus. In national taxing and spending, this is the Treasury and the national budget.[4] At the environmental level, the best way to entrench and manage the separation is in the creation of a Nature Fund.

Looking after the future

The helpful analogy here is with the sovereign wealth funds that many countries that are depleting non-renewable resources have set up. The poster example is Norway. It has abundant oil and gas that it is extracting now. These resources will run out, or if we decarbonise effectively, the market for them will fall away.[5] It would be unfair for the current generation to reap all the benefits of the oil and gas production and for the next generation to get the global warming that results. It is a non-renewable resource. It can be used only once. So the Norwegians put the surplus economic rents into their sovereign wealth fund for the benefit of future generations. Norway spends about 3 per cent of the fund each year, which it argues is the return that its investments can be expected to make. In other words, 3 per cent is the maximum spending consistent with maintaining the value of the fund intact over time.

The contrast with Britain and its North Sea oil and gas could not be greater. Here there is no fund. The money has been spent over the last four decades and there is nothing to bequeath future generations, except the liabilities.

When it comes to a Nature Fund, the arguments for protecting the interests of future generations are even stronger because the natural capital that we can bequeath is renewable. Recall it can go on delivering its bounty for ever, provided we don't deplete it beyond a critical threshold after which it becomes non-renewable. The value at stake is not just the immediate benefits, but also the benefits for all the future too. That is why keeping renewables above a safe limit from the thresholds is of paramount importance.

The Norwegian example gets us some way to taking into account the interests of future generations. It is, however, quite a simple problem compared with that of a Nature Fund. The Norwegian fund has one revenue flow only, easily measured and easily banked. The money is then invested, primarily in stocks and shares, and mainly globally. It is now worth around $1 trillion.[6] In contrast, a Nature Fund would have multiple revenue sources and it would not hold onto a portfolio of investments. Rather, it would be holding onto the precious stewardship of our natural capital. It is more like the Treasury, with money in and money out. The revenues are turned into enhanced natural assets, and it is these that are passed down the generations, not the portfolio of general investments in the Norwegian example.

How to take future generations' interests into account throws up lots of philosophical and also practical questions. A fund to protect and enhance natural capital has at its heart the idea that we are holding these precious assets *in trust*. But how seriously should we take their future into account against our needs now? The philosophical answer is all about whether we should discount the future and, as noted in chapter 10, it has a practical analogy when it comes to long-term carbon sequestration in trees, soils and peat bogs. Is the utility of future people more or less important than our own? Should we care as much about people in 100 years' time, 1,000 years or even 100,000 years?

Some argue that it is immoral to treat people differently because of the time they live, since this discrimination cannot be anything to do with choices they make. It is an accident. We should not discount utility. This is the line that Nicholas Stern takes in his famous 'Economics of Climate Change'.[7] Yet it is an impossible ethical demand. Think just how radical the idea would be to treat everyone at any time the same. Having no say in when you are born is just one example of luck, as is where in the world you are born.[8] If we treat everyone everywhere and at any time as the same, we would radically redistribute all wealth, and we would of course not give priority to our own children or to our fellow country inhabitants.

The very idea does violence to human nature. We are partial, not impartial, animals. We should of course care about people in the future, but not to this impossible extent. We should care about global environmental impacts, but we should not divert all the revenues identified above to the protection of the tiger or the Amazon rainforests. Some, yes; all, no.

This focus on utility and ethics cannot be avoided. But even if utility is not discounted, there is, as noted above, another dimension to take into account in viewing the future, and hence how we might spend the Fund's revenues. For the last 200 years, it has been reasonable to assume that people tomorrow will be better off than people today because of economic growth. You are probably better off than your parents, and it is assumed that your children will be better off than you will be. In consequence, the argument goes, we should discount the future by the economic growth rate, whatever we do about utility discounting.

There is one good reason for assuming your children will be better off than you, and one dubious one. The ultimate driver of economic growth is technology, and technological progress is advancing, perhaps faster than it has in the past. In the last 20 years, the digital communications revolution has changed almost all economic activity, and most personal behaviours too. The smartphone, Facebook, Twitter and Instagram are a world away from the fixed telephone line, letters drafted on a typewriter and photographic slides. Ahead lies genetics as a technology for all, robotics, 3D printing, new materials and AI. It is safe to assume that future generations will have more and much better technologies than we do. For this reason we should discount their future – a bit.

A less convincing reason relates to whether in fact we and our predecessors will have done so much damage to the environment that they will be worse off. They will inherit the climate change and the loss of biodiversity. They will not have the natural beauty of unindustrialised landscapes, and many more green spaces will have been concreted over. Indeed, the environmental damage may be so great as to offset the technological gains, leaving them in a net worse position.

How do we solve this problem? By bequeathing them a natural environment which is better than that which we inherited. We start to put right the damage we and our predecessors have done. We set about enhancing natural capital. We act as good stewards of natural capital so they can choose how to live their lives – rather than trying to make sure they are happy.

This needs to be the primary duty of a Nature Fund: to invest in our national natural capital so that it increases in aggregate value over time. To be more precise, it is the *renewable* natural capital that needs to get better, and we need to make sure that the non-renewable depletion is not done at the expense of future generations.[9] It is this latter requirement that the Norwegian fund meets.

Designing a Nature Fund

A national Nature Fund requires: a credible institutional structure and governance arrangements that can withstand short-term pressures to raid it; a short- and medium-term budgeting framework; and a mechanism for deciding how to spend the money.

The most difficult bits are its statutory status and its governance. It is where almost all sovereign wealth funds fall down, for the simple reason that in adversity it is politically almost always expedient to plunder it. The Saudi Arabian oil fund has already been depleted by around half since the oil prices fell in 2014, and the Russian fund has been similarly depleted for short-term purposes. Indeed, Norway is probably the only example of a sovereign wealth fund that has avoided being raided for short-term expediency, and it is a special case in that there are only around 4 to 5 million Norwegians, and 3 per cent per annum provides for a lot of government general expenditure relative to this small population.

There are two ways in which the Nature Fund could be protected. The first is to give it statutory independence and hence to require primary legislation to interfere with it. This is a step well beyond the current environmental bodies – the Environment Agency and Natural England, which are regularly described as 'parts of the DEFRA family'. It is more like the independence of the Bank of England.

Yet even in the case of the Bank of England, 'independent' is a relative concept. The government of the day appoints the Governor and the deputies, and the members of the Monetary Policy Committee. Real independence requires an independent appointment process. This is a detail of immense importance. It might give rise to concerns about democracy and democratic control, all the more complicated by the fact that the future generations are not around to vote now to protect their interests against those of the current selfish generation. The issue is about the objectives that the Nature Fund should pursue. The objective of the 25 Year Environment Plan – to leave the natural environment in a better state for future generations – is a good starting point. This is something parliament should legislate into place.

The risks are obvious. Consider the 'public money for public goods' argument advanced in DEFRA's consultation paper 'Health and Harmony: The Future for Food, Farming and the Environment in a Green Brexit' and in the 2018 Agriculture Bill that followed it.[10] The Treasury will understandably want to minimise the subsidies, and hence the temptation is to play with the public goods definition to get other items of possible public expenditure inside this definition. It has happened with the National Lottery. So far, we have already had the suggestion that post-CAP subsidies might be spent on rural broadband (part of the Department for Digital, Culture, Media and Sport budget) and to pay farmers not to dock pigs' tails. It is a short step to include rural 'development', rural tourism and even rural buses. These are included in pillar 2 of the CAP spending. Add in all the local interests, and the politics of geographically defined parliamentary constituencies, and the Nature Fund will face enormous pressures to bend to political, social and especially media campaigns and interests.

To ensure that this sort of interference is not possible (or is at least limited), parliament would need to set out a clear remit for the Nature Fund, under the umbrella of the overall objective of the 25 Year Environment Plan. This could be general, listing out areas where the money could be spent, or it could be specific and tied to the 10 goals of the Plan. Either approach requires legislation.

There is a precedent: the Climate Change Act 2008. It set a target for 2050, and a process for determining how to achieve it (the carbon budgets that set the limits for five-year periods). It has not been without its problems, and it has inevitably succumbed to mission creep, but it has seen off attempts to prune back its carbon budgets.[11] Indeed, it has been tightened up from its 80 per cent target to net zero.

It is much more complicated in the case of natural capital and the natural environment. Biodiversity is multidimensional and location-specific, whereas climate change is about a small number of relatively easily measured gases, and is independent of location. But even if it is more difficult, it is essential to enshrine the objectives of the Fund in legislation. We will return to this in the next chapter.

The second protection is to make sure the Nature Fund does not accumulate cash, but rather spends it. If the revenue is spent and committed then it is not available to be syphoned off for other purposes. The Saudi Arabian and Russian problems noted above do not then arise. The objectives of the Fund would be similar to those of charities: to spend their resources on specific purposes. The Nature Fund might accumulate reserves, especially where there are long-term projects to be supported – in some cases over decades – but these can nevertheless be earmarked and committed. Again it helps if there is an overarching framework

within which the projects fit, a credible rolling 25-year environment plan, rather than a single plan ending in 2043.

The governance of the Nature Fund is obviously crucial to its
independence and success. Wherever a public body handles
money, there needs to be a series of safeguards, reporting and
auditing processes. These may seem boring matters of detail,
but they are anything but. They really matter. A credible Fund
would have credible people and a mix of expertise. It needs a
chair, an advisory council, a chief executive, a finance officer and
an expert panel of scientists, accountants and economists. It
needs formal consultative processes, links to national and local
government, the National Parks, city authorities and formal links
to the owners of natural capital. Its personnel need fixed terms
to limit the emergence of dominant figures.

A Nature Fund would need to formally report to parliament,
analogous to the reporting by the Committee on Climate Change.
It would need to present its accounts to the National Audit Office,
and this process would be aided if the rolling 25-year environment
plan were to be updated at five-year intervals, again for formal
approval by parliament.

The Nature Fund budget

The Nature Fund would have a budget comprising income and
expenditure. These should balance out over time. Improving
natural capital is not typically a short-term activity – some projects
take years and even decades to come to fruition. Reconstructing
wildlife corridors may involve a series of steps rather like building
a high-speed railway line. Creating new wetlands will require
initial construction projects, and then a process of engineering
the necessary changes. Capital maintenance will follow.

The revenues would flow into the Fund on a continuous basis,
and there will be mismatches with the expenditure. The revenue

line might comprise some or all of the following: environmental charges and taxes *plus* the CAP successor monies *plus* net environment gain compensation payments. It might also receive some of the economic rents from the depletion of the non-renewables, depending on whether these are to be put in a sovereign wealth fund and, if this is the case, whether they are to be spent on improving renewables in compensation for the depletion of the non-renewables, or on the general economy as in the case of Norway.

The difference between including and not including the non-renewable economic rents would amount to a lot of revenue. It would not be as much as it would have been had the sovereign wealth fund concept been used from the outset for North Sea oil and gas, but still it would be a significant revenue flow. It would also include other mineral depletions from mining and quarrying.[12] Some of this activity should be stopped anyway, such as peat extraction, so the revenues would be net of the ending of harmful activities, and over time the North Sea reserves will be further depleted.[13]

A fund with this sort of revenue would be transformational: it would ensure that the natural environment is enhanced. The temptation for the Nature Fund management will be to go further and to borrow against its future revenues, as it is for government generally. This temptation will be given an extra gloss by pointing to the opportunity to issue green bonds. Buying the Nature Fund's bonds will have two attractions for investors: they will be 'green', and hence good for corporate social responsibility accounting; and they will be 'safe' in that the revenues will be ultimately protected by government, which will either provide an explicit guarantee, or an implicit one because government will ultimately determine the legal framework under which the Fund receives its money.

Despite the obvious attractions of green bonds, not least because they would add more firepower to the Nature Fund, there are reasons to be cautious. Borrowing has the nasty habit of requiring that interest is paid on the bonds, and that there is repayment of the principal in the future. In a conventional economic activity, the borrowing is paid back from the returns to the investments that it has financed. In the case of nature borrowing, it is far from clear what the future revenues from the projects would be and, in particular, whether they can be monetarised. A new wetland brings a great deal of economic benefit and well-being to the people who enjoy it, and it strengthens ecosystems and their resilience. But it does not produce obvious additional revenues, and it is not easy to monetarise.

As a result, the revenue to pay the interest and repay the debt is just future income from the main revenue lines. Green bonds are, in effect, a mortgage on the future, with the result that more spending now means less spending later. This is really like government borrowing, and may be treated as such by the Office for National Statistics (ONS). It is probably best avoided.

Owning assets

So far the Nature Fund is a channel to take revenues and translate them into spending on the natural environment. It is like an arm's-length DEFRA, with the added advantage of hypothecating the revenues and having a ring-fenced independence from government.

It could be more: it could *own* natural capital. This is what the National Trust, the RSPB and the Wildlife Trusts do. The Land Trust is a recent addition.[14] They own assets-in-perpetuity, held in the trust on behalf of their members and for the benefit of future generations.

The trust concept is an intuitively appealing one for the natural environment. We, the current generation, are the stewards of the assets, which keep on being passed down through the genera-tions. We have no right to trash them. Ownership conveys the right to exclude certain activities that might damage precious natural assets, and the right to give access to what are critical public goods.

The Nature Fund could take on ownership too. In re-creating a wetland, it could buy the land and then hold it in perpetuity. It is an appealing idea, in effect a new and grander National Trust. Yet it also runs into difficulties. These would ultimately be state-owned assets, and the Fund would then not only finance these assets, but have to run them too. Just as banks are kept separate from the management of the companies they lend to, so too does it make good sense to keep the two apart for natural assets.

To keep this separation in place, the Nature Fund would need partners to hand over the enhanced assets to, and to coordinate their activities. In the example of the new wetland, the Nature Fund could buy the land, create the new wetland, and hand it on to, say, a Wildlife Trust; or it could get the Wildlife Trust to buy the asset with money granted to it by the Nature Fund.

To the Wildlife Trust in this example, the question would be who is going to pay for the maintenance of the wetland once the key works have been carried out? Trusts rely on memberships for revenue, as well as grants and other donations. The core problem for any trust is how to pay for ongoing commitments.

This brings into play the concept of capital maintenance, and the role of the Nature Fund in guaranteeing the revenue to pay for it. Natural assets of the renewable variety are assets-in-perpetuity. They are not like factories and machinery that have limited lives and depreciate over time. Natural capital assets cannot be allowed to depreciate, because that means risking falling below the critical thresholds beyond which they cannot renew themselves.

As there can be no depreciation, money must be found to keep the value of the natural assets at least intact over time. This is capital maintenance, and for any new assets like the wetland example, the financing requires a commitment to the ongoing capital maintenance in perpetuity, on top of the initial cost in creating the new natural asset in the first place.

For the Nature Fund, the budget should show a line for capital maintenance as a first claim on its revenue, and then the balance sheet should show the new assets being created. There is a plus – an asset – and also a liability, which is the capitalisation of the future required capital maintenance. As the assets are passed from the Nature Fund to trusts and other bodies, the slate is wiped clean of these assets, but not the capital maintenance requirement, which remains in the accounts.

There is nothing in principle against the state, via the Nature Fund or directly, continuing to own natural capital assets. It already owns military land with great natural capital, notably Salisbury Plain, and a large number of public spaces and forests. The Crown Estate plays a pivotal role in all this. Yet this has not generally proved a sustainable role for the state because of all the other pressing claims on its revenues. To own the assets risks them being traded off against other claims, like health and education, the police and the military, and so on. This is doubly dangerous, because natural capital is typically longer-term and crosses the generations, and hence is about our duty to the future, whereas many of the other claims on government are to meet immediate needs and – crucially – to persuade the current electorate to keep them in power.

The overwhelming evidence is that the politics favours the current generation over the future, and that is precisely what the Nature Fund is trying to avoid. That is why the Nature Fund is an example of institutional hypothecation – to prevent the natural environment being sacrificed in the name of immediate short-term considerations. Trusts are typically much better owners, committed to the assets-in-perpetuity, expert in their understanding of how to manage the assets, and free from the immediate political influences.

Deciding how to spend the money

How should the Nature Fund spend its money and prioritise the many claims made upon it? It would be the biggest spender in town for the natural environment, especially since it might include the post-CAP agricultural subsidies. When there is a honeypot of money to spend, the lobbyists will swarm. In the case of farming, we already have one of the most effective lobby groups in Britain, the NFU.[15] Although it has only around 50,000 members, and not even the majority of farmers, it punches massively above its weight. It is going to remain a big vested interest. In chapter 4 we saw how impressive its lobbying has been. Consequentially, it will be important to avoid having 'stakeholders' on the board of the Nature Fund.

Then there are the environmental groups, the Trusts and the NGOs. There is a risk that they become dependent on the Nature Fund, analogous to the dependency of the NFU members on the CAP. They will develop their own teams to deal with the Nature Fund, and will want to capture it for the purposes of their specific objectives and preferred projects. The risks are all the greater here because of the size disparity between environmental organisations, with the National Trust and the RSPB towering over the local community groups and the specialist organisations. This dependency can be two-way: there is also the risk that the Nature Fund becomes dependent on these organisations to deliver its objectives.

There are several ways of dealing with this capture problem. The first is the expert approach, which involves careful scientific and economic assessment of the host of proposals that the interested parties will bring forward. The NFU is always in the business of proposing what government should spend money on. Its proposals could and should be subject to detailed scrutiny. The Nature Fund would need an assessment capability. The analogies are with the ONS, the Office for Budget Responsibility and the Monetary Policy Committee of the Bank of England.

There would have to be a cadre of genuinely independent experts, but these too could bring the risk of capture by particular ideas, like rewilding, technological fixes and the long-held views of key individuals. There should be no revolving doors. The big agrichemical companies would need to be kept at bay. Independent experts are necessary, but the history remains one of repeated attempts at capture. The lesson is that the Nature Fund would need to lean against this wind and not be blown away by it.

An alternative route is to have a *plan*, and a view about what will and what will not pass the tests set out in the plan and the assessment criteria. This is what a proper rolling 25-year environment plan should be, to which we turn in the next chapter.

With a plan in place, the Nature Fund monies could be parcelled out to our five main categories in aggregate: the river catchments, the agricultural lands, the uplands, the marine areas and the urban areas. Within each of these, the various parties could bid the environmental improvement they can offer, both large-scale and small. These bids would then be sifted to find the greatest environmental benefits for the monies, all in the context of the overarching rolling 25-year environment plan. It is where farmers, conservation and local groups come to the party. It would necessarily be a decentralised and local process. For each of the five categories, there would need to be particular institutions to handle the bidding processes. For the rivers there would be catchment system operators; for the uplands the National Parks might play a core role. For the marine areas there might be new institutions, while for the cities it might be the elected authorities. All of these require a credible rolling 25-year environment plan, on a statutory basis. This is the final part needed to create a greener and more prosperous land, fitting all the parts together.

12

THE PLAN

There is a strong economic case for enhancing the natural environment. It would make us more prosperous. It is good economics. It can be financed by redirecting the CAP subsidies, by making polluters pay and by ensuring that damage done to the environment by developers is paid for. All of these steps improve economic performance relative to business-as-usual.

The gap that remains to be filled is how to join up the financial support, the Nature Fund described in the previous chapter and the specific improvements outlined in part two. That is where the plan comes in. But if you are expecting a detailed project specification, set out as a detailed blueprint, and are looking to see if your preferred projects are included, then you are going to be disappointed.

Before anyone can start to do this, the nature of the plan and how it is put together need to be properly defined. It is then up to those delivering the plan to fill in these details, at the river catchment level, for the agricultural public goods, for the National Parks and the uplands, for the marine areas around our coasts, and for each city, town and village.

Why we need a top-down plan

A plan is more than the sum of its parts. It is an algorithm for sorting out how interlocking systems fit together, each dependent on the others. The reason it is necessary for enhancing the natural environment is that habitats and ecosystems all fit together.

Put it the other way around: what happens when each environmental policy area is treated as a silo? Take the EU Water Framework Directive and river quality. If there is no parallel action to reduce the pollution and soil run-off from agriculture, then the costs of the river clean-up are going to be all the greater. In effect, by allowing polluters not to pay for the pollution they cause, and hence not to face the true economic costs of their activities, they will carry on discharging too much into the rivers. The result is that water companies will have an incentive to invest in clean-up solutions, including concrete ones, in extra water-treatment works. Costs are higher and environmental outcomes worse.

The inefficiency of such an outcome can be seen in the development of trading systems to pay farmers not to pollute. These not only reflect the fact that it is cheaper to reduce the source of pollution than try to remove it once it is there, but also how difficult it is to get the incentives right. How much will the water companies have to pay? That depends on how bad the situation is *ex ante*. From the farmers' narrow commercial perspective, best to make it worse so more is paid for cleaning it up.

The European and global dimensions

It could of course be argued that all these systems interact with all the systems worldwide, and what is needed is a global natural capital plan. There is much to commend this idea, and there are some attempts towards this level of planetary planning. There are agreements like the Convention on Biological Diversity and the Convention on International Trade in Endangered Species, and there is the Paris Agreement on climate change.

All of these have a contribution to make. Europe-wide natural capital plans have greater traction than those designed just for Britain, and much of the current environmental policy frameworks, the nature designations, agricultural and water regimes and social subsidies have been developed by the EU. Britain proposes to match the level of environmental protection that it has inherited from the EU when it is no longer a member and, in transition, bound by its rules. But it remains very unclear how a 'third country' can be an integral part of developing environmental plans in Europe if it is not part of the core. If the aim is to integrate the environment into the heart of the Europe-wide economy and economic policy, then Britain will struggle to get attention since it is not able to be part of the overall economic decision-making of which the environment is a part. All those migrating birds, including the turtle doves shot in Malta as they migrate, will have even less protection if Britain is not at the table to pressurise the Maltese government.[1]

For the specific sectors too, it matters what the next phase of the CAP will look like to the environment of Britain, as it does what the next iterations of the Water Framework Directive look like and how the European regulation of pesticides, herbicides and fertilisers develops. The 22 miles across the English Channel may limit land migration and hence the topping-up of some of our native terrestrial species, but they are trivial when it comes to birds, insects and the marine life around our coasts. What happens in Europe needs to be taken into account in the British plan. In the past it was endogenous: we helped to shape environmental policies and we were bound by the European legislation and support schemes that resulted. A post-Brexit world presents a much more exogenous constraint.

How do the bits fit together?

Within the overriding objective to leave the natural environment in a better state than we inherited it, the overall natural environment plan needs first principles against which to identify the key elements and account for progress. Everything in the plan should follow these principles.[2]

Where principles are concerned, there are both obvious candidates and a limited scope for agreement. The obvious candidates are: public money for public goods; the polluter-pays principle; and net environmental gain. The first makes sure that the public goods are provided. The second internalises the costs of pollution, and the third ensures that natural capital does not decline in aggregate. The goals listed in the government's 25 Year Environment Plan should comprise those measures necessary to meet the principles. And the principles matter because they embed the plan's key objectives: to be economically efficient, and to prevent a net loss in natural capital.

The public money for public goods principle depends on the identification of the public goods, which will not be provided by private markets, and it makes the plan concentrate on these. Its early application will be to agriculture as the CAP drops away. But then it will be a principle that guides the revision of the plan towards the harder-to-reach public goods, and it dictates the form and content of interventions in the cities and the marine environments.

Applying the polluter-pays principle to all and every dimension of the natural environment is very radical: it changes the nature of farming, land management, the management of rivers and the marine context. It means not just that there would be fertiliser and pesticide charges, but that the use of plastics would be taxed, as would water companies for their discharges to rivers. As the plan evolves and goes through implementation there would be a rolling programme of polluter-pays interventions.

The net environmental gain is, like the polluter-pays principle, a universal requirement, and allows the plan to respond to the other activities in the economy. It is not possible to know in advance what will be developed where. We do not even know what the infrastructure in 25 years' time will look like. Will there be electric transport charging networks? Where will houses be built? Where will companies develop new offices and factories? The principle of net environmental gain applied to each and every development through the planning laws allows the plan to be implemented in line with the dynamics of the economy. In its application it will shape the economy, as will the polluter-pays principle. It will not be so attractive to build where the environmental damage is large. It will not be an all-or-nothing planning decision.

The accounting basis and metrics

To make sense of the plan, it needs an accounting base. We need to be able to measure whether or not the environment is getting in a better shape. There are two ways of doing this, and they address two somewhat different but related questions. The first is to ask: has the state of natural capital assets improved? The second is: have the environmental outputs gone up?

The first is about whether, as time goes by, people have more and better natural assets on which to base their choices, and how they want to live their lives. It is also about whether industry has more renewable natural capital on which to base decisions about when to produce and invest. The asset approach asks about the state of our rivers, farmland and soils, the uplands, the urban environments and coasts and marine areas. It asks whether the stock of fish, birds, mammals and insects has gone up or down, and whether the ecosystems within which they live are in better or worse condition. The metrics follow, and answer questions like: how much carbon is there in the soils? Are the populations of farmland birds going up? How many peregrines are there in our cities?

These assets can be listed on a balance sheet, and particular attention can be paid to those renewables at most risk of falling below critical thresholds. This leads to a risk register. We can then ask what capital maintenance is required to make sure the aggregate set of assets – the overall natural environment – does not decline, and then finally what enhancements would be most beneficial to the overall environmental systems.

The second approach looks at the outputs and asks questions like: how clean is the air and water? How clean are the beaches? How many children have been to the seaside? The 25 Year Environment Plan's initial 10 goals are all about these sorts of outputs. The outputs approach focuses on a tight relationship between what ecosystems services are provided and human valuations of them in utility terms. Ecosystem services are placed alongside other goods and services in the economy.

A natural capital approach lends itself to the former, while a core conventional cost–benefit analysis lends itself to the latter. It is hard to ask what a particular asset is worth independent of the system within which it is contextualised, and it is impossible to sensibly value ecosystems as a whole. We just need them, and the right question to ask is: what would be the consequences of not having them? What are their deprival values?

While both approaches are useful, and both should be pursued, it is the assets that are the primary concern, and in particular what state they are in. When it comes to enhancements – the sorts of improvements discussed in part two – the main issue is the extent to which particular improvements lend themselves to the whole; and again a plan is needed. While we might, for example, convert an intensively farmed arable field into a wild flower meadow, with benefits in terms of outputs, it would be of much greater value if it were added to an existing set of wild flower meadows. The key point is that scale and location matter, and matter a lot.

Compare this asset approach with the government's 25 Year Environment Plan. It sets some high-level outputs targets – to improve air quality, to improve water quality and so on – and some of these may become legally binding. But then it blends in some asset objectives, such as for soils. What it does not yet do is provide for a balance sheet, against which to adjudicate progress and to incorporate new assets. It needs to, in order to provide the comprehensive basis for the action it wants to deliver.

How do we prioritise?

There are a host of improvements that could be made. Every environmental organisation has a wish list. Which to choose and in what order? In the absence of a plan, the answer is to consider each on its merits. If we have a plan that contains, say, new Marine Protected Areas, a new coastal Green Belt, new woodlands and forests and new wildlife corridors, then the answer is that we should prioritise those projects that best meet the objectives of the plan.

That is not what we do now, because until very recently we have not had a plan, and each project has indeed been considered on its own merits. Where public money is involved, the Treasury's Green Book is the manual.[3] Where applications are made to the Heritage Lottery Fund, it is its criteria that apply. This is broadly an output-based approach, not an asset one. The benefits – the ecoservices – are valued, the costs of the project subtracted and the net returns are then discounted by the government's discount rate – typically around 3 per cent. It is the same approach applied to bridges, roads, schools and hospitals, and it is probably what will happen to schemes that fall under the subsidies for agriculture post-CAP, the public money for public goods approach.

To put the priorities in order, there needs to be an assessment of the current assets. This is not an ecosystems services exercise, but a State of Nature Review. The assets at risk of falling below the critical thresholds are the priority, starting at the national level, and then working through the key domains identified in part two. For each river catchment, for each city, for each upland area and for each marine area there would be an assessment, repeated, say, every five years.

Who would do this assessment? For the river catchments there needs to be an assessment at the catchment level. This is where the system operators described in chapter 3 come in. They would have a catchment balance sheet, identifying the main catchment assets, working out the necessary capital maintenance, and then focusing on specifics. It might include natural capital flood defences, and reduced soil erosion with revised farming policies; it could include all sorts of access to nature for the public.

For the uplands it could be the National Parks. For the land areas generally devoted to agriculture much can be covered by catchments and catchment system operators, but probably not all. It would probably need a new land management and subsidy body for the rest. The land body would need a plan of how to get the greatest environmental asset benefits from the subsidies. It might be crafted out of Natural England. Cities are well ahead in one sense: they all have local governments of one form or another, and city planning is a well-understood concept. For the marine areas, a new body might be required, with the fisheries quotas and other elements of fishing policies.

Revising the plan

A battle plan, it is sometimes remarked, fails with the first contact with the enemy. Any general natural capital plan is bound to run into trouble as soon as it hits a river catchment or other natural asset. Why? Because the clash with reality reveals all sorts of information not previously known. Ecosystems are always throwing up surprises.

This means that a plan needs both a timetable and milestones, and at the same time it has to be flexible and open to revisions. Within the envelope of the overall objective – a better natural environment for the next generation, driven by the three principles of public money for public goods, polluter pays and net gain – the plan can be broken down into bite-sized bits. Although there is no particular reason for choosing a specific number of intervals, there is merit in having five-year periods, rather than a continual rolling system of revisions. Five years ties in neatly with the typical parliamentary period; it is long enough to appraise progress, and short enough to make sensible revisions. It also happens to be the length of most utility regulation periods. Lots of projects would take more than one period, but taking stock of progress on these every five years would be a useful exercise nonetheless.

Each period can be set well in advance. So the design of, for example, the third five-year plan can be set every five years, leaving 15 years always determined at least in outline. This is analogous to the way the carbon budgets work on the pathway to the Climate Change Act's 2050 net zero target.

Each of the periods would have a target for the improvement in the overall natural capital, and a set of output targets for things like air and water quality. The first would be captured in the ONS natural capital accounts. Aggregate natural capital would have to go up by a specified amount over each of the periods, and the outputs would be set on a ratchet, with each period improving on the last.

With these in place, there would be specific priority enhancements in each period, using the monies from the national Nature Fund, set out in the previous chapter. There would be a practical sequence in the five-year periods, so for example it might be easier to develop new forests earlier on because the land is available, and later it might be possible to develop wildlife corridors. Action on marine conservation areas could be immediate because the Crown Estate owns the seabed. Similarly, improving urban parks could be immediate where these are owned by trusts and local government, but it might perhaps be slower to get uptake on taking out marginal land from agriculture. It may take time to get acceptance for the reintroduction of the lynx, and there may need to be trials and pilots, but it would be easier to quickly extend the range of beaver reintroductions. Planting crops amenable to corn buntings can be done in the annual agricultural cycle, and getting maize off the sensitive soils could also be achieved within the very short term. Creating new salt marshes takes longer. All of this also has to consider the capacity of the key organisations to cope with multiple projects, and there is nothing to stop voluntary bodies jumping the gun and getting on with specific tasks. The constraint of the plan is that it determines the timing and flow of the funding.

As long as the principles are strictly adhered to, and as long as the aggregate natural capital is going up, the precise order of developments may not matter so much. The exception is where there are renewable natural assets close to the thresholds and in danger of becoming non-renewable. Here, immediate and urgent action may be the only strategy to prevent sub-sustainable populations. Action on the hen harriers in England is one such example, as is the rescue of key farmland birds. The turtle dove is close to extinction in Britain and needs more amenable habitats quickly.

Big data, GPS and genomics

The principles, the initial plan and the periodic approach provide the framework for the gradual implementation of the plan. They require a great deal of information, and a lot of detailed ecosystem knowledge. This is a daunting task, and one that has largely defeated conservationists to date. There has been no way of providing a schedule of priorities or for the revisions outlined above on a detailed, comprehensive, scientific and economic basis.

This is changing. Conservationists need to catch up with the data revolution all around them, and the ability to link up big datasets in an intelligent way. Satellites have already given us detailed maps so we can see our planet in ways that eluded previous generations of conservationists. From satellites we can see what is going on in pretty much any part of the planet. We can see the algae blooms from the run-off through estuaries out into the North Sea, the impact of the burning of heather moors and the scale of light pollution.

This is but a start on the information revolution that is putting new tools in the hands of conservationists and enables us to see in minute detail what is really going on. Take an agri-environmentalist scheme on a farm. What exactly are the farmers up to? Are they keeping to both the spirit and the letter of their agreements? A drone sorts this out pretty quickly. We can see down to the square metre what is happening. The same goes for field margins and whether they are being properly maintained. We can see whether farmers are actually abiding by the cross-compliance rules. Compliance is likely to increase massively with this level of scrutiny.

The technology gives us this ability to make sure that what is paid for gets delivered. But it is about much more than enforcement. The new data technologies enable us to see into the vegetation, to detect species numbers and even peer into the soils themselves. They enable farmers to use precision in the chemicals they apply, to be able to track run-offs, and for river catchment managers to follow the flow of chemicals. Much of this is already happening.

The data can come from lots of sources, including citizen science. All those garden bird-watch surveys and the photos uploaded via apps to researchers can go into the big data melting pot, to which the long history of recording Britain's wildlife by its extraordinary naturalists over the last two centuries provides a calibrating set of benchmarks. The flora and fungi atlases, the bird atlases, the insect data – all can be brought by the swipe of a screen to those running the plan and all those interested in it. It is a new, data-rich world.

To this, something entirely new is being added: genetics. Where once brown trout and sea trout were thought to be different species, we can now see that they are actually one. Instead of thinking about their conservation as separate problems, we can now see them as integrated. The interesting questions are about what triggers some trout to go to sea and others to remain. Returning salmon can be genetically traced to see if they really do return only to their rivers of birth. The behaviour of sparrows can be better understood to help work out how they do and do not thrive in urban environments.[4]

This sort of extra knowledge is but a small start of what is to come. Sequencing genomes is no longer a rare and expensive task: soon all of us could have access to our own personal genome. For the conservation of nature, genetics will become a normal tool, with possibly even field identification kits. Indeed, for many it already is.

The coming masses of data will enable us to understand our natural environment so much better, to learn more about what works, and to design more effective and cheaper ways of understanding how to conserve at the micro level. It will also enable the splicing of all this data on an ecosystem basis, to have models of the key ecosystems, and to pack these models with data.

To do this, one more technological innovation is needed: AI. AI brings the capacity to look for patterns and trends in all the data in a matter of seconds. Suppose you want to know how best to protect the brent geese that come to Britain's coastal marshes every winter. AI can provide a real-time map of where they are and how they get here; it can also provide an understanding of how successful the breeding season in Siberia was. AI can help integrate the population data on snowy owls and their predation on the goslings, which in turn is strongly influenced by the population of lemmings as the alternative and preferred food for the owls (and the arctic foxes and other predators). This data can then be set against information on the eel grass in, for example, the Blackwater Estuary or the Solway Firth, as well as data on rising sea levels and what these are doing to the coastal marshes and their grasses on which the brent geese graze.

Naturalists who have spent years studying the brent geese know a lot of this, but cannot easily put all the information together to form a complete picture. If the problem is the lemmings, then it might not be the state of the coastal marshes, and it may not be worth putting time, money and subsidies into the marshes. If, however, the lemmings are doing just fine, then the causes of the changes in the population in the last couple of decades may be closer to home. Most likely it is all of these factors working together in complex ways.

All of this information also helps to inform the economics. Think back to the river catchment problem for the water companies, and their extraction and purification of water for drinking. What would be the most cost-effective way of getting drinking water to us? Would it be a general policy to tax fertilisers, and other agrichemicals, or would it be better to target specific forms of pollution in particular localities? Could AI integrate the databases and send signals to the tractor applying fertiliser on a particular field? Think of the savings, not only for the water company but also for the farmer. This is smart environmental technology with smart efficiency savings.

These economic gains brought about by big data and AI also help us to work out where the benefits to us humans are greatest from the enhancements in the plan. Imagine there are two proposed projects: to enhance the air quality in a town along a particular part of a river, or to improve the wildness and beauty of an upper catchment area. One gives immediate relief to the lungs, and the other increases our sense of well-being and hence our mental health. You might be thinking: do both. Ideally we would indeed do all these projects. But now suppose that the Nature Fund has only limited money to spend. Where should it spend it? Both projects enhance natural capital, and both therefore contribute to achieving the plan's objectives.

A lot of progress can be made given genomes and big data about air quality and the impacts on well-being from the enhanced beauty. Suppose now that a lot of people live in the area affected by poor air quality, and that we can estimate pretty accurately the impact on both life expectancy and the quality of life. It should be possible to come up with a fairly good estimate of the benefits of improvements in air quality. It might turn out that big gains are made from initial improvements, but they tail off quickly. Suppose too that the data can tell us what the causes of this pollution are, and how much it costs to reduce them. The net present value of the project to improve air quality is then estimated quite accurately, and it can be put into effect.

Is this a better project than the upper-river beauty enhancements? Should it be given priority? The beauty problem is typically presented as something that is not amenable to data and evidence and costs and benefits. It is an aesthetic. All of this is true, but it does not get us very far. The question is not about the abstract concept of beauty; it is about whether we should prioritise it over other projects, and spend money in the plan on it.[5] It is relevant to ask how many people do, and might, benefit from the enhanced beauty; whether the particular enhancements are likely to increase the numbers who benefit; and, among the many ways of enhancing beauty, which are likely to have the most immediate impacts. New technologies allow us to map what is going on in very great detail: not only where people go, but more deeply from the clicks they make on their smart devices, from the cookies that track them, and from their uploaded photos.

This sort of calculation may make many conservationists shudder, but the question of what to spend the funds on, and how much, is inescapable. There are choices. There is not an infinite budget for the plan, and prioritisation is inevitable.

In this highly contrived example, the two projects have been treated as separate, but they may not be. The air pollution could be caused by agriculture, and the modification of agriculture might also improve the upper river and its biodiversity. This is where the full understanding of the whole catchment comes into play.

What the new technologies can do is revolutionise the way we tackle the plan's objectives, to know much more about what might work, what might have the greatest benefits and to monitor the consequences so we can change tack if things turn out differently. Big data and new AI technologies enable us to track pollution, monitor the state of natural capital assets, target the Nature Fund's spending and hold the government to account for the delivery of the plan. There are not going to be so many places for pollutants to hide.

Embedding the plan

Only the subject of accounting is more likely to make environmentalists' eyes glaze over more than a discussion of the institutions. Yet, as noted, the plan has little chance of success unless it is protected against the pressures of day-to-day political and economic life, and has a body capable of independently revising and updating it. Put simply, someone has to be in charge, with a legal duty to ensure that the objective – more natural capital – is delivered. Revisions need someone to do the revising, and the ability to respond flexibly within the principles is dependent on the institutional structures and institutional discretion.

The trouble with anything to do with government is that, in a democracy, what matters is the immediate programme of the elected ministers and the day-to-day responses to events as they unfold. Democracy focuses on the present, and the electorate does not directly include the future generations to whom the plan is directed.[6]

This problem for democracy of taking account of future people is an endemic one, and in practice the future is frequently sacrificed to the present. For the last 200 years it has been reasonable to assume that future people will be better off than we are; the assumption that follows is that they can take care of themselves. That no longer stands up when it comes to nature and natural capital. Future people will have much better technologies, but climate change and biodiversity loss are big liabilities we are bequeathing them. Nature might not care, since there are always new ecological niches for evolution to fill, but future people almost certainly will.

The political trick in tackling short-termism has been to create constitutions – rules that constrain immediate political interests – and arm's-length institutions. In the case of natural capital and the 25 Year Environment Plan, the current government decides the overall objective, and then the institution's job is to deliver it. The general objective that the natural environment should be left in a better shape for future generations translates into an aggregate natural capital rule, and then a body is charged with making sure that natural capital keeps going up. The 25 Year Environment Plan is given statutory backing in part by setting the objectives, duties and responsibilities of the institutions charged with delivering it.

Some of the institutional architecture is already in place. The ONS has begun compiling statistics on various types of natural capital to create natural capital accounts, and from these we can see that renewable natural capital is still in decline.[7] The ONS is a credible independent body charged with producing credible statistics. But what is missing is a body that owns the *delivery* of the 25 Year Environment Plan.

There are some obvious candidates. The Environment Agency, Natural England and the NCC come to mind. But none of these is currently set up for this new purpose. The Environment Agency is charged with a host of responsibilities, inherited from the way it was cobbled together from the old Her Majesty's Inspectorate of Pollution and the National Rivers Authority (NRA), plus some of the local authorities' waste responsibilities.[8] It ended up a very lopsided organisation with a big labour force (over 10,000) concentrated on flood defences and catchments. Natural England, after endless reorganisation and budget cuts, ended up with the agri-environment schemes and natural nature reserves, SSSIs and other land activities. The marine side has been largely left out, and the uplands are covered by the uneasy mix of the National Parks and the AONBs, agri-environmental schemes and trusts and other bodies. The NCC in its current incarnation does not have the resources, being an expert advisory committee.

The 25 Year Environment Plan is never going to fly in this complex, overlapping and competing context. Why? Because there is money on the table, and all organisations are attracted to the light of further resources to bolster their organisations. Everyone wants a slice of the natural capital action.[9]

Take the Cumbria pioneer as an example. The approach has been to try to corral the various bodies and hope that the 'stakeholders' come up with implementable answers. But on what can and should the Environment Agency with its focus on flooding, the farmers with an eye to the subsidies, Natural England with an eye to the areas under its protection, the grouse moor game interests, and the local authorities and the water company agree? No one is in charge. No one can decide.

A better way forward is to start with a blank piece of paper. The plan is a radical departure from the past. It requires new thinking, a new integrated approach, lots of data, and a specialist ability to model and appraise environmental systems.

The delivery body needs a statutory framework, and this has to give it the remit to ensure that the natural environment is enhanced. Like the Climate Change Act, a well-designed Nature Act would set a simple statutory duty, and not be hedged about with hosts of caveats. The vested interests need to be kept at bay. No doubt the NFU would want to add 'in particular in respect of food production', or even 'while ensuring a profitable farming industry'. The grouse shooters might want to add 'respecting the traditional game shoots'. And so on.

In addition to the overall duty, the new delivery body should have to have regard to the principles outlined above: public money for public goods; the polluter-pays principle; and net environmental gain.

The clean and simple overarching duty needs to be backed up with money. This is where the Nature Fund comes into play. The delivery body is about how it is spent. The Fund needs a clear duty on trustees to ensure that it is properly managed.

The Nature Fund and the new delivery body need to be centres for environmental big data and AI. To enhance the credibility of the new body, and to ensure it is open and transparent, the information should be available on public databases and readily accessible so that citizens and citizen science can play their parts. This openness and transparency is crucial to undermining vested interests and lobbying, which plague anything to do with our natural environment. Claims that money should be spent on this or that should be open to testing against the databases and the models, and by the bidding process and calculations run by, for example, the catchment system operator.

The ecosystem models should be continuously updated, and anyone should be able to run these models to examine proposals made by themselves or by others wanting alternative projects to triumph.

Resistance to capture needs to be hardwired into the new body. The integration of data is a new and exciting opportunity. It helps to protect the organisation from the forces that will no doubt seek to undermine it. Enhancing our natural environment is good for the economy, but not for all the polluters. There will be losers as well as gainers, and losers usually shout louder than gainers. It is therefore critical that the public benefits, and the overall economic benefits, are clear for all to see. If there is clear damage, as evidenced in the data from satellites and drones and against the model runs, those responsible must pay, as must polluters generally. Claims for money that advances private interests are ruled out accordingly.

The body would have to report on its performance against the plan and recommend to parliament the updating of the plan over the five-year periods. It would not be possible to make proposals that allow the aggregate natural capital to decline in any period, and it would not be up to parliament to come up with alternatives that did not meet the aggregate natural capital rule, without first repealing the Nature Act itself.

There would be accounts: a national natural capital balance sheet, which incorporates capital enhancements, and capital maintenance. The flow of monies from the Nature Fund would be recorded, and the spending clearly identified, along with the expected gains. There would be an auditing process.

With this blank piece of paper approach, Britain would end

up with coherent institutions capable of delivering the plan and revising it over time. The role of existing bodies would change. In the case of the river catchments, the catchment system operator would coordinate activities on a catchment-by-catchment basis, taking on the role of regulating the water companies, and opening up flood defences to alternative solutions, including natural flood management. Urban natural capital system operators could play a part, and there is a clear role for a marine system operator too.

These decentralised bodies would interface with the national delivery body, and they would be obvious parties to help in the delivery process. The national body would own the plan: the system operators would make it happen on the ground in the specific contexts.

There would remain the tasks of regulation, prosecution and enforcement. Post-Brexit, a new Office for Environmental Protection (OEP) has been proposed to hold the government to account, so that standards do not slip or regulation become weakened.[10] It is not yet really clear where this fits in relative to the other existing bodies in this crowded institutional space, unless as a tight legal entity with its own inspectorates and legal functions. The obvious way to handle this would be to create a proper Environment Protection Agency, charged with regulating, licensing, prosecuting and enforcing across both the public and private sectors, and with a broader domain and more legal teeth than the OEP. This more focused institutional map, with an Environment Protection Agency, a Nature Fund and a delivery body, would be underpinned by system operators, and the Environment Agency and Natural England would be absorbed by these various structures.

The clean sheet is the best approach, but the chances of it happening are not good. In addition to the proposed post-Brexit OEP, the Environment Agency, Natural England and the others will no doubt fight their own corners. The NFU will play its part too. The result is likely to be a muddle, and a muddle that blurs the institutional responsibilities and loses the integrated approach. It does not have to be like this, but it probably will be.

Making governments stick to the plan

Whether or not the above structures would weather the inevitable storms and pressures of short-term political interests, and the hail of lobbying arrows that would be fired at them, ultimately depends on the deeper democratic forces and on a bedrock of public support. Conservationists talking to themselves may remain convinced, but it is the wider, largely urban, public that counts.

To make the plan stick, there has to be something in it for people now, and something tangible and very visible, to build the credibility and commitment of the plan. Most people see the environment on television and social media. They need to see tangible benefits, to be seen to be better off as a result, if they are to continue to support it through the ballot box.

This is anathema to conservationists. What should be done is what is scientifically right and meets their conservationist mindsets. But, for perfectly understandable reasons, the average urban citizen probably could not identify a swallow, has never seen a spotted flycatcher, and may think a brent goose is something for Christmas dinner that comes from the Brent Cross shopping centre. They don't have the detailed knowledge base of committed conservationists – and why should they? What they do know is that there is nowhere for their children to play, that the air is damaging their lungs and that they display an innate biophilia, a seemingly universal human trait.

Making the plan stick depends on keeping the bulk of the population on side. Fortunately this is not difficult to achieve. It means that the urban part of the plan is, at least in the short term, probably the most important. It means concentrating on the urban parks and the greening of the cities. It means education, and getting the children out into nature. Children have a right to clean air, to green spaces and access to the countryside. They are the next generation at which the plan is ultimately aimed. The final way of entrenching the plan is to make its key parts a *universal right for citizens*, just as there is for the provision of clean drinking water and electricity. The current and future generations are entitled to access to green spaces, to nature and the country-side, full stop.

Conclusions

SECURING THE PRIZE

When people in 2050 look back on us now, what will they say? Will they say that we met our obligations, were good stewards of the natural environment, and bequeathed them a better set of natural capital assets? That we achieved net zero? Or will they say we promised but did not deliver? Will the 97 per cent of wild flower meadows that had already gone by 2020 have become 100 per cent, but for a few nature reserves and extended gardens? Will they ask why we let the farmland birds and the seabirds perish, and turned what could have been a green and prosperous land into a browner and greyer land punctuated with a few nature reserves? Will they ask where the Green Belt went and why the children have nowhere green to play? Will they ask why carbon emissions kept going up?

It is up to us, and it is not that difficult. It is in our collective economic interests. Yet the opposing forces are powerful and organised, while the conservationists are less so. Facing up to the intensive farmers, the agrichemical companies, the house-building companies and the transport businesses, the mass membership of nature organisations punches way below its weight. In theory, the conservationists should sweep the board, but in practice they are often ineffective. Why?

There are at least two reasons for this collective failure.

Conservationists are fractious, and for understandable reasons they can sometimes see everything with the word 'economic' associated with it as part of the conspiracy against nature. For centuries, economic progress has been detrimental to nature. Economic progress has been associated with taming the rivers by straightening them out and adding weirs and locks, and with using them as open sewers. It has been about killing off competitors to the crops and livestock; about turning the uplands over to sheep and cattle; catching as many fish as possible; and concreting over the cities. In all this, economic progress has been incredibly successful in the battle against nature.

But now it has gone too far. The climate is being changed by the burning of fossil fuels that have provided the energy for the great economic transformation of the nineteenth and especially the twentieth centuries, and that have powered the tractors and the diesel fishing boats. The land has been chemicalised, destroying soils, flora and fauna. The meadows have gone, as have many of the birds. The debasement of the soils, of the air quality, of our abundant supplies of fresh water, and of our ability to enjoy physical and mental health will ultimately result in lung disease, scarce water supplies, obesity and mental illnesses. Indeed, all of these are already happening. The fact that GDP doesn't measure most of these costs does not make them go away. We are less prosperous as a result.

The conservationists realise all this and more besides. They can see what is happening. The trouble is that they tend to talk among themselves, and meticulously record the inevitable declines, but they do not consider the economics.

Take a look at the books that conservationists regard as their guides, such as Bill Adams's *Future Nature* and Peter Marren's *Nature Conservation*, or the pages of the excellent *British Wildlife* journal.[1] You won't find much about economics in any of them. Indeed, in Mark Cocker's *Our Place*, natural capital does not even appear in the index.[2] This is a mistake, and one with consequences. We know that things are going downhill. But what we want, to paraphrase Marx, is to change the world, to make it a better place for nature.

Once the Rubicon is crossed, environmentalists will find that there is much to be gained by taking a seriously economic view of what is going on. While there are lots of good reasons to conserve nature beyond economics, nature comprises very special scarce resources and economics is all about allocating them efficiently. It is patently obvious that that is not what we are currently doing. We should.

There is in one sense nothing radical about the measures proposed in this book. The 25 Year Environment Plan, the Nature Fund and the applications of sound mainstream economic principles like public money for public goods, polluter pays and net environmental gain, are all pretty straightforward, economically efficient things to do, and to do now. But there are two senses in which the proposals here are really radical. They call for us to confront the vested interests that stand in the way; and they require the conservationists to do a U-turn on their approach to economics and the centrality of the environment in the economy.

When people look back in 2050, it is possible that they will see this as the time we stopped going backwards and got firmly on the front environmental and economic foot. They could look back at the 2011 White Paper on 'The Natural Choice' as the moment when two core ideas took root: that it is the duty of any generation to look after its natural capital so that it is passed on in better shape to the next; and that no economic policy makes sense unless the environment is at the heart of it, rather than as a separate silo of nice things that might be afforded if the growth of the rest of the economy makes us rich enough to care about them. We have become richer over the last 200 years, and on aggregate the environment has become poorer.

The 2011 White Paper was pretty toothless. It was full of aspiration, but not content. Yet it has kick-started a positive process that may yet bear considerable fruit. It has provided the pioneers and now the 25 Year Environment Plan, which embeds the three key principles – public money for public goods, polluter pays and net environment gain – and these have now been advanced for agricultural policy too.

Will these radical steps deliver? The jury is out, as it almost always is with such fine words coming from the mouths of politicians, who inevitably come and go. There have been several DEFRA secretaries of state since the 2011 White Paper. Yet the 25 Year Environment Plan could turn into a new agricultural policy, a new fisheries policy, a new air quality policy, a new framework for the National Parks and a new catchment approach to our rivers.

The good news is that there are practical proposals of the sort set out in this book to turn the aspirations into reality. There is no doubt all this can be done. The bad news is that in every case there are deep vested interests, powerful and rich, that stand in the way, and the conservationists remain divided. The battle lines are drawn, but the sides are unevenly matched. The battle is about entrenching the 25 Year Environment Plan, using forceful legislation, with new credible institutions, with an independent Nature Fund, and with system operators for the river catchments, landscapes, uplands, cities and coastal areas.

In their engagement in this battle for nature, the conservationist organisations are still hesitating. There are those who see the whole idea of natural capital as a 'neo-liberal conspiracy', and who take a fundamentalist view that it is only by a wholesale renunciation of economic growth that we can live sustainably. They see natural capital and economics as one and the same utilitarian plot to further undermine nature in the name of progress.

They could not be more wrong, and they could not take any other line which will do more to undermine the 25 Year Environment Plan. Plans to go back to nature, to rewild the countryside and to turn Britain into a zoo of reintroductions allow those opposed to enhancing the natural environment to isolate the environmental interests as part of what gets called the 'green crap' that stands in the way of house-building, infrastructure, jobs and wages.

Although it should be obvious, there is no state of nature to go back to, a world without us. The environment is now irrevocably man-made, and we have an active, not a passive, duty to do something about it, to make a better man-made world. Conservationists sometimes appear to be against humans, preferring a non-human world of their imagination, a sort of 'presenting nature without any people'. Rewilding too often means just abandoning, and that of course has the merit for governments that it is at least cheap. Doing nothing in the uplands, for example, might appeal to some cash-strapped National Parks and to the Treasury, but the results may not be quite as environmentally benign as some of the advocates suggest. Getting the sheep numbers down is sound economic policy. There are too many, and they are not economic once all the subsidies and the environmental damage are taken into account. But that does not mean that we shouldn't manage upland grazing, with cattle and some sheep and even Exmoor ponies too.

In order to get the respect of those looking back in 2050, to be good stewards, we need a clear practical programme and to implement it with a sense of urgency. We need to bring the full force of the environmental movement together behind the 25 Year Environment Plan. We need to get serious about making polluters pay, to introduce appropriate green charges. We – and the EU – need to put an end to paying £3 billion to farmers, mostly to provide private goods and reward them for owning land. We need to focus on the public goods, and make sure that the money is well spent on them. We need to encourage farmers and others to bid for these funds, and to compete to offer the best public outcomes. We need them to work together to offer wider landscape projects, and to do this at the river catchment and upland levels in particular. We need flood defences to be the outcome of a competition between concrete and natural capital solutions. We need Marine Protected Areas to ban fishing in the interests of fishers.

Above all, what is needed is a new approach to the rights of citizens to a green and prosperous future. Citizens have entitlements and they have obligations. They should be entitled to access green spaces, like the rights to electricity, water, transport and now broadband. People need green space in order to be able to prosper, to participate in society, to be healthy in body and mind. Humans are not really human without nature. It is built into what we are, and into what constitutes a good life. Humans cannot be prosperous in a purely concrete jungle.

Do all these things and there is no reason why the future can't be brighter. Carry out our responsibilities to pay for the necessary capital maintenance to stop the declines of natural capital; make sure developments have green outcomes and compensate for further damage; and make sure the polluters face up to their responsibilities to make good the damage they cause by paying the costs they impose on the rest of us. Make sure the great green public goods – the landscapes that shape what we are, the parks and gardens and the ultimate public good, *nature* – are properly funded. It is not that difficult; it is economically wise; and it will leave those in 2050 with a greener and more prosperous land.

ACKNOWLEDGEMENTS

This is my own take on the prize of a green and prosperous land and how to get there, and not that of the NCC or of its individual members. In writing this book, I have been greatly influenced by my fellow NCC colleagues: Melanie Austen, Ian Bateman, Christopher Collins, Diane Coyle, Maja Kent, Paul Leinster, Georgina Mace, Colin Mayer, Maniv Pathak and Kathy Willis. Nick Barter and Julian Harlow drafted the 25 Year Environment Plan, and both have helped me enormously. Between them they have made a major impact on Britain's environmental policies, in the best traditions of the civil service.

There are many others who have helped shape my understanding, regardless of whether they will agree with my conclusions. Among these are Abigail Barker and Beccy Wilebore who, together with Kathy Willis, are advancing the data and modelling dimensions of natural capital. Shaun Spiers, now heading up Green Alliance, has been a significant influence. I have discussed many of these themes with members of the Environment Group I chair: Simon Bimpson, Stephen Bird, Owen Brennan, Richard Clay, Adrian Dolby, David Elliot, Julie Fourcade, Philip Gready, James Hall, Jo Harrison, Jacob Hayler, John Kimmance, Ed Mitchell, Darren Moorcroft, Adam Read, Kitty Rose, Guy Thompson, Steven Thompson, John Varley and Philip

Wyndham. Again, none can be assumed to agree with what I write.

A number of people have been kind enough to comment on early drafts. I am particularly grateful to Nick Barter, Richard Benwell, Yvette de Garis, David Elliott, Charles Godfray, Julian Harlow, Paul Leinster, Kim Wilkie and Kathy Willis.

I have greatly benefited from discussions with Minette Batters, James Bevan, Katie Bolt, Ian Boyd, Helen Browning, Chris Curran, Karin Ellis, Shaun Gallagher, Joe Grice, Emma Howard Boyd, Stanley Johnson, Neil Kenward, Andrea Ledward, Tom Le Quesne, Tim Leunig, Robin Milton, Ronan Palmer, Alan Parker, Jane Parker, Arlin Rickard, Lizzie Rogers, Chris Stark, Roger Scruton, Nigel Stone and Ueli Zellweger.

Sue Helm read and commented on various drafts and provided many valuable examples. She has been the inspiration for writing the book.

Myles Archibald has been a superb editor at HarperCollins, greatly improving my text, ably assisted by Hazel Eriksson. Kerry Hughes has copy-edited with her usual professionalism, and Jenny Vaughan has helped keep the show on the road and greatly assisted with a succession of drafts and my appalling handwritten scribbles.

The Warden and Fellows of New College, Oxford, have continued to indulge my many absences in focusing on NCC matters, and have provided me with the perfect backdrop to develop the ideas in this book. It would be an added bonus if this book encourages the College (and indeed all the Oxford colleges) to hold back on the chemicals and encourage more wildlife in their wonderful gardens.

ENDNOTES

PREFACE

1 James Wentworth Day wrote extensively on the marshes, and was a frequent visitor to my grandfather's farm. He was also acutely aware of what postwar farming was doing to the land and its wildlife. On shooting, see his *The Modern Fowler: With a Guide to Some Principal Coastal Wildfowling Resorts of Today* (Longman, Green & Co., 1934); and on the environmental damage, see his *Poison on the Land: The War on Wild Life, and Some Remedies* (Eyre & Spottiswoode, 1957).

2 Department for Environment, Food and Rural Affairs, 'The Natural Choice: Securing the Value of Nature', White Paper, June 2011.

3 The prime minister, David Cameron, was sympathetic and quite green-minded. He came to BBOWT, the Berkshire, Buckinghamshire and Oxfordshire Wildlife Trust, of which I have the privilege of being a vice president, to see what the volunteers were doing to turn Chimney Meadow Farm on the banks of the Upper Thames into a haven for wild flowers in its wetland meadows, encouraging the return of the curlews and the barn owls, and even perhaps some lapwings.

4 Wilson, E. O., *Biophilia*, Harvard University Press, 1986. See also his *The Diversity of Life* (Harvard University Press, 1992).

5 Department for Environment, Food and Rural Affairs, 'A Green Future: Our 25 Year Plan to Improve the Environment', January 2018.

6 Helm, D., *Natural Capital: Valuing the Planet*, London: Yale University Press, 2015.

INTRODUCTION

1 This number excludes the costs of the Common Agricultural Policy (CAP), the bulk of which goes on the basic farm payment, the budget

of the Environment Agency (much of which is used for flood defences), and Natural England's budget.

2 Carson, R. *Silent Spring*, Boston: Houghton Mifflin, 1962.

3 Wildlife corridors were promoted in the Lawton report. Lawton, J. 'Making Space for Nature: A Review of England's Wildlife Sites and Ecological Network', prepared for Department for Environment, Food and Rural Affairs, September 2010.

4 On the efforts of the Norfolk Wildlife Trust, see www.edp24.co.uk/news/rabbits-are-the-key-part-of-500-000-project-to-help-breckland-s-rare-wildlife-species-1-4988850.

5 See www.bbowt.org.uk/nature-reserves/upper-ray-meadows.

6 The timing of this withdrawal of the subsidy for owning land depends on how Brexit, the transition and subsequent UK–EU agricultural relationships play out over the next decade and beyond. In due course, regardless of Brexit, the EU will probably reduce this part of the subsidies in any event – and it should do so for the sake of the EU members' environments.

7 Department for Environment, Food and Rural Affairs, 'A Green Future: Our 25 Year Plan to Improve the Environment', January 2018.

8 Department for Environment, Food and Rural Affairs, 'The Natural Choice: Securing the Value of Nature', White Paper, June 2011.

1: THE PRIZE

1 David Goulson points out that there is little direct benefit from the great yellow bumblebee which hangs on in the machair of the Uists. While this might be true, the loss of the machair habitat and its ecosystem does matter, and preserving the great yellow bumblebee would require preserving the machair. Goulson, D., *Bee Quest*, London: Vintage, 2017.

2 The 'tragedy of the commons' arises because, for a commonly owned natural asset, each commoner (a grazier on land or a fisher at sea) will always have an incentive to add more cattle or take more fish, even though if they all do this the result will be to destroy the asset. This theory was originally set out in Hardin, G., 'The Tragedy of the Commons', *Science*, 162, 1968, pp. 1243–8.

3 Peat loss in the Fens has been estimated at between 1.5 and 2.1 cm

per year. Holman, I. P., 'An Estimate of Peat Reserves and Loss in the East Anglian Fens', Cranfield University, October 2009, commissioned by the RSPB.

4 National Infrastructure Commission, 'National Infrastructure Assessment', July 2018. Interestingly, *natural* infrastructure hardly gets a look-in.

5 The Plan sets out its high-level objectives as follows: '1. Clean air. 2. Clean and plentiful water. 3. Thriving plants and wildlife. 4. A reduced risk of harm from environmental hazards such as flooding and drought. 5. Using resources from nature more sustainably and efficiently. 6. Enhanced beauty, heritage and engagement with the natural environment. In addition, we will manage pressures on the environment by: 7. Mitigating and adapting to climate change. 8. Minimising waste. 9. Managing exposure to chemicals. 10. Enhancing biosecurity.' Department for Environment, Food and Rural Affairs, 'A Green Future: Our 25 Year Plan to Improve the Environment', January 2018.

6 For a review, see House of Lords Economic Affairs Committee, 'The Economics of High Speed 2', 1st Report of Session 2014–15, HL Paper 134, March 2015.

7 See Brown et al., 'Natural vs Anthropogenic Streams in Europe: History, Ecology and Implications for Restoration, River-rewilding and Riverine Ecosystem Services', *Earth-Science Reviews*, 180, May 2018, pp. 185–205.

8 This is disputed by the Environment Agency and its cost–benefit analysis. Yet Oxford has to date not had the hard concrete alleviation, and natural approaches must improve the marginal risks. On the Upper Thames plans see, for example, www.thamesriverstrust.org.uk/natural-flood-management/. See also: www.bbowt.org.uk/what-we-do/living-landscapes/upper-thames.

9 On the natural flood defences for Pickering, see www.bbc.co.uk/news/uk-england-york-north-yorkshire-36029197.

10 See Holman, I. P., 'An Estimate of Peat Reserves and Loss in the East Anglian Fens', Cranfield University, October 2009; and Holman, I. P. and Kechavarzi, C., 'A Revised Estimate of Peat Reserves and Loss in the East Anglian Fens', Cranfield University, January 2011. Both studies were commissioned by the RSPB.

11 See Thompson, K. and Head, S., 'Gardens as a Resource for Wildlife',

www.wlgf.org/The%20garden%20Resource.pdf. There may be as much as 1 million acres of gardens.

2: BUSINESS-AS-USUAL

1 For an account of one of Britain's greatest naturalists, Derek Ratcliffe, see Thompson, J., Birks, H. and Birks, J. (eds), *Nature's Conscience: The Life and Legacy of Derek Ratcliffe*, Langford Press, 2015. See also Marren, P., *The New Naturalists*, London: HarperCollins, 2005.

2 Lee, L., *Cider with Rosie*, Hogarth Press, 1959; Thompson, F., *Lark Rise to Candleford*, Oxford: Oxford University Press, 1945.

3 See Environment Agency, 'The State of the Environment: Water Quality', February 2018, https://assets.publishing.service.gov.uk/government/uploads/system/uploads/attachment_data/file/709493/State_of_the_environment_water_quality_report.pdf

4 For the key charts, see www.climate.gov/news-features/understanding-climate/climate-change-atmospheric-carbon-dioxide.

5 Hayhow et al., 'The State of Nature 2016', the State of Nature Partnership, 2016, updated 2018.

6 Some non-renewables do get recycled, at additional cost. This, however, does not make them 'renewable'. Most non-renewables are used only once.

7 Whether or not this is the case, the Thames is one of the most intensively used river systems in the world, and around 55 per cent of effective rainfall is used for public supplies.

8 The National Infrastructure Commission was set up in 2015. It provides a national infrastructure assessment in each parliament.

9 National Infrastructure Commission, 'Preparing for a Drier Future: England's Water Infrastructure Needs', April 2018.

10 During the 2018 summer drought conditions, demand for water shot up in some regions very significantly. Despite rainfall across many regions being far less than the long-term average over the summer months, it was the heat and increased demand that caused the problems rather than the lack of rain.

11 Cleaning palm oil tanks will not be banned until 2021. Palm oil has repeatedly washed up on beaches, notably in the Blackpool and Fylde coastal areas.

12 The difference between greenfield and brownfield sites is that the former have not been built upon, whereas the latter have been, and are typically now abandoned industrial sites.

13 See Office for National Statistics, 'Migration Statistics Quarterly Report: August 2018', www.ons.gov.uk/peoplepopulationandcommunity/populationandmigration/internationalmigration/bulletins/migrationstatisticsquarterlyreport/august2018.

14 See Office for National Statistics, 'National Population Projections: 2016-based Statistical Bulletin', www.ons.gov.uk/peoplepopulation andcommunity/populationandmigration/populationprojections/bulletins/nationalpopulationprojections/2016basedstatisticalbulletin.

15 Ownership does, however, go against a broader trend, which is for citizens to own less, and rent or hire more. Cars are now no longer bought for cash, but leased. Customers buy the services, not the asset. This is being extended through a culture of apps and digital technologies. Airbnb, Uber and the like are examples. Suppliers who sell the services will quite soon own heating systems, and the boiler will belong to them and not the homeowner.

16 The average occupancy rate has fallen from 2.4 to 2.3 over the last decade. This trend may have quite a way further to run. See www.gov.uk/government/statistics/dwelling-stock-estimates-in-england-2017.

17 See www.gov.uk/government/topics/planning-and-building, and also Spiers, S., *How to Build Houses and Save the Countryside*, Policy Press, 2018.

18 See Office for National Statistics, 'Making Ends Meet: Are Households Living Beyond Their Means?', July 2016, https://www.ons.gov.uk/economy/nationalaccounts/uksectoraccounts/articles/makingendsmeetarehouseholdslivingbeyondtheirmeans/2018-07-26.

19 See Helm, D., *Natural Capital: Valuing the Planet*, London: Yale University Press, 2015.

20 'Big Yellow Taxi', written and composed by Joni Mitchell, 1970.

3: RESTORING RIVERS

1   See Bright et al., 'Measuring Natural Capital: Towards Accounts for the UK and a Basis for Improving Decision-making', *Oxford Review of Economic Policy*, 35(1), January 2019, pp. 88–108.

2   Silt also comes from the Severn Estuary, churned up by the tide. On

the Environment Agency's approach, see Environment Agency, 'Somerset Levels and Moors: Reducing the Risk of Flooding', August 2015, www.gov.uk/government/publications/somerset-levels-and-moors-reducing-the-risk-of-flooding/. See also Flooding & Coastal Erosion Risk Management Network, 'Why Dredging Our Rivers Shouldn't Be a First Response to Flooding', July 2015, http://fcerm.net/Thorne-Dredging.

3 See Palmer, R. C. and Smith, R. P., 'Soil Structural Degradation in SW England and its Impact on Surface Water Runoff Generation', *Soil Use and Management*, 2013, 29(4), pp. 567–75. See also Harrabin, R., 'Careless Farming Adding to Floods', 7 March 2014, www.bbc.co.uk/news/science-environment-26466653.

4 The rules on spreading slurry and other manures are very clear, but widely flouted. See 'Rules for farmers and land managers to prevent water pollution' at www.gov.uk/guidance/rules-for-farmers-and-land-managers-to-prevent-water-pollution.

5 See the Guidance Code, which requires a certificate of competence: 'Sheep dip: groundwater protection code', at www.gov.uk/guidance/sheep-dip-groundwater-protection-code.

6 The Coal Authority receives £30 million per annum from government to manage £4.3 billion of legacy cost liabilities, not paid for by the polluters at the time. See The Coal Authority, 'Annual Report and Accounts, 2017–18', HC 1168, https://assets.publishing.service.gov.uk/government/uploads/system/uploads/attachment_data/file/722535/Coal_Authority_annual_report_and_accounts_2017-2018_web.pdf.

7 See Barbier, E., *The Water Paradox: Overcoming the Global Crisis in Water Management*, Yale University Press, 2019.

8 Water companies are not the only abstractors and polluters. Other industrial practices are of concern to the natural environment; they can use lots of water and pollute the rivers. Power stations take a lot of water for cooling purposes, and its return to water courses can increase water temperatures. But in most cases the pollution is regulated (and usually prohibited) and hence it is a case of enforcement. Fortunately, coal mining and coal power stations are closing down. Like coal mining, the direction of travel in electricity generation is becoming more benign.

9 See the Pitt Review on some of the consequences of current flood defence measures. Pitt, M., 'Learning Lessons from the 2007 Floods', the Pitt Review, June 2008.

10 This is one of the headline proposals in Helm, D., 'The Cost of Energy Review', report prepared for the Department of Business, Energy and Industrial Strategy, October 2017.

11 These are on a pay-as-you-go basis, limiting longer-term funding options.

12 This is set out in Helm, D., 'Water Catchment Management, Abstraction and Flooding: The Case for a Catchment System Operator and Coordinated Competition', May 2015, www.dieter-helm.co.uk/natural-capital/water/water-catchment/.

13 For details, see www.wessexwater.co.uk/Nitrogen-offsetting-project/.

4: GREEN AGRICULTURE

1 The Hill Farming Act of 1946 was aimed at the expansion of pastoral farming and made available grants for improving upland farms. The government sustained a drive to use marginal land for stock farming into the 1950s, resulting in a substantial increase in the upland acreage used for farming into the 1950s. The National Archives, 'Farming and the Agriculture Acts: The Agriculture Act of 1947', www.nationalarchives.gov.uk/cabinetpapers/themes/farming-agriculture-acts.htm.

2 See Edmondson et al., 'Urban Cultivation in Allotments Maintains Soil Qualities Adversely Affected by Conventional Agriculture', *Journal of Applied Ecology*, 24 April 2014, https://besjournals.onlinelibrary.wiley.com/doi/abs/10.1111/1365-2664.12254.

3 See Helm, D., 'The Cost of Energy Review', report prepared for the Department of Business, Energy and Industrial Strategy, October 2017.

4 Committee on Climate Change, 'Net Zero: The UK's contribution to stopping global warming', May 2019.

5 The Haber-Bosch process was developed in the early twentieth century, and fixes nitrogen with hydrogen to produce ammonia, thereby facilitating the mass production of fertilisers.

6 For a summary, see House of Commons Library, 'The UK Bee Population', CDP 2017/0226, 10 November 2017.

7 The classic peregrine study is *The Peregrine Falcon* by Derek Ratcliffe (Poyser, 1980; expanded second edition 1993).

8 *Nature*, 'Flying Insects Are Disappearing from German Skies', 18 October 2017, www.nature.com/articles/d41586-017-04774-7.

9 For background, see the Woodlands.co.uk blog at www.woodlands.co.uk/blog/flora-and-fauna/hedgerow-loss/.

10 Farmers continue to press for derogations so they can cut hedges early. The pages of *Farmers Weekly* report the lobbying for these derogations. See, for example, 'Hedgecutting Ban: One Rule for Farmers, One for Councils?', 5 June 2017, www.fwi.co.uk/news/hedgecutting-ban-one-rule-for-farmers-one-for-councils.

11 See Lobley, M. and Winter, M., '"Born out of crisis": Assessing the Legacy of the Exmoor Moorland Management Agreements', *Rural History*, 20(2), 2009, pp. 229–47. Even the Punchbowl above Winsford was at one stage ploughed up.

12 One relationship whose discovery led to groundbreaking conservation has been extensively researched by Jeremy Thomas. For one twist in this story see Thomas, J. A. and Setele, J., 'Butterfly Mimics of Ants', *Nature*, 432, December 2004, pp. 283–4.

13 The 2018 'Bovine TB Strategy Review' stated that bovine TB is 'the most pressing animal health problem in the UK with increasing numbers of affected herds. Tackling bovine TB in England is estimated to cost the taxpayer around £70 million a year, with costs to farmers running to a further £50 million.' Godfray et al., 'Bovine TB Strategy Review', Department for Environment, Food and Rural Affairs, October 2018.

14 The Carbon Price Floor was introduced in 2013 to underpin the EU Emissions Trading Scheme. It creates a minimum carbon price to both encourage switching from high-carbon polluting technologies (such as coal-fired electricity generation) to less-polluting ones (such as gas and renewables), and to incentivise low-carbon investments.

15 See Lightfoot et al., *Farming Tomorrow: British Agriculture after Brexit*, Policy Exchange, 2017.

16 For an early attempt to systematically categorise and estimate the full external costs of UK agriculture, see Pretty et al., 'An Assessment of the Total External Costs of UK Agriculture', *Agricultural Systems*, 65, 2000, pp. 113–16.

17 For a description of some of the effects of mechanisation on farm labour and rural villages, see Newby, H., *Green & Pleasant Land? Social Change in Rural England*, Hutchinson & Co., 1979.

18 See the classic history of our attitude to nature and the countryside: Thomas, K., *Man and the Natural World: Changing Attitudes in England 1500–1800*, London: Penguin Books, 1984.

19 The classic statement of Gilpin's thesis was set out in his 'Three

Essays: On Picturesque Beauty, on Picturesque Travel, and on Sketching Landscapes: To which is Added a Poem on Landscape Painting', 1794. See www.royalcollection.org.uk/collection/1151698/three-essays-on-picturesque-beauty-on-picturesque-travel-and-on-sketching.

20 See Buzard, J., 'The Grand Tour and After (1660–1840)' in Hulme, P. and Youngs, T. (eds), *The Cambridge Companion to Travel Writing*, Cambridge: Cambridge University Press, 2001.

21 See Reynolds, F., *The Fight for Beauty: Our Path to a Better Future*, Oneworld Publications, 2016.

22 For a historical overview, see Linklater, A., *Owning the Earth: The Transforming History of Land Ownership*, London: Bloomsbury, 2014.

23 The 25 Year Environment Plan has a target of doubling farm productivity. What it should say – and doesn't – is 'while maintaining and enhancing natural capital'. It is *natural* productivity that matters.

24 The Californian almond industry takes around half of all American honey bees. See Traynor, J., 'A History of Almond Pollination in California', *Bee World*, 94(3), 11 August 2017, pp. 69–79.

25 GM and gene editing are not the same thing, but both can have an effect on resistance.

26 At a March 2015 conference on Climate Smart Agriculture, the French agriculture minister, Stéphane Le Foll, proposed the ambitious target of increasing French soil carbon content by 0.4 per cent year on year ('4 pour mille'). This 4-per-1,000 target has caught on. See Baveye et al., 'The "4 per 1000" Initiative: A Credibility Issue for the Soil Science Community?', *Geoderma*, 309, June 2017.

27 For a guide to cross-compliance rules, see DEFRA's 2017 report, 'The Guide to Cross Compliance in England 2017', https://assets.publishing.service.gov.uk/government/uploads/system/uploads/attachment_data/file/579836/Cross_Compliance_2017_rules_FINAL.pdf.

28 Simberloff, D. S. and Wilson, E. O., 'Experimental Zoogeography of Islands: The Colonization of Empty Islands, *Ecology*, 50(2), 1969, pp. 278–96. See also Lawton, J., 'Making Space for Nature: A Review of England's Wildlife Sites and Ecological Network', prepared for Department for Environment, Food and Rural Affairs, September 2010.

29 www.spacefornature.net/monitoring.

30 The Wildlife Trusts' 'Living Landscape' proposals are a good example.

31 See Macfarlane, R., *The Old Ways: A Journey on Foot*, London: Penguin, 2012.

32 'Use and Delight' is a chapter in T. C. Smout's excellent book *Nature Contested*. Smout, T. C., *Nature Contested: Environmental History in Scotland and Northern England Since 1600*, Edinburgh: Edinburgh University Press Ltd, 2000.

33 www.brown-co.com/articles/new-nfu-president-minette-batters-tells-lincolnshires-farmers-we-must-speak-with-one-voice-on-brexit-in-speech-to-annual-farming-conference.

34 On carbon border adjustments see Helm et al., 'Trade, Climate Change, and the Political Game Theory of Border Carbon Adjustments', *Oxford Review of Economic Policy*, 28(2), July 2012.

5: THE UPLANDS

1 Around only 5 per cent is left of the original 1.5 million hectares. See Wilson, S. M., *The Native Woodlands of Scotland: Ecology, Conservation and Management*, Edinburgh: Edinburgh University Press, 2015.

2 The Netherlands example at Oostvaardersplassen has been controversial. See https://truenaturefoundation.org/ecological-restoration/future-oostvaardersplassen-ecological-corridors-predation/. For Knepp, see https://knepp.co.uk/.

3 www.alladale.com/tag/wolves.

4 For a definition and chilling account of the accident and its aftermath, see Plokhy, S., *Chernobyl: History of a Tragedy*, Allen Lane, 2018.

5 Rebanks, J., *The Shepherd's Life: A Tale of the Lake District*, Allen Lane, 2015.

6 See also Stewart, R., *The Marches*, London: Jonathan Cape, 2016.

7 Rackham, O., *The History of the Countryside*, J.M. Dent, 1986.

8 For a summary, see John Muir Trust, 'Too Many Deer and Too Few Trees', 23 December 2015, www.johnmuirtrust.org/about/resources/761-too-many-deer-and-too-few-trees.

9 There is much controversy over the cause of the moorland fires in the hot dry summer of 2018, and whether the game bird management techniques contributed to their severity.

10 See sections 6 and 7 on deer and grouse management, respectively, in Hughes et al., 'Land Stewardship: A Blueprint for Government Policy', Edinburgh, Scottish Wildlife Trust, 2017.

11 See Avery, M., *Inglorious Conflict in the Uplands*, London: Bloomsbury, 2015.

12 In 2018, more tagged hen harriers (and their tags) again disappeared over large grouse-shooting estates. For a detailed analysis, see the RSPB's 'Birdcrime Report' at www.rspb.org.uk/birds-and-wildlife/advice/wildlife-and-the-law/wild-bird-crime/the-birdcrime-report/?utm_source=short_url&utm_campaign=birdcrime.

13 Ibid.

14 The precise number is not known because game shoots will not reveal them.

15 The overall economic value (before externalities) of shooting in the UK may be of the order of £2 billion, with almost half a million people participating. This is only partially subsidised indirectly through the CAP, and stands in comparison to the £9 billion total output of UK farming. Not all of this of course is in the uplands.

16 See Worster, D., *A Passion for Nature: The Life of John Muir*, Oxford: Oxford University Press, 2008.

17 The relevant papers are available at http://discovery.nationalarchives.gov.uk/details/r/C8788.

18 For a leading example, see Deane, R. and Walker, A., 'Towards a Register of Exmoor's Nature Capital: Report prepared for the Exmoor Society', June 2018.

19 Glover, J., 'Landscapes Review: Final Report', September 2019, https://assets.publishing.service.gov.uk/government/uploads/system/uploads/attachment_data/file/833726/landscapes-review-final-report.pdf

20 Details are provided at www.nationalparks.gov.uk/students/ourchallenges/tourism.

21 On the opposition to the proposal, see, for example, www.friendsofthelakedistrict.org.uk/News/zip-wire-development-across-thirlmere-threatens-the-lake-district.

22 An example of bracken control for a specific conservation purpose is the attempt to maintain and enhance the high brown fritillary butterfly population at Heddon's Mouth in Exmoor. www.nationaltrust.org.uk/heddon-valley/features/butterfly-conservation-in-heddon-valley.

23 From Winsford Hill in Exmoor there is a fabulous 360° view over the moors, blighted by a large wind farm near South Molton. Note also the disputes over the Flow Country in Sutherland, first for plantations and then for wind farm developments.

24 Peterken, G., *Meadows*, London: Bloomsbury, 2013. See in particular chapter 5.

6: THE COASTS

1 See Natural England, 'Monitor of Engagement with the Natural Environment: The National Survey on People and the Natural Environment – Visits to Coastal England', NECR226, 24 October 2016.

2 Ten series of *Coast* were broadcast between 2005 and 2015, with some episodes attracting more than 5 million viewers.

3 A classic is John Fowles's *The French Lieutenant's Woman* (Jonathan Cape, 1969), set at the Cobb in Lyme Regis.

4 It is only now that beaches are being comprehensively surveyed. Lots of local groups are taking responsibility, such as Plastic Free Falmouth.

5 https://mcsuk.org/press/scrapbook_map_update.

6 http://ec.europa.eu/environment/water/water-bathing/summary.html.

7 Millions watched the BBC's *Autumnwatch* programme broadcast from the reserve. The *Springwatch* and *Autumnwatch* programmes have gained between 1 million and almost 3 million viewers per episode, depending on the day broadcast.

8 www.wwt.org.uk/wetland-centres/steart-marshes/about/.

9 See Chatters, C., *Saltmarsh*, London: Bloomsbury, 2017. For an artist's take, see Lichtenstein, R. *Estuary: Out from London to the Sea*, Penguin, 2016.

10 Dumping dredged muds and silts without consideration of the wider ecological consequences is a classic example of 'out of sight, out of mind'.

11 Despite a very poor and partial review of the project by the former energy minister, Charles Hendry, the government wisely rejected the project's request for a high guaranteed price in 2018.

12 The invasive Pacific oysters complicate the options.

13 Flushing tanks is technically illegal, but enforcement is minimal.

14 See House of Commons Environmental Audit Committee, 'Environmental Impact of Microplastics', HC 179, July 2016.

15 Hardin, G., 'The Tragedy of the Commons', *Science*, 162, 1968, pp. 1243–8. For a discussion see Helm, D., *Natural Capital: Valuing the Planet*, London: Yale University Press, 2015.

16 See Kurlansky, M., *Cod: A Biography of the Fish that Changed the World*, Vintage Publishing, 1999.

17 There have been recent signs of the gradual return of the bluefin tuna. See Hortin et al. 'Bluefin Tuna Off Britain and Ireland: Return of the Giant Tunny?', *British Wildlife*, 402, August 2018.

18 Now referred to as mariculture. For a number of references and sources, see www.sciencedirect.com/topics/agricultural-and-biological-sciences/mariculture.

19 For a flavour of the controversy, see Blue Planet Society, 'Where Have all the Sandeels Gone?', 24 June 2009, http://blueplanetsociety. org/2009/06/where-have-all-sandeels-gone/; and *The Sunday Times*, 'Puffins Starve as Danes Grab UK Sand Eels', 22 July 2018, www.thetimes.co.uk/article/puffins-starve-as-danes-grab-uk-sand-eels-srwrfgdrs.

20 The exceptions include the oil and gas industrial complexes in the Orkneys and Shetland.

21 Islands in theory lend themselves to isolation, and the smaller the land area, the lower the biodiversity. Yet Britain's islands are the site of mobile populations (seabirds) and the distances from the mainland are limited, so Britain's islands have the advantages with few of the downsides.

22 For more information on the economics of the UK fishing industry, see Ares et al., 'The UK Fishing Industry', CDP 2017/0256, House of Commons Library, 6 December 2017.

23 Both too are dangerous activities with high health and safety risks, and both have among the highest mortality rates compared with other employments.

24 See various papers by Callum Roberts, including Roberts et al., 'Effects of Marine Reserves on Adjacent Fisheries', *Science*, 294(5548), 2001, pp. 1920–3.

25 See Institute for Government, 'Common Fisheries Policy', www. instituteforgovernment.org.uk/explainers/common-fisheries-policy. For the latest round of quota-setting see Marine Manage-

ment Organisation, 'How Fish Quotas for 2018 are Set', 5 December 2017, https://marinedevelopments.blog.gov.uk/2017/12/05/december-council-eu-fish-quotas-cfp-uk/.

26 On discards see Hirst, D., 'Ending Fish Discards: Implementing the Fish-landing Obligation of the Common Fisheries Policy (CFP)', Annex to CBP-05957, House of Commons Library, 17 August 2015.

27 On Marine Protected Area policies and history, see www.ukmpas.org/index.php. See also The Wildlife Trusts, 'The Way Back to the Living Seas', www.wildlifetrusts.org/sites/default/files/2018-07/the_way_back_to_living_seas_the_wildlife_trusts.pdf.

28 For a discussion, see Salmon & Trout Conservation Scotland, 'BBC's "Fish Farms of the Future" – Our Comments on Closed Containment', www.salmon-trout.org/2017/10/27/bbc-fish-farms-of-the-future-our-comments/.

29 See details of the recent Scottish government inquiry at www.parliament.scot/parliamentarybusiness/CurrentCommittees/107588.aspx.

30 See www.wildlifetrusts.org/past-campaigns/blue-belt; and Natural England, 'A Blue Belt in Marine Protection for Seabirds', 7 September 2017, https://naturalengland.blog.gov.uk/2017/09/07/a-blue-belt-in-marine-protection-for-seabirds/.

31 National Trust, 'Mapping Our Shores: 50 Years of Land Use Change at the Coast', 2015.

32 See Stace, C. A. and Crawley, M. J., Alien Plants, London: HarperCollins, 2015.

33 http://www.nonnativespecies.org/index.cfm?sectionid=55

34 The UK government published a new strategy on biosecurity in 2018 in its policy paper, 'Biological Security Strategy: How We are Protecting the UK and its Interests from Significant Biological Risks', The Home Office, 30 July 2018.

7: NATURE IN THE TOWNS AND CITIES

1 See National Audit Office, 'Air Quality', Environmental Audit Committee, Environment, Food and Rural Affairs Committee, Health Committee and Transport Committee, HC 529, 16 November 2017.

2 For details on London's green spaces, see www.gigl.org.uk/keyfigures/.

3 For an engaging guide, see Elborough, T., *A Walk in the Park: The Life and Times of a People's Institution*, London: Jonathan Cape, 2016.

4 House of Commons Communities and Local Government Committee, 'Public Parks: Seventh Report of Session 2016–17', 30 January 2017.

5 On the controversy, see BBC, 'Sheffield tree-felling: Gove will "do anything" to end row', 23 March 2018, www.bbc.co.uk/news/uk-england-south-yorkshire-43492887.

6 Vollaard et al., *Making Urban Nature*, nai010, 2017; Dunnett, N. and Kingsbury, N., *Planting Green Roofs and Living Walls*, Timber Press, 2008; and Gunnell *et al.* (2013), *Designing for Biodiversity: A Technical Guide for New and Existing Buildings*, 2nd edn., RIBA Publishing, 2013.

7 London and Newcastle continued to rely on rivers (and eventually the Kielder Dam would be built for the north-east – just as its industrial water demands begun to fall sharply).

8 See Schilthuizen, M., *Darwin Comes to Town: How the Urban Jungle Drives Evolution*, London: Quercus, 2018.

9 Swifts remain over the skies of many European cities. They can be seen (and heard as the small groups patrol the skies with their acrobatics) all across Europe. But less so in London or the other cities here in Britain. Swifts very rarely nest in postwar buildings. The London skyline has become a desert for them.

10 Redstarts were common on bombsites after the war – another example of a bird well adapted to urban locations. It needed nesting sites – abundant in bombsites – and it needed insects to feed on. Imagine creating new urban stone walls and having an insect-rich flower meadow around and about. The point here is that, with a little forethought and planning, the urban potential for nature could be radically increased, without much cost and with lots of benefits.

11 One study found that viewing actual plant foliage significantly increased oxyhaemoglobin concentrations in the prefrontal cortex, and that even projected images of foliage had positive effects. Igarashi et al., 'Effect of Stimulation by Foliage Plant Display Images on Prefrontal Cortex Activity: A Comparison with Stimulation Using Actual Foliage Plants', *Journal of Neuroimaging*, 25(1), 2014, pp. 127–30.

12 See for a survey Fong et al., 'A Review of Epidemiological Studies on Greenness and Health: Updated Literature Review through 2017', Current Environmental Health Report 5, 2018, pp. 77–87.

13 In terms of environmental benefits, European and Mediterranean garden plants are much better than exotics. See Stace, C. A. and Crawley, M. J., *Alien Plants*, London: HarperCollins, 2015.

14 On Kingsbrook and the RSPB contribution, see www.rspb.org.uk/our-work/conservation/projects/kingsbrook-housing/.

15 His poem 'Slough' (1937) famously bemoans 'the mess they call a town'.

16 See again Shaun Spiers's excellent exposition of postwar planning ambitions. Spiers, S., *How to Build Houses and Save the Countryside*, Policy Press, 2018.

17 Liz Truss, as Chief Secretary to the Treasury, for example, stated that it is 'either building on the Green Belt or Corbyn'. Chief Secretary to the Treasury Liz Truss speech to the London School of Economics, 'Liberation nation: how to free the economy and reinvent the state', 26 June 2018.

18 See a description of the Welsh example in Bateman et al., *Applied Environmental Economics: A GIS Approach to Cost–Benefit Analysis*, Cambridge: Cambridge University Press, 2003. For a more recent application across Britain, see Bateman et al., 'Bringing Ecosystem Services into Economic Decision making: Land Use in the UK', *Science*, 341(6141), 2013, pp. 45–50.

19 It was the 1961 Land Compensation Act that did the damage. It required local authorities to pay a price that assumed the land had planning permission, rather than the agricultural market value.

20 On Section 106 requirements see www.local.gov.uk/pas/pas-topics/infrastructure/s106-obligations-overview.

21 Professor Kathy Willis has promoted the idea of a natural environmental census, and it is one that the NCC has taken up.

8: PUBLIC GOODS

1 For a history of landownership and insight into how recent the private assets of the great global commons are, see Linklater, A., *Owning the Earth: The Transforming History of Land Ownership*, London: Bloomsbury, 2014.

2 The classic exposition on the theory of public goods is Samuelson, P. A., 'The Pure Theory of Public Expenditure', *Review of Economics and Statistics*, 36(4), 1954, pp. 387–9.

3 On clubs, see Buchanan, J. M., 'An Economic Theory of Clubs', *Economica*, 32(125), February 1965, pp. 1–14. For an optimistic take on how local communities can overcome public goods problems, see Ostrom et al., 'Covenants with and without a Sword: Self-Governance is Possible', *American Political Science Review*, 86(2), June 1992, pp. 404–17.

4 The privatisation proposals led to a review. See Department for Environment, Food and Rural Affairs, 'Independent Panel on Forestry: Final Report', July 2012. See also Bennett, O. and Hirst, D., 'The Forestry Commission and the Sale of Public Forests in England', House of Commons Library Standard Note: SN/SC/5734, 28 November 2014.

5 https://hansard.parliament.uk/commons/2018-03-14/debates/5BAA7D11-174C-4670-BBFA-37DD3FA1B521/Engagements

6 www.gov.uk/government/speeches/a-brighter-future-for-farming

7 On the integrated systems, see Barbier, E., *Capitalizing on Nature: Ecosystems as Natural Assets*, Cambridge: Cambridge University Press, 2011.

8 See, for example, Exmoor National Park's 'Exmoor's Ambition' at www.exmoor-nationalpark.gov.uk/living-and-working/info-for-farmers-and-land-managers/exmoor-ambition.

9 https://canalrivertrust.org.uk/.

9: PAYING FOR POLLUTION

1 It is sometimes argued that it is not important who pays, the polluter or the polluted, as long as they bargain. This is captured in the Coase theorem. It neglects the impact on output: if the polluter is paid not to pollute, output and therefore the level of pollution will be too high. See Baumol, W. J. and Oates, W. E., *The Theory of Environmental Policy*, 2nd edn., Cambridge: Cambridge University Press, 1988.

2 See the account of the Knepp experiment in Tree, I., *Wilding: The Return of Nature to a British Farm*, London: Picador, 2018.

3 See Review on Antimicrobial Resistance, 'Tackling Drug-resistant

Infections Globally: Final Report and Recommendations', chaired by Jim O'Neill, May 2016.

4 Methicillin-resistant staphylococcus aureus: a group of bacteria responsible for several infections in humans that are very difficult to treat.

5 See Stephen Smith's excellent *Taxation: A Very Short Introduction*, Oxford: Oxford University Press, 2015.

6 The Voluntary Initiative that has been adopted (voluntarily) instead does not charge for the pollution, and there is a world of difference between 'best practice' in the use of pesticides and reducing inputs in response to a higher price, which includes the pollution costs. Without a price for the pollution, applications will remain excessive, leaving the polluted to pay for the resulting harm.

7 For a summary and assessment, see Elliott, T., 'Landfill Tax in the United Kingdom', Eunomia and Institute for European Environmental Policy, https://ieep.eu/uploads/articles/attachments/e48ad1c2-dfe4-42a9-b51c-8fa8f6c30b1e/UK%20Landfill%20Tax%20final.pdf?v=63680923242.

8 Helm, D. 'The Cost of Energy Review', report prepared for the Department of Business, Energy and Industrial Strategy, 2017.

9 Case, P., 'Dairy Farm Hit with £14,000 Penalty for Slurry Pollution', *Farmers Weekly,* 21 September, https://www.fwi.co.uk/news/environment/dairy-farm-hit-with-14000-penalty-for-slurry-pollution.

10 See Helm, D., *Natural Capital: Valuing the Planet*, pp. 124–6, and Bryant, B., *Twyford Down: Roads, Campaigning and Environmental Law*, London: Routledge, 1995.

11 See, for example, Savills, 'GB Agricultural Land: Spotlight 2018', 2018, which shows that this followed the EU membership referendum.   https://pdf.euro.savills.co.uk/uk/rural---other/gb-agricultural-land-2018.pdf.

10: NATURAL CAPITAL MARKETS, AUCTIONS AND THE NET ZERO EXAMPLE

1 Committee on Climate Change, 'Net Zero: The UK's contribution to stopping global warming', May 2019.

2 See Helm, D., Hepburn, C. and Ruta, G., 'Trade, Climate Change, and the Political Game Theory of Border Carbon Adjustments', *Oxford Review of Economic Policy*, 28(2), July 2012, pp. 368–94.

3   www.shell.com/media/news-and-media-releases/2019/shell-in-vests-in-nature-to-tackle-co2-emissions.html

4   For a more detailed discussion about discounting, see chapter 3 of Helm, D., *The Carbon Crunch: How We're Getting Climate Change Wrong – And How to Fix it*, Revised and Updated. London: Yale University Press, 2015.

11: A NATURE FUND

1   On tax design see the Mirrlees Review: Institute for Fiscal Studies, 'Reforming the Tax System for the 21st Century: The Mirrlees Review', www.ifs.org.uk/publications/mirrleesreview.

2   The Carbon Price Floor raises over £1 billion. See House of Commons Library, 'Carbon Price Floor (CPF) and the Price Support Mechanism', Briefing Paper, 8 January 2018, https://researchbriefings.parliament.uk/ResearchBriefing/Summary/SN05927.

3   It is small compared with Stamp Duty. There is an opportunity to reduce Stamp Duty and use some of the reduction for the compensation payments, therefore leaving the total cost constant to the house buyer (but not to the developer).

4   Even local taxation is determined to a considerable extent by the Treasury.

5   In *Burn Out* I explain how the oil price is likely to fall as decarbonisation takes effect. Helm, D., *Burn Out: The Endgame for Fossil Fuels*, London: Yale University Press, 2017.

6   www.nbim.no/.

7   Stern, N., 'The Economics of Climate Change: The Stern Review', HM Treasury, Cambridge: Cambridge University Press, January 2007. For my discussion of the objections to Stern's approach to discounting, see Helm, D., *The Carbon Crunch: How We're Getting Climate Change Wrong – And How to Fix it*, Revised and Updated, London: Yale University Press, 2015.

8   See Williams, B., *Moral Luck*, Cambridge: Cambridge University Press, 1981.

9   Two versions of aggregate natural capital rules are set out in my book *Natural Capital*. Helm, D., *Natural Capital: Valuing the Planet*, London: Yale University Press, 2015, p. 64.

10 Department for Environment, Food and Rural Affairs, 'Health and

Harmony: The Future for Food, Farming and the Environment in a Green Brexit', Consultation, February 2018.

11 The chancellor at the time, George Osborne, called for a review of the Fourth Carbon Budget but ultimately had to give way.

12 See Office for National Statistics at www.ons.gov.uk/economy/ nationalaccounts/uksectoraccounts/methodologies/naturalcapital.

13 A non-oil-and-gas example is the mining of phosphorus on the edge of the North Yorkshire National Park. These economic rents for depletion should be in addition to the net environmental gain compensation payments.

14 https://thelandtrust.org.uk/.

15 Prior to the CAP, the NFU directly negotiated food prices with government.

12: THE PLAN

1 In the song 'The Twelve Days of Christmas' there may not be even two turtle doves left, whatever we do here, if the guns of Malta carry on their spring slaughters.

2 The list of principles in the Environmental Audit Committee's report on the 25 Year Environment Plan can be seen at www. parliament.uk/business/committees/committees-a-z/commons-select/environmental-audit-committee/news-parliament-2017/ governments-25-year-plan-report-publication-17-19/. House of Commons Environmental Audit Committee, 'The Government's 25 Year Plan for the Environment: Eighth Report of Session 2017–19', 24 July 2018.

3 HM Treasury, 'The Green Book: Central Government Guidance on Appraisal and Evaluation', 2018, https://assets.publishing.service. gov.uk/government/uploads/system/uploads/attachment_data/file/ 685903/The_Green_Book.pdf.

4 Peach et al., 'Depleted Suburban House Sparrow *Passer domesticus* Population Not Limited by Food Availability', *Urban Ecosyst*, 11 July 2018, https://link.springer.com/article/10.1007%2Fs11252-018-0784-4.

5 This is arguably not taken fully into account in Fiona Reynolds's book, *The Fight for Beauty*. Reynolds, F., *The Fight for Beauty: Our Path to a Better Future*, Oneworld Publications, 2016.

6 It is tempting for people to put faith in particular politicians. For example, Michael Gove's speech setting out his ambitions for the 25 Year Environment Plan is one that many environmentalists can cheer. But then look at his predecessors and think about his successors. One predecessor recently criticised the 'hot air' at DEFRA. See 'The Unfrozen Moment – Delivering a Green Brexit', 21 July 2017, www.gov.uk/government/speeches/the-unfrozen-moment-delivering-a-green-brexit.

7 Bright et al., 'Measuring Natural Capital: Towards Accounts for the UK and a Basis for Improving Decision-making', *Oxford Review of Economic Policy*, 35(1), January 2019, pp. 88–108.

8 Helm, D. R., 'Environmental Regulation: The Environment Agency Proposal', *Fiscal Studies*, 13(2), 1992, pp. 66–83.

9 The Committee on Climate Change tried to get in on the 25 Year Environment Plan act, bidding for more resources and making recommendations for most of the 10 goals. The NCC responded forcefully to this attempt to turn the plan into an adjunct of climate change. See Committee on Climate Change, 'Letter to Michael Gove: Environmental Principles and Governance after EU Exit Consultation', 24 July 2018, www.theccc.org.uk/publication/letter-to-michael-gove-environmental-principles-and-governance-after-eu-exit-consultation/.

10 The government published its consultation document, and the prime minister then indicated that there will be a comprehensive Environment Bill to incorporate this.

CONCLUSIONS: SECURING THE PRIZE

1 Adams, W. M., *Future Nature: A Vision for Conservation*, Revised Edition, Abingdon: Earthscan, 2003; Marren, P., *Nature Conservation*, London: HarperCollins, 2002.

2 Cocker, M., *Our Place: Can We Save Britain's Wildlife Before it is Too Late?*, London: Jonathan Cape 2018.

BIBLIOGRAPHY

Adams, W. M., *Future Nature: A Vision for Conservation*, Revised Edition. Abingdon: Earthscan, 2003

Ares, E., Rhodes, C. and Ward, M., 'The UK Fishing Industry', CDP 2017/0256, House of Commons Library, 6 December 2017

Avery, M., *Inglorious Conflict in the Uplands*. London: Bloomsbury, 2015

Barbier, E. *The Water Paradox: Overcoming the Global Crisis in Water Management*. London: Yale University Press, 2019

Barbier, E., *Capitalizing on Nature: Ecosystems as Natural Assets*. Cambridge: Cambridge University Press, 2011

Bateman, I. J., Harwood, A., Mace, G. M., Watson, R., Abson, D. J., Andrews, B., Binner, A., Crowe, A., Day, B. H., Dugdale, S., Fezzi, C., Foden, J., Haines-Young, R., Hulme, M., Kontoleon, A., Lovett, A. A., Munday, P., Pascual, U., Paterson, J., Perino, G., Sen, A., Siriwardena, G., van Soest D. and Termansen, M., 'Bringing Ecosystem Services into Economic Decision Making: Land Use in the UK', *Science*, 341(6141), 5 July 2013, pp. 45–50

Bateman, I. J., Lovett, A. A. and Brainard, J. S., *Applied Environmental Economics: A GIS Approach to Cost–Benefit Analysis*. Cambridge: Cambridge University Press, 2003

Bates, H. E., *The Darling Buds of May*. Michael Joseph, 1958

Baumol, W. J. and Oates, W. E., *The Theory of Environmental Policy*, 2nd edn. Cambridge: Cambridge University Press, 1988

Baveye, P., Berthelin, J., Tessier, D. and Lemaire, G., 'The "4 per 1000" Initiative: A Credibility Issue for the Soil Science Community?', *Geoderma*, 309, June 2017

BBC, 'Sheffield tree-felling: Gove will "do anything" to end row', 23 March 2018, www.bbc.co.uk/news/uk-england-south-yorkshire-43492887

Bennett, O. and Hirst, D., 'The Forestry Commission and the Sale of Public Forests in England', House of Commons Library Standard Note: SN/SC/5734, 28 November 2014

Blue Planet Society, 'Where Have all the Sandeels Gone?', 24 June 2009, http://blueplanetsociety.org/2009/06/where-have-all-sandeels-gone/

Bright, G., Connors, E. and Grice, G., 'Measuring Natural Capital: Towards Accounts for the UK and a Basis for Improving Decision-making', *Oxford Review of Economic Policy*, forthcoming 2019

Brown, A. G., Lespez, L., Sear, D. A., Macaire, J-J., Houben, P., Klimek, K., Brazier, R. E., Van Oost, K. and Pears. B., 'Natural vs Anthropogenic Streams in Europe: History, Ecology and Implications for Restoration, River-rewilding and Riverine Ecosystem Services', *Earth-Science Reviews*, 180, May 2018, pp. 185–205

Bryant, B., *Twyford Down: Roads, Campaigning and Environmental Law*. London: Routledge, 1995

Buchanan, J. M., 'An Economic Theory of Clubs', *Economica*, 32(125), February 1965, pp. 1–14

Buzard, J., 'The Grand Tour and After (1660–1840)' in Hulme, P. and Youngs, T. (eds), *The Cambridge Companion to Travel Writing*. Cambridge: Cambridge University Press, 2001

Carson, R., *Silent Spring*. Boston: Houghton Mifflin, 1962

Case, P., 'Dairy Farm Hit with £14,000 Penalty for Slurry Pollution', *Farmers Weekly*, 21 September 2018, www.fwi.co.uk/news/environment/dairy-farm-hit-with-14000-penalty-for-slurry-pollution

Case, P., 'Hedgecutting Ban: One Rule for Farmers, One for Councils?', *Farmers Weekly*, 5 June 2017, www.fwi.co.uk/

news/hedgecutting-ban-one-rule-for-farmers-one-for-councils

Chatters, C., *Saltmarsh*. London: Bloomsbury, 2017

Cocker, M., *Our Place: Can We Save Britain's Wildlife Before it is Too Late?* London: Jonathan Cape, 2018

Committee on Climate Change, 'Net Zero: The UK's contribution to stopping global warming', May 2019

Committee on Climate Change, 'Letter to Michael Gove: Environmental Principles and Governance after EU Exit Consultation', 24 July 2018, www.theccc.org.uk/publication/letter-to-michael-gove-environmental-principles-and-governance-after-eu-exit-consultation/

Day, Wentworth, J., *Poison on the Land: The War on Wild Life, and Some Remedies*. London: Eyre & Spottiswoode, 1957

Day, Wentworth, J., *The Modern Fowler: With a Guide to Some Principal Coastal Wildfowling Resorts of Today*. Longman, Green & Co., 1934

Deane, R. and Walker, A., 'Towards a Register of Exmoor's Nature Capital: Report prepared for the Exmoor Society', June 2018

Department for Environment, Food and Rural Affairs, 'Health and Harmony: The Future for Food, Farming and the Environment in a Green Brexit', Consultation, February 2018

Department for Environment, Food and Rural Affairs, 'A Green Future: Our 25 Year Plan to Improve the Environment', January 2018

Department for Environment, Food and Rural Affairs, 'The Guide to Cross Compliance in England 2017', 2017, https://assets.publishing.service.gov.uk/government/uploads/system/uploads/attachment_data/file/579836/Cross_Compliance_2017_rules_FINAL.pdf

Department for Environment, Food and Rural Affairs, 'Independent Panel on Forestry: Final Report', July 2012

Department for Environment, Food and Rural Affairs, 'The Natural Choice: Securing the Value of Nature', White Paper, June 2011

Dunnett, N. and Kingsbury, N., *Planting Green Roofs and Living Walls*. Timber Press, 2008

Edmondson, J. L., Leake, J. R., Davies, Z. G. and Gaston, K. J., 'Urban Cultivation in Allotments Maintains Soil Qualities Adversely Affected by Conventional Agriculture', *Journal of Applied Ecology*, 24 April 2014, https://besjournals.onlinelibrary.wiley.com/doi/abs/10.1111/1365-2664.12254

Edwards, T., Hughes, J., Keegan, M., Pike, J. and Wilson, B., 'Land Stewardship: A Blueprint for Government Policy'. Edinburgh Scottish Wildlife Trust, 2017

Elborough, T., *A Walk in the Park: The Life and Times of a People's Institution*. London: Jonathan Cape, 2016

Elliott, T., 'Landfill Tax in the United Kingdom', Eunomia and Institute for European Environmental Policy, https://ieep.eu/uploads/articles/attachments/e48ad1c2-dfe4-42a9-b51c-8fa8f6c30b1e/UK%20Landfill%20Tax%20final.pdf?v=63680923242

Environment Agency, 'The State of the Environment: Water Quality', February 2018, https://assets.publishing.service.gov.uk/government/uploads/system/uploads/attachment_data/file/709493/State_of_the_environment_water_quality_report.pdf

Environment Agency, 'Somerset Levels and Moors: Reducing the Risk of Flooding', August 2015, www.gov.uk/government/publications/somerset-levels-and-moors-reducing-the-risk-of-flooding/somerset-levels-and-moors-reducing-the-risk-of-flooding

Flooding & Coastal Erosion Risk Management Network, 'Why Dredging Our Rivers Shouldn't Be a First Response to Flooding', July 2015, http://fcerm.net/Thorne-Dredging

Fong, K., Hart, J. and James, P., 'A Review of Epidemiological

Studies on Greenness and Health: Updated Literature Review through 2017', Current Environmental Health Report 5, 2018, pp. 77–87

Fowles, J., *The French Lieutenant's Woman*. London: Jonathan Cape, 1969

Gilpin, W., 'Three Essays: On Picturesque Beauty, on Picturesque Travel, and on Sketching Landscapes: To which is Added a Poem on Landscape Painting', 1794, www.royalcollection.org.uk/collection/1151698/three-essays-on-picturesque-beauty-on-picturesque-travel-and-on-sketching

Glover, J., 'Landscapes Review: Final Report', September 2019, https://assets.publishing.service.gov.uk/government/uploads/system/uploads/attachment_data/file/833726/landscapes-review-final-report.pdf

Godfray, C., Donnelly, C., Hewinson, G., Winter, M. and Wood, J., 'Bovine TB Strategy Review', Department for Environment, Food and Rural Affairs, October 2018

Goulson, D., *Bee Quest*. London: Vintage, 2017

Gunnell, K., Murphy, B. and Williams, C., *Designing for Biodiversity: A Technical Guide for New and Existing Buildings*, 2nd edn. RIBA Publishing, 2013

Harrabin, R., 'Careless Farming Adding to Floods', 7 March 2014, https://www.bbc.co.uk/news/science-environment-26466653

Hayhow, D. B., Burns, F., Eaton, M. A., Al Fulaij, N., August, T. A., Babey, L., Bacon, L., Bingham, C., Boswell, J., Boughey, K. L., Brereton, T., Brookman, E., Brooks, D. R., Bullock, D. J., Burke, O., Collis, M., Corbet, L., Cornish, N., De Massimi, S., Densham, J., Dunn, E., Elliott, S., Gent, T., Godber, J., Hamilton, S., Havery, S., Hawkins, S., Henney, J., Holmes, K., Hutchinson, N., Isaac, N. J. B., Johns, D., Macadam, C. R., Mathews, F., Nicolet, P., Noble, D. G., Outhwaite, C. L., Powney, G. D., Richardson, P., Roy, D. B., Sims, D., Smart, S.,

Stevenson, K., Stroud, R. A., Walker, K. J., Webb, J. R., Webb, T. J., Wynde, R. and Gregory, R. D., 'State of Nature 2016', The State of Nature Partnership, updated 2018

Helm, D., 'The Cost of Energy Review', report prepared for the Department of Business, Energy and Industrial Strategy, October 2017

Helm, D., *Burn Out: The Endgame for Fossil Fuels*. London: Yale University Press, 2017

Helm, D., *Natural Capital: Valuing the Planet*. London: Yale University Press, 2015

Helm, D., *The Carbon Crunch: How We're Getting Climate Change Wrong – And How to Fix it*, Revised and Updated. London: Yale University Press, 2015

Helm, D., 'Water Catchment Management, Abstraction and Flooding: The Case for a Catchment System Operator and Coordinated Competition', May 2015, www.dieterhelm.co.uk/natural-capital/water/water-catchment/

Helm, D. R., 'Environmental Regulation: The Environment Agency Proposal', *Fiscal Studies*, 13(2), 1992, pp. 66–83

Helm, D., Hepburn, C. and Ruta, G., 'Trade, Climate Change, and the Political Game Theory of Border Carbon Adjustments', *Oxford Review of Economic Policy*, 28(2), July 2012

Hirst, D., 'Ending Fish Discards: Implementing the Fish-landing Obligation of the Common Fisheries Policy (CFP)', Annex to CBP-05957, House of Commons Library, 17 August 2015

HM Government, 'Biological Security Strategy: How We are Protecting the UK and its Interests from Significant Biological Risks', The Home Office, 30 July 2018

HM Treasury, 'The Green Book: Central Government Guidance on Appraisal and Evaluation', 2018, https://assets.publishing.service.gov.uk/government/uploads/system/uploads/attachment_data/file/685903/The_Green_Book.pdf

Holman, I. P., 'An Estimate of Peat Reserves and Loss in the East

Anglian Fens', Cranfield University, October 2009. Commissioned by the RSPB

Holman, I. P. and Kechavarzi, C., 'A Revised Estimate of Peat Reserves and Loss in the East Anglian Fens', Cranfield University, January 2011. Commissioned by the RSPB

Hortin, T., Hamkes, L. and Witt, W., 'Bluefin Tuna Off Britain and Ireland: Return of the Giant Tunny?', *British Wildlife*, 402, August 2018

House of Commons Communities and Local Government Committee, 'Public Parks: Seventh Report of Session 2016–17', 30 January 2017

House of Commons Environmental Audit Committee, 'Environmental Impact of Microplastics', HC 179, July 2016

House of Commons Environmental Audit Committee, 'The Government's 25 Year Plan for the Environment: Eighth Report of Session 2017–19', 24 July 2018

House of Commons Library, 'Carbon Price Floor (CPF) and the Price Support Mechanism', Briefing Paper, 8 January 2018, https://researchbriefings.parliament.uk/ResearchBriefing/Summary/SN05927

House of Commons Library, 'The UK Bee Population', CDP 2017/0226, 10 November 2017

House of Lords Economic Affairs Committee, 'The Economics of High Speed 2', 1st Report of Session 2014–15, HL Paper 134, March 2015

Igarashi, M., Song, C., Ikei, H. and Miyazaki, Y., 'Effect of Stimulation by Foliage Plant Display Images on Prefrontal Cortex Activity: A Comparison with Stimulation Using Actual Foliage Plants', *Journal of Neuroimaging*, 25(1), 2014, pp. 127–30

Institute for Fiscal Studies, 'Reforming the Tax System for the 21st Century: The Mirrlees Review', www.ifs.org.uk/publications/mirrleesreview

Institute for Government, 'Common Fisheries Policy', www.instituteforgovernment.org.uk/explainers/common-fisheries-policy

John Muir Trust, 'Too Many Deer and Too Few Trees', 23 December 2015, www.johnmuirtrust.org/about/resources/761-too-many-deer-and-too-few-trees

Kurlansky, M., *Cod: A Biography of the Fish that Changed the World*. London: Vintage Publishing, 1999

Lawton, J., 'Making Space for Nature: A Review of England's Wildlife Sites and Ecological Network', prepared for Department for Environment, Food and Rural Affairs, September 2010

Lee, L., *Cider with Rosie*. London: Hogarth Press, 1959

Lichtenstein, R., *Estuary: Out from London to the Sea*. London: Penguin, 2016

Lightfoot, W., Burke, J., Craig-Harvey, N., Dupont, J., Howard, R., Lowe, R., Norrie, R. and Taylor, M., *Farming Tomorrow: British Agriculture after Brexit*. Policy Exchange, 2017

Linklater, A., *Owning the Earth: The Transforming History of Land Ownership*. London: Bloomsbury, 2014

Lobley, M. and Winter, M., '"Born out of crisis": Assessing the Legacy of the Exmoor Moorland Management Agreements', *Rural History*, 20(2), 2009, pp. 229–47

Macfarlane, R., *The Old Ways: A Journey on Foot*. London: Penguin, 2012

Marine Management Organisation, 'How Fish Quotas for 2018 are Set', 5 December 2017, https://marinedevelopments.blog.gov.uk/2017/12/05/december-council-eu-fish-quotas-cfp-uk/

Marren, P., *The New Naturalists*. London: HarperCollins, 2005

Marren, P., *Nature Conservation*. London: HarperCollins, 2002

National Audit Office, 'Air Quality', Environmental Audit Committee, Environment, Food and Rural Affairs Committee, Health Committee and Transport Committee, HC 529, 16 November 2017

National Infrastructure Commission, 'National Infrastructure Assessment', July 2018

National Infrastructure Commission, 'Preparing for a Drier Future: England's Water Infrastructure Needs', April 2018

National Trust, 'Mapping Our Shores: 50 Years of Land Use Change at the Coast', 2015

Natural England, 'A Blue Belt in Marine Protection for Seabirds', 7 September 2017, https://naturalengland.blog.gov.uk/2017/09/07/a-blue-belt-in-marine-protection-for-seabirds/

Natural England, 'Monitor of Engagement with the Natural Environment: The National Survey on People and the Natural Environment – Visits to Coastal England', NECR226, 24 October 2016

Nature, 'Flying Insects Are Disappearing from German Skies', 18 October 2017, www.nature.com/articles/d41586-017-04774-7

Newby, H., *Green & Pleasant Land? Social Change in Rural England*. Hutchinson & Co., 1979

Office for National Statistics, 'Making Ends Meet: Are Households Living Beyond Their Means?', July 2016, www.ons.gov.uk/economy/nationalaccounts/uksectoraccounts/articles/makingendsmeetarehouseholdslivingbeyondtheirmeans/2018-07-26

Office for National Statistics, 'Migration Statistics Quarterly Report: August 2018', 23 August 2018, www.ons.gov.uk/peoplepopulationandcommunity/populationandmigration/internationalmigration/bulletins/migrationstatisticsquarterlyreport/august2018

Office for National Statistics, 'National Population Projections: 2016-based Statistical Bulletin', 26 October 2017, www.ons.gov.uk/peoplepopulationandcommunity/populationandmigration/populationprojections/bulletins/nationalpopulationprojections/2016basedstatisticalbulletin

Ostrom, E., Walker, J. and Gardner, R., 'Covenants with and

without a Sword: Self-Governance is Possible', *American Political Science Review*, 86(2), June 1992, pp. 404–17

Palmer, R. C. and Smith, R. P., 'Soil Structural Degradation in SW England and its Impact on Surface Water Runoff Generation', *Soil Use and Management*, 29(4), 2013, pp. 567–75

Peach, W. J., Mallord, J. W., Ockendon, N., Orsman, C. J. and Haines, W. G., 'Depleted Suburban House Sparrow *Passer domesticus* Population Not Limited by Food Availability', *Urban Ecosyst*, 11 July 2018, https://link.springer.com/article/10.1007%2Fs11252-018-0784-4

Peterken, G., *Meadows*. London: Bloomsbury, 2013

Pitt, M., 'Learning Lessons from the 2007 Floods', The Pitt Review, June 2008

Plokhy, S., *Chernobyl: History of a Tragedy*. London: Allen Lane, 2018

Pretty, J. N., Brett, C., Gee, D., Hine, R. E., Mason, C. F., Morison, J. I. L., Raven, D., Rayment, M. D. and van der Bijl, G., 'An Assessment of the Total External Costs of UK Agriculture', *Agricultural Systems*, 65, 2000, pp. 113–16

Rackham, O., *The History of the Countryside*. J.M. Dent, 1986

Ratcliffe, D., *The Peregrine Falcon*. Poyser, 1980 (expanded 2nd edn 1993)

Rebanks, J., *The Shepherd's Life: A Tale of the Lake District*. London: Allen Lane, 2015

Review on Antimicrobial Resistance, 'Tackling Drug-resistant Infections Globally: Final Report and Recommendations', chaired by Jim O'Neill, May 2016

Reynolds, F., *The Fight for Beauty: Our Path to a Better Future*. Oneworld Publications, 2016

Roberts, C. M., Bohnsack, J. A., Gell, F., Hawkins, J. P. and Goodridge, R., 'Effects of Marine Reserves on Adjacent Fisheries', *Science*, 294(5548), 2001, 1920–192–3

Salmon & Trout Conservation Scotland, 'BBC's "Fish Farms of

the Future" – Our Comments on Closed Containment', www.salmon-trout.org/2017/10/27/bbc-fish-farms-of-the-future-our-comments/

Samuelson, P. A., 'The Pure Theory of Public Expenditure', *Review of Economics and Statistics*, 36(4), 1954, pp. 387–9

Savills, 'GB Agricultural Land: Spotlight 2018', 2018, https://pdf.euro.savills.co.uk/uk/rural---other/gb-agricultural-land-2018.pdf

Schilthuizen, M., *Darwin Comes to Town: How the Urban Jungle Drives Evolution*. London: Quercus, 2018

Simberloff, D. S. and Wilson, E. O., 'Experimental Zoogeography of Islands: The Colonization of Empty Islands, *Ecology*, 50(2), 1969, pp. 278–96

Smith, S., *Taxation: A Very Short Introduction*. Oxford: Oxford University Press, 2015

Smout, T. C., *Nature Contested: Environmental History in Scotland and Northern England Since 1600*. Edinburgh: Edinburgh University Press, 2000

Spiers, S., *How to Build Houses and Save the Countryside*. Policy Press, 2018

Stace, C. A. and Crawley, M. J., *Alien Plants*. London: HarperCollins, 2015

Stern, N., 'The Economics of Climate Change: The Stern Review', HM Treasury. Cambridge: Cambridge University Press, January 2007

Stewart, R., *The Marches*. London: Jonathan Cape, 2016

The Coal Authority, 'Annual Report and Accounts, 2017–18', HC 1168, https://assets.publishing.service.gov.uk/government/uploads/system/uploads/attachment_data/file/722535/Coal_Authority_annual_report_and_accounts_2017-2018_web.pdf

The National Archives, 'Farming and the Agriculture Acts: The Agriculture Act of 1947', www.nationalarchives.gov.uk/cabinetpapers/themes/farming-agriculture-acts.htm

The Sunday Times, 'Puffins Starve as Danes Grab UK Sand Eels', 22 July 2018, www.thetimes.co.uk/article/puffins-starve-as-danes-grab-uk-sand-eels-srwrfgdrs

The Wildlife Trusts, 'The Way Back to the Living Seas', www.wildlifetrusts.org/sites/default/files/2018-07/the_way_back_to_living_seas_the_wildlife_trusts.pdf

Thomas, J. A. and Setele, J., 'Butterfly Mimics of Ants', *Nature*, 432, December 2004, pp. 283–4

Thomas, K., *Man and the Natural World: Changing Attitudes in England 1500–1800*. London: Penguin Books, 1984

Thompson, F., *Lark Rise to Candleford*. Oxford: Oxford University Press, 1945

Thompson, J., Birks, H. and Birks, J. (eds), *Nature's Conscience: The Life and Legacy of Derek Ratcliffe*. Langford Press, 2015

Thompson, K. and Head, S., 'Gardens as a Resource for Wildlife', www.wlgf.org/The%20garden%20Resource.pdf

Traynor, J., 'A History of Almond Pollination in California', *Bee World*, 94(3), 11 August 2017, pp. 69–79

Tree, I., *Wilding: The Return of Nature to a British Farm*. London: Picador, 2018

Vollaard, P., Vink, J. and de Zwarte, N., *Making Urban Nature*. nai010, 2017

Williams, B., *Moral Luck*. Cambridge: Cambridge University Press, 1981

Wilson, E. O., *The Diversity of Life*. Cambridge, MA: Harvard University Press, 1992

Wilson, E. O., *Biophilia*. Cambridge, MA: Harvard University Press, 1986

Wilson, S. M., *The Native Woodlands of Scotland: Ecology, Conservation and Management*. Edinburgh: Edinburgh University Press, 2015

Worster, D., *A Passion for Nature: The Life of John Muir*. Oxford: Oxford University Press, 2008

INDEX